MODERN METHODS
OF INDUCING ABORTION

Modern Methods of Inducing Abortion

EDITED BY

David T. Baird MB ChB, DSc
MRC Clinical Research Professor
of Reproductive Endocrinology
Centre for Reproductive Biology
Department of Obstetrics and Gynaecology
University of Edinburgh
Edinburgh, UK

David A. Grimes MD
Chief, Department of Obstetrics, Gynecology
and Reproductive Sciences
San Francisco General Hospital
San Francisco, California, USA

Paul F.A. Van Look MD, PhD
Associate Director, Special Programme of Research, Development
and Research Training in Human Reproduction
World Health Organization
Geneva, Switzerland

FOREWORD BY
Malcolm Potts

**Blackwell
Science**

© 1995 by
Blackwell Science Ltd
Editorial Offices:
Osney Mead, Oxford OX2 0EL
25 John Street, London WC1N 2BL
23 Ainslie Place, Edinburgh EH3 6AJ
238 Main Street, Cambridge
    Massachusetts 02142, USA
54 University Street, Carlton
    Victoria 3053, Australia

Other Editorial Offices:
Arnette Blackwell SA
    1, rue de Lille, 75007 Paris
    France ⁻

Blackwell Wissenschafts-Verlag GmbH
    Kurfürstendamm 57
    10707 Berlin, Germany

    Feldgasse 13, A-1238 Wien
    Austria

First published 1995

Set by Semantic Graphics, Singapore
Printed and bound in Great Britain
by Hartnolls Ltd, Bodmin, Cornwall

DISTRIBUTORS

    Marston Book Services Ltd
    PO Box 87
    Oxford OX2 0DT
    (*Orders:* Tel: 01865 791155
              Fax: 01865 791927
              Telex: 837515)

North America
    Blackwell Science, Inc.
    238 Main Street
    Cambridge, MA 02142
    (*Orders:* Tel: 800 215-1000
              617 876-7000
              Fax: 617 492-5263)

Australia
    Blackwell Science Pty Ltd
    54 University Street
    Carlton, Victoria 3053
    (*Orders:* Tel: 03 9347-0300
              Fax: 03 9349-3016)

A catalogue record for this title
is available from the British Library

ISBN 0-86542-819-0

Library of Congress
Cataloging-in-Publication Data

Library of Congress
Cataloging-in-Publication Data

Modern methods of inducing abortion/
edited by David T. Baird, David A. Grimes,
    Paul F.A. Van Look; foreword by
    Malcolm Potts.
            p.   cm.
    Includes bibliographical references
    and index.
    ISBN 0-86542-819-0
    1. Abortion, Therapeutic.
    I. Baird, David T.
    II. Grimes, David A.
    III. Look, P.F.A. Van.
    [DNLM: 1. Abortion, Induced.
    2. Abortion, Induced—methods.
    WQ 440 T398   1995]
    RG734.T48   1995
    618.8'8—dc20
    DNLM/DLC
    for Library of Congress   95-14056
                                          CIP

Contents

List of Contributors

David T. Baird MB, ChB, DSc, MRC Clinical Research Professor of Reproductive Endocrinology, Centre for Reproductive Biology, Department of Obstetrics and Gynaecology, University of Edinburgh, Edinburgh, UK

Traci L. Baird MPH, Program Associate, IPAS, Carrboro, North Carolina, USA

Marc Bygdeman MD, PhD, Professor, Medical Director, Department of Obstetrics and Gynaecology, Karolinska Hospital, Stockholm, Sweden

Rebecca J. Cook JD, LLM, JSD, Professor (Research), Faculty of Law, University of Toronto, Toronto, Canada

Bernard M. Dickens PhD, LLD, Professor, Faculty of Law, University of Toronto, Toronto, Canada

Anna Glasier BSC, MD, Director/Consultant, Family Planning and Well Woman Services, Dean Terrace Centre, Edinburgh, UK

Forrest C. Greenslade PhD, President, IPAS, Carrboro, North Carolina, USA

David A. Grimes MD, Chief, Department of Obstetrics, Gynecology and Reproductive Sciences, San Francisco General Hospital, San Francisco, California, USA

Helena von Hertzen DDS, MD, Medical Officer Special Programme of Research, Development and Research Training in Human Reproduction, World Health Organization, Geneva, Switzerland

Pak Chung Ho MD, FRCOG, Reader, Department of Obstetrics and Gynaecology, University of Hong Kong, Queen Mary Hospital, Hong Kong

Brooke R. Johnson PhD, Research Associate, IPAS, Carrboro, North Carolina, USA

Ann H. Leonard RN, MSPH, Vice President for International Programs, IPAS, Carrboro, North Carolina, USA

Ruth Macklin PhD, Professor of Bioethics, Department of Epidemiology and Social Medicine, Albert Einstein College of Medicine, New York, New York, USA

Malcolm Potts MB, BChir, PhD, Bixby Professor of Population and Family Planning, School of Public Health, University of California, Earl Warren Hall, Berkeley, California, USA

Mokhtar Toppozada MD, Professor, Department of Obstetrics and Gynaecology, Shatby Maternity Hospital, University of Alexandria, Egypt

Paul F.A. Van Look MD, PhD, Associate Director, Special Programme of Research, Development and Research Training in Human Reproduction, World Health Organization, Geneva, Switzerland

Beverly Winikoff MD, MPH, Program Director, Reproductive Health, The Population Council, One Dag Hammarskjold Plaza, New York, New York, USA

Judith Winkler MEd, Director of Communications Division, IPAS, Carrboro, North Carolina, USA

Foreword

Abortion is a subject that raises strong emotions. Some hold that it is unethical and that termination of pregnancy impairs physical and mental health. In reality, abortion performed early in pregnancy is remarkably safe, has few physical and no demonstrable long-term psychological side effects and commonly brings profound relief.

Practically all communities from the Stone Age culture of Hawaii prior to Western contact, to post-industrial Europe practice abortion. Methods vary in safety and rates may be high or low, but in the final analysis, the pressure that drives a woman to end her pregnancy crosses historical, geographical and cultural boundaries: at that particular moment in her life the woman involved does not feel that she can give the child, if born, the love and security she would wish.

While the decision to end a pregnancy is never a happy or easy one, once it is made many women are willing to pay an extremely high economic or physical price to achieve their goal. Until the middle of this century abortion was usually dangerous and painful. Methods included the insertion of a foreign body through the cervix, with the risk of infection and haemorrhage, and the use of various poisons, which in low doses did not work and in high doses either risked damaging the mother or causing abnormalities to the child. Some techniques have remained virtually unchanged for a millennium. The twelfth century bas reliefs on the great Temples of Ankor Wat, Kampuchea, illustrate a massage abortion and the technique remains a relatively common practice in the Orient today. A skeleton of a woman in her twenties discovered in a Gallo-Roman cemetery in the Netherlands had a bone stylet at the site of the uterus and is interpreted as evidence of death associated with the insertion of a foreign body. Cervical dilators and curettes of remarkably modern appearance exist from Roman times. Possibly the oldest historical mention of abortion is that in the Bible and it concerns physical injury to the pregnant woman (Exodus 21:22). 'If men strive and hurt a woman with child, so that her fruit depart from her, and yet no mischief follow: he shall be punished as the judges and as the woman's husband shall lay upon him: and shall pay a fine as the judges determine.' As the Judeo-Christian tradition has had such a powerful effect on abortion, it is interesting that this, the only reference to the legality of abortion in the Bible, does not regard abortion as murder, but as a crime to be punished by a fine. The commentors in the Talmud interpreted this verse to mean life began with the baby's first breath.

Community and cultural attitudes to abortion have varied enormously and continue to do so. In preliterate societies, abortion was generally a matter of personal decision-making. In the Orient, abortion was regarded as a crime against the family, but not àgainst society. The Early Fathers of the Christian Church, however, condemned abortion almost as vehemently as they did contraceptive practices. Until 1800, abortion before quickening was legal under English common law and in all States of the Union in America. But, abortion was not common and no satisfactory technology existed. In the USA, as the medical and midwifery professions struggled to separate themselves from barber surgeons and other traditional practitioners, so they began to condemn abortion as unacceptable and dangerous. In 1861 in England, without any public or parliamentary debate, the law was modified to exclude abortion before quickening. Even the intention to perform an abortion became a felony. It was only with anaesthesia and asepsis that safe abortion became achievable towards the end of the nineteenth century, but by this time the condemnation of the technique was so strong and universal that even when appropriate technologies were devised and proved to work, they could not make progress against the combined opposition of physicians and clergy.

So strong was the opposition that the modern technique of vacuum aspiration abortion was invented independently on at least three occasions and on the first two, use of the technique seems to have withered away in a hostile environment. James Young Simpson described what he called 'dry cupping' in 1863. Bykov in Russia described a similar procedure in 1927. Again, the method, although excellent, was not adopted by others. In 1958 Wu and Wu described vacuum aspiration for the third time, on this occasion in China. This time the method did spread, but in a halting and irregular fashion, being taken up in only some parts of the then Soviet Union and Eastern Europe. It was brought to Britain by Dortheria Kerslake.

In the 1960s, Berislav Beric and his father in Novi Sad and Subitica, Yugoslavia, brought together vacuum aspiration and out-patient routines. This highly effective combination was observed and copied in the

1970s and has become the standard technique for most of the world. Benjamin Branch took day-care abortion techniques from Yugoslavia to the USA and Rustom Soonawalla to Bombay, India. The technique of out-patient vacuum aspiration abortion has been used in millions of cases over several decades and has proved exceptionally safe. Mortality from early vacuum aspiration abortion is up to five times less than that of delivery.

The relationship between abortion and contraception is often misunderstood. On the one hand, every method of contraception has a sufficiently high failure rate that it is impossible to control fertility without access to abortion, even though the number of induced abortions may be relatively few. On the other hand, when a community first begins to use contraception there are often many mistakes which lead to the need for a relatively large number of abortions, even though family size is also moderately high. As the prevalence of contraceptive usage rises, the number of abortions falls.

Calculation suggests that if every unwanted pregnancy in the world could be prevented—and that could only be done by universal access to safe abortion—then human numbers would stabilize at approximately 7.5 billion. In the absence of safe abortion and universal access to contraceptive services, human population could grow to 15 billion before it stabilizes.

While abortion is the most controversial aspect of fertility control the technology is so simple and the demand for the procedure so well defined that, given appropriate training and cheap hand-held equipment, it could become the first element of fertility regulation to become totally self sufficient, even amongst the poorest nations. As a rule of thumb, many women when pressed can find 1 week's disposable income to pay for an abortion. By contrast, experience suggests that individuals will spend perhaps 1% of their disposable income on contraception and this will not pay the full cost of modern services. Do those who oppose abortion appreciate and support the higher cost of contraceptive services? Where abortion is part of the mainstream of medial practice it should be associated with post-abortion contraceptive care. In the long run, recognizing the reality of abortion and helping couples use contraception after an abortion may lead to less overall destruction of embryos than forbidding access to safe procedures and leaving the couple without help in the difficult but essential task of limiting family size.

Malcolm Potts

Preface

The urge to reproduce is the most fundamental human instinct on which the survival of the species depends. Patterns of sexual behaviour have evolved to ensure that men and women are attracted to one another and for the most part establish a stable relationship within which children can be reared successfully. However, because the number of times that any one woman can become pregnant greatly exceeds the number of children she can raise without detriment to their and her own well-being, all societies have developed patterns of reproductive behaviour which control the growth of their populations. The rate of growth of the population of the world has increased exponentially during this century and has added a global dimension to this individual problem.

Traditionally, contraceptive methods (both natural and artificial) have concentrated on women on whom the burden of child bearing and rearing falls heaviest. Family planning movements rose from the wish of individual women to limit the number of their children. However, women in many countries of the world do not yet have access to effective and affordable methods of contraception. Even where such methods are available, unwanted and unplanned pregnancies still occur either because the methods are not used or because they fail. Many women will decide that terminating the pregnancy by abortion is the only realistic way of coping with their circumstances. Faced with the prospect of an unwanted pregnancy, many women will submit to potentially dangerous and unpleasant procedures aimed at procuring abortion. In many countries where abortion is illegal, the major cause of maternal death and morbidity is a result of attempts to terminate the pregnancy in circumstances which are far from optimal. Easy access to safe abortion should be the goal of any civilized society.

Modern methods of inducing abortion in early pregnancy are now extremely effective and safe. The chance of dying following vacuum aspiration in the first trimester of pregnancy is five- to 10-fold lower than if the pregnancy continues. In the last decade medical methods involving anti-progestogens and prostaglandins have been developed as an effective and safe alternative to surgical methods. This book which was based on a meeting convened by the World Health Organization in Geneva in April 1994 considers the relative merits of these modern methods and the social and political constraints to their widespread availability.

Abortion is an emotive subject about which widely differing views are held. But, at the end of the day, it is of most concern to individual women who are faced with an unwanted pregnancy. The decision whether or not to terminate a pregnancy is never easy; surely we should provide the most effective and safe methods for those women who decide that abortion is the only option?

1   Induced Abortion: a Global Perspective*

Paul F.A. Van Look & Helena von Hertzen

Introduction

The global statistics on the causes and numbers of induced abortions, particularly those performed under unsafe conditions, and on the consequences of such unsafe abortions for women's health make worrying reading. According to estimates of the World Health Organization (WHO) [1] the approximately 100 million acts of sexual intercourse that take place each day result in some 910 000 conceptions. About 50% of these conceptions are unplanned and some 25% of them are definitely unwanted. Between 100 000 and 150 000 unwanted pregnancies every day, or 36–53 million in 1 year, are terminated by induced abortion. One-third of these abortions are performed under unsafe conditions, in an adverse social and legal climate. Complications resulting from such unsafe abortions are responsible for an annual death toll of about 70 000 [2]. Unsafe abortion is, therefore, the cause of an estimated 13%, or one in eight, of the approximately 500 000 maternal deaths that occur annually. Most of these deaths occur in developing countries, where access to safe abortion is restricted either by law or because services are inadequate. Furthermore, the number of deaths is only one facet of the grim picture; for every woman dying many more suffer injuries and complications that can be life-threatening in the short term or the cause of permanent disabilities in the long term. As stated in the WHO report, 'Unsafe abortion is one of the great neglected problems of health care in developing countries and is a serious concern to women during their reproductive lives' [1].

Even before more reliable information about the number and distribution of abortions became available in the 1970s, the public health aspects of induced abortion were already a matter of concern to many nations. As early as 1967, the World Health Assembly of the WHO passed

* The views expressed in this chapter are those of the authors and do not necessarily represent the opinions or the stated policy of the World Health Organization.

1

a Resolution (WHA 20.41) which stated that, 'abortions...constitute a serious public health problem in many countries...' and it requested '...the Director-General...to continue to develop the activities of the World Health Organization in the field of health aspects of human reproduction...' [3]. The International Conference on Population, held in Mexico City in 1984, urged governments 'to take appropriate steps to help women avoid abortion, which in no case should be promoted as a method of family planning, and—whenever possible—to provide for the humane treatment and counselling of women who have had recourse to abortion' [4]. The recently held International Conference on Population and Development in Cairo also approved a Programme of Action that states, 'In no case should abortion be promoted as a method of family planning. All Governments and relevant inter- and non-governmental organizations are urged to strengthen their commitment to women's health, to deal with the health impact of unsafe abortion as a major public health concern and to reduce the recourse to abortion through expanded and improved family planning services. Prevention of unwanted pregnancies must always be given the highest priority and every attempt should be made to eliminate the need for abortion' [5].

While, from the standpoint of public policy, few would disagree that reducing the number of unintended pregnancies and abortions worldwide is a desirable goal, opinions differ as to the most effective measures of achieving that goal. As is evident from the statements quoted above, international gatherings of a primarily political nature emphasize prevention through wider provision of family planning services rather than decriminalization or 'liberalization' of existing restrictive legislation. This emphasis on prevention rather than on legislative change reflects the divergent views—and the consequent need for political compromise—on a subject that religious and moral beliefs keep at the centre of an intense public controversy about the status of the fetus and a woman's right to make choices about pregnancy and motherhood (see Chapters 10 and 11 and Jacobson [6]).

Expanding access to family planning services and widening the range of methods offered by these services should result in a reduced number of unplanned pregnancies. However, it would be unrealistic to expect that the need for pregnancy termination can be eliminated entirely by better family planning services. Even in countries such as the Netherlands where there are no barriers to obtaining contraceptives, even for high-risk groups such as adolescents, about 20% of native Dutch women who request pregnancy termination did not use contraception during the

6 months prior to the abortion [7]. Amongst a similar group of 769 women in the UK, 210 (27%) did not use contraception at the time of conception [8]. For women not using contraception and for women who have a contraceptive mishap, such as a torn condom, timely use of emergency contraception can avoid unplanned pregnancy in most cases [9]. Regrettably, however, this option is not known to many family planning providers and, hence, is unavailable to their clients. Yet, the currently most common methods of emergency contraception, namely the combined oestrogen–progestogen pill regimen and intrauterine contraceptive device (IUCD) insertion, use technology that has been around for some 30 years. Conversely, use of a contraceptive method is no absolute guarantee against unplanned pregnancy. Many of the current methods of family planning are difficult for some couples to use, and no method is completely effective. The annual number of pregnancies resulting from contraceptive failure has been estimated at between 8 and 30 million [10]. It is uncertain how many of these pregnancies are terminated, but they must contribute substantially to the total number of abortions carried out worldwide each year.

This chapter reviews the incidence of abortion and some of the factors that contribute to differences in the use of abortion between countries and between different population groups within the same country. The amount and reliability of information available for any given country is largely determined by the legal status of abortion, so a brief overview of abortion laws and policies currently in force throughout the world has also been included. More detailed discussions of these legal and other aspects of induced abortion can be found in the other chapters of this book, in the comprehensive publications on the subject by Henshaw and associates at the Alan Guttmacher Institute [11,12], and in a number of other recent reviews [13,14].

Laws, policies and practices

The legal and ethical status of the fetus has been debated at least since written records began [15]. The Greek and Roman civilizations accepted the deliberate termination of early pregnancy. The developing Christian and Islamic cultures disapproved strongly of the destruction of the fetus but, at least until the end of the seventeenth century, followed the Greek philosophers in tolerating abortion during the early part of pregnancy (usually up to quickening—the time at which the first movements of the fetus were felt by the woman, usually around 16–18 weeks of gestation), but made it a crime at later gestations. The attitudes of church and state became more restrictive during the nineteenth century, partly as a result of the professionalization of medicine and the suppression of unqualified practitioners and, partly, because increasing knowledge of intrauterine development suggested that there was no precise gestation at which a fetus could be said to become a person.

Under common law, which is the basis of the British legal system, abortion was not an indictable offence in Great Britain until 1803. At that time it became a felony, but doctors who performed an abortion prior to 'quickening' were punished less severely than those who did so later in gestation. The Offences Against the Person Act of 1861 made 'unlawfully' induced abortion a felony regardless of the duration of pregnancy. The Act did not define 'unlawfully' and made no provision for the termination of pregnancy on medical grounds. However, in the 1938 case of *Rex* v. *Bourne*, the judge ruled that abortion need not be unlawful if it is performed in good faith to preserve the mother's life [11].

In the USA, the tradition of English common law also prevailed well into the nineteenth century: abortion was not considered a crime before 'quickening' and a woman who had had an abortion was immune from prosecution. But, after 1860, as a result of anti-abortion campaigns by, *inter alia*, the medical profession which used the abortion issue in its power struggle against unqualified lay practitioners, most of the states started to enact much more restrictive abortion laws that remained in force with little change for the next century.

Apart from the UK and USA, most, if not all, of the countries in the Western hemisphere had restrictive abortion laws during the latter part of the nineteenth century and well into the twentieth century. The many millions who migrated from Europe in the nineteenth and early twentieth centuries took their laws and their moral and religious attitudes with them, and these are the basis of the restrictive abortion legislation that still exists in many developing countries (Fig. 1.1), particularly in Africa and Latin America.

During the twentieth century, an increasing number of countries became concerned about the harm caused by illegal abortion and the distress experienced by women and their families from unwanted pregnancy. The first country to make abortion available for social reasons was the former USSR in 1920 (some restrictions were introduced in 1936). Subsequently, several European countries introduced laws that gave doctors limited freedom to perform abortion to protect the health of women. This happened in Iceland in 1935, Sweden in 1938, Denmark in

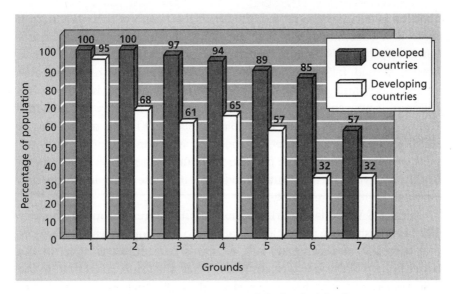

Fig. 1.1 Grounds on which abortion is permitted, by level of development (percentage of population): (1) to save the life of the woman; (2) to preserve physical health; (3) to preserve mental health; (4) rape or incest; (5) fetal impairment; (6) economic or social reasons; and (7) available on request. Based on United Nations data [16–18].

1939 and Great Britain in 1967 [19]. These laws could be interpreted liberally, so that a threat to health could be judged to be present when the pregnancy would result in serious stress from adverse social circumstances. However, except in the Soviet law of 1920, the power to make the abortion decision was left with the doctors or with a special committee rather than with the woman herself. The bureaucracy associated with many of these laws made the process of obtaining an abortion slow, so that some were delayed until the second trimester [20]. 'Liberalization' of abortion laws occurred in most of the countries of Central and Eastern Europe in the 1950s, and in almost all the remaining developed countries during the 1960s and 1970s. A few developing countries, most notably China and India, also relaxed their restrictions on abortion at that time [11].

The British Abortion Act of 1967 (which came into force on 27 April 1968) governs the practice of abortion in England, Wales and Scotland, but not in Northern Ireland where the Act does not apply and abortion continues to be restricted. Apart from Northern Ireland, only the Republic of Ireland and Malta still have restrictive legislation in Europe. The 1967 British Act allows abortion only if two doctors certify that the abortion is necessary to protect the life or the health of the woman, or if there is a substantial risk that the child, if born, would be seriously handicapped. It also states that the doctors, in considering the risk to health, should take into account the woman's actual or foreseeable environment and the effect of the pregnancy on the health of her children. Some changes to this law were made recently through the Human Fertilization and Embryology Act 1990 which provides a statutory limit of 24 weeks for inducing abortion except to save the mother's life, prevent grave permanent injury to her physical or mental health or avoid serious fetal handicap. In these rare instances the 24-week limit does not apply.

In the USA, two landmark decisions of the Supreme Court in January 1973 established the principle that access to abortion, at least during the first trimester of pregnancy, is a woman's constitutional right. In the better known of these two cases, *Roe* v. *Wade*, the Court ruled that, in the first trimester, 'the abortion decision and its effectuation must be left to the medical judgement of the pregnant woman's attending physician', in consultation with the woman herself. The principle laid down in *Roe* v. *Wade* that access to abortion is a constitutional right was reaffirmed by the Supreme Court in a series of subsequent decisions during the period between 1973 and 1986. However, due to changes in the Court's composition, which now has a greater number of more conservative judges nominated during the Reagan and Bush eras, more recent Court decisions have tended to weaken the constitutional guarantees of abortion rights. For example, in the recent cases of *Webster* v. *Reproductive Health Services* (1989) and *Planned Parenthood* v. *Casey* (1992) the Court upheld individual state laws containing a number of restrictions on abortion. By doing so the Court in effect authorized states to impose requirements that could significantly affect a woman's access to abortion (e.g. discontinuation of public funding of abortion services, parental or husband notification requirements, obligatory waiting period between first consultation and the abortion, and so on).

A similar trend towards more restrictive regulations of abortion provision has also emerged during the last few years in some countries of Central and Eastern Europe, notably Poland and Hungary. In Romania and Albania, on the other hand, the existing restrictive laws, which permitted abortion only on narrowly defined grounds, were revoked. In Romania, after the December 1989 revolution, one of the first acts of the provisional government abrogated the 1966 law banning abortion and contraception and made abortion available on request [21]. The new

Albanian directive issued in June 1991 by the Ministry of Health makes
abortion available on request up to 12 weeks, for social reasons up to 15
weeks, and on medical grounds without time limit. In contrast, in
Germany, in May 1993, the Constitutional Court declared unconstitutional a law designed to strike a compromise between abortion provisions
prevailing in East and West Germany before unification. The Court held
that Parliament had violated a constitutional guarantee protecting the life
of the fetus. Until Parliament passes new legislation, abortion remains
illegal, except for narrowly specified situations involving rape, incest or
fetal malformation. However, no punishment is imposed on the woman
or her physician if abortion is carried out in the first 12 weeks of
pregnancy, provided she attends mandatory counselling, which, the
justices ruled, 'must be oriented to the protection of unborn life'.
Abortion services can no longer be provided in state facilities and cannot
be subsidized by social assistance funds or by statutory or private
insurance plans (except for cases permitted under the ruling) [22].

Currently, abortion is available either on request or for social reasons
to 63% of women in the world [12] (Fig. 1.2). About 25% of women live in
countries in which abortion is prohibited, except when the woman's life
would be endangered if the pregnancy continued. For the remaining 12%,
abortion can be obtained when the pregnancy is a risk to the woman's
health rather than to her life and, in some countries, to avoid the birth of
a malformed child or when conception resulted from rape or incest.

However, the legal status of abortion does not always ascertain access
to services. Rather, it is the interpretation and application of the laws
that determine whether a woman will have a safe or an unsafe abortion
(see Chapter 11 and Cook [23]). Interpretation of similar laws can vary
widely between countries and sometimes even within a country. For
example, in Switzerland, the provision that a pregnancy can be termi-

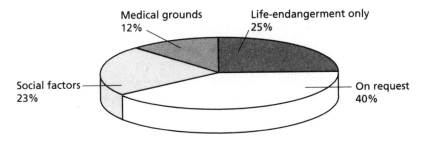

Fig. 1.2 Legal status of abortion throughout the world and proportion of women in
the world affected. From Van Look and von Hertzen [14].

nated for a medical reason is interpreted very liberally in some cantons and very narrowly in others. Furthermore, the existence of a 'liberal' law does not necessarily guarantee that services are widely available and accessible and that all abortions are induced under safe conditions. Conversely, in countries with restrictive legislation, safe abortion may nevertheless be available to women, particularly those from higher socioeconomic groups. In Brazil, for instance, safe abortion can be obtained at numerous clandestine clinics by those who can afford to pay. In Indonesia, where abortion is illegal, pregnancy terminations are done in teaching hospitals as part of medical training. In Bangladesh, government clinics provide menstrual regulation before pregnancy is confirmed even though abortion is, as in most Muslim countries, strictly forbidden. However, though abortion is legal in India and Zambia, many women are driven to clandestine procedures since abortion services are inadequate to meet the demand. Insufficient resources for services, complicated procedures for application and shortages of qualified, approved personnel are the main obstacles. Furthermore, the regulations may not be known to the women in need of services or to the health workers who should apply them. Many women have to rely on unskilled assistance and cannot even count on medical care for complications [13]. Thus, from a public health perspective, the generally used distinction between 'legal' and 'illegal' abortion is not always very meaningful and the number of 'legal' abortions may only be a poor reflection of the use of abortion by the population as a whole. For women and societies the more relevant and important distinction is between 'safe' and 'unsafe' abortions [14].

Abortion incidence

Annual number of abortions

The number of pregnancies aborted each year throughout the world is unknown. Even in countries where induced abortion is 'legal' and widely accepted, statistics are not always reliable due to under-reporting. Not all procedures performed by physicians are reported, and those provided by traditional, non-medical practitioners do not appear in the official statistics. Estimating the number of clandestine abortions is, of course, even more difficult; various approaches have been proposed over the years, but complete accuracy will probably remain elusive [2]. Indirect methods that have been—and are being—used include surveys of the numbers of women admitted to hospital with conditions that can be attributed to clandestine abortion, such as pelvic infection or reproductive tract injury, information on death certificates and surveys of samples of women [24,25]. None of these methods is likely to be accurate for several reasons. First, induced abortion cannot always be distinguished medically from miscarriage. Second, an unknown minority of women have sufficiently severe complications from clandestine abortion to require hospital treatment and only a small fraction actually die. Third, women are reluctant to admit to having had an abortion and doctors may conceal this information, both in their case notes and on death certificates, to protect the reputation of the woman and her family and to guard them from prosecution.

Henshaw [12] has estimated that, in 1987, the number of legal abortions performed worldwide was approximately 28 million, but may have ranged from 26 to 31 million. The number of clandestine abortions during that year was estimated at 15 million (range: 10–22 million), giving an estimated worldwide total of between 36 and 53 million. Demographers calculate that from one-third to half of all women undergo at least one induced abortion during their lifetime [12].

Rates and ratios

The occurrence of abortion is usually measured either by rates, which relate the number of abortions to defined populations, or ratios, which relate the number of abortions to the number of births or pregnancies. The types of information obtainable by these two main approaches are different but complementary, and both are needed for the understanding of abortion from a demographic perspective.

Abortion rates can be expressed in several ways [26]. The crude abortion rate is the number of abortions per year per 1000 total population at mid-year; it corresponds to other crude rates in vital statistics, such as the crude birth rate. A more refined, and more preferable, measurement is the general abortion rate per 1000 women of reproductive age (usually defined as 15–44 years), analogous to the general fertility rate. Age-specific abortion rates, like age-specific fertility rates, can be cumulated to successive ages, usually at 5-year intervals. Cumulation over the entire reproductive period gives the total abortion rate per 1000 women during their lifetime, in the same way as the total fertility rate is calculated. The total abortion rate thus represents the number of abortions that would be experienced by 1000 women during their reproductive lifetimes, assuming the present age-specific abortion rates (from which the total abortion rate is calculated) remain unchanged. Cumulative and total rates may be computed either on a 'period' basis, for one or several years, or on a 'cohort' basis, for women born during a given year or period.

Abortion ratios may be computed per 100 (or 1000) live births or deliveries or per 100 (or 1000) known pregnancies. The abortion ratio per 1000 deliveries is most often used in studies of legal abortions, especially if such abortions are relatively infrequent. Age-specific abortion ratios per 100 (or 1000) pregnancies are usually computed in terms of age at conception, but age-specific abortion ratios per 100 (or 1000) live births are often based on when the pregnancy ends. The latter method may introduce a substantial error for the youngest age group and smaller errors for all other age groups if a significant proportion of conceptions amongst women of the youngest age group occurs towards the end of the age period. For example, women who conceive between 19 years and 3 months and 19 years and 9 months of age will most likely appear in the 'under-20' age group if the pregnancy ends in abortion, while most of them will be in the '20–24' age group if they continue the pregnancy and give birth. The displacement of births into the next higher age group produces an inflation of the abortion ratio for the youngest age group. Conversely, the abortion ratios for all higher age groups are reduced, especially that for the highest age group. An illustrative example of the distortion of age-specific abortion ratios appears in Table 1.1. A similar distortion may also affect the abortion ratios for successive calendar years if the annual number of pregnancies is changing rapidly [26].

Examples of abortion rate, abortion ratio and, where known, total abortion rate are shown for selected countries in Table 1.2. Differences between countries are the result of a complex interaction between several factors that include, *inter alia*, desired family size, cultural attitudes to—and the status of—women in societies, the use of contraception and the provision and availability of family planning services.

Amongst countries thought to have complete and reliable statistics, the Netherlands has the lowest reported abortion rate in the world, which contradicts the claim made by most groups opposed to abortion that a non-restrictive abortion law inevitably results in a large number of abortions and a reliance on abortion as a method of family planning. The low abortion rate in the Netherlands has been ascribed to the open attitude in that country *vis-à-vis* sexuality which expresses itself through, amongst other things, universal sex education in schools and easily accessible family planning services, with special services for adolescents

Table 1.1 Live births and legal abortions related to maternal age; Czechoslovakia, 1964. Adapted from World Health Organization data [26]

Age (years)	By maternal age at birth or abortion		By estimated maternal age at conception	
	Live births	Legal abortions	Live births	Legal abortions
Numbers				
≤ 19	28 100	4 304	43 779	4 825
20–24	101 683	13 033	97 676	13 242
25–29	60 272	15 272	54 884	15 379
30–34	33 003	17 337	29 829	17 323
35–39	14 277	14 095	12 309	13 818
≥ 40	3 953	6 240	2 811	5 694
Total	241 288	70 281*	241 288	70 281*
Abortion ratios				
≤ 19	—	153.2	—	110.2
20–24	—	128.2	—	135.6
25–29	—	253.4	—	280.2
30–34	—	525.3	—	580.7
35–39	—	987.3	—	1 122.6
≥ 40	—	1 578.5	—	2 025.6

* Excludes abortions for which information on maternal age was not available.

and the provision of emergency contraception [14]. The high rates and ratios in Central and Eastern European countries reflect a desire for smaller families in societies that had—and continue to have—limited access to modern contraceptives. In the former USSR, the official data for 1987 indicated a rate of 112 per 1000 women aged 15–44 years but estimates derived from survey data suggested that the rate may have been as high as 181. Abortion rates in most of the other developed countries range from 10 to 20 per 1000 women of reproductive age, but the USA rate is somewhat higher at 28 per 1000. In the UK, the rate for Scotland is only about two-thirds that of England and Wales and, like the rate for the Netherlands, is below the range found in most developed countries.

Trends

Because of incomplete statistics and uncertainty about the number of clandestine abortions, it is not known whether the worldwide total number of induced abortions is decreasing or increasing. In fact, even

Table 1.2 Number of abortions, abortion rate per 1000 women aged 15–44 years, abortion ratio per 100 known pregnancies and total abortion rate for selected countries. From Henshaw [12]

Country (year)	No. of abortions	Rate	Ratio	Total rate
Complete statistics				
Australia (1988)	63 200	16.6	20.4	484
Bulgaria (1987)	119 900	64.7	50.7	u
Canada (1987)	63 600	10.2	14.7	299
China (1987)	10 394 500	38.8	31.4	u
Czechoslovakia (1987)	156 600	46.7	42.2	1 400
Denmark (1987)	20 800	18.3	27.0	548
England and Wales (1987)*	156 200	14.2	18.6	413
Finland (1987)	13 000	11.7	18.0	356
Hungary (1987)	84 500	38.2	40.2	1 137
The Netherlands (1986)	18 300	5.3	9.0	155
New Zealand (1987)	8 800	11.4	13.6	323
Norway (1987)	15 400	16.8	22.2	493
Scotland (1987)†	10 100	9.0	13.2	255
Singapore (1987)	21 200	30.1	32.7	840
Sweden (1987)	34 700	19.8	24.9	600
USA (1985)	1 588 600	28.0	29.7	797
Incomplete statistics				
France (1987)	161 000	13.3	17.3	406
India (1987)	588 400	3.0	2.2	u
Ireland (1987)‡	3 700	4.8	5.9	139
Italy (1987)	191 500	15.3	25.7	460
Japan (1987)	497 800	18.6	27.0	564
Soviet Union (1987)	6 818 000	111.9	54.9	u

* Residents only.
† Including abortions obtained in England.
‡ Based on Irish residents who obtained abortions in England.
u, unknown.

within a given country changes in annual abortion statistics may be difficult to interpret. For example, in countries where reporting is less than optimal and both the numerator and denominator used in calculating a rate or ratio are subject to substantial errors, a change in the extent of under-reporting can have a large effect. Likewise, increases or decreases in abortion rates and ratios can be caused by simple shifts in the age structure of a population rather than by a profound change in women's attitudes to—and requests for—abortion. An illustrative example of such a situation is provided by the abortion statistics for England and Wales (Fig. 1.3).

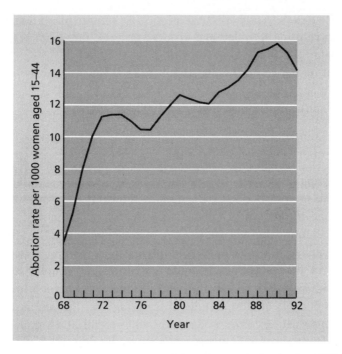

Fig. 1.3 Abortion rate among women aged 15–44 years in England and Wales. Based on Office of Population Censuses and Surveys data [27,28].

The initial rapid rise of the abortion rate from 3.5 per 1000 women aged 15–44 years in 1968 (the year in which the Abortion Act became operative) to a level rate of about 11 in the 1970s can be attributed to the increasing availability of legal termination of pregnancy and the corresponding decrease in clandestine abortion as women and their doctors learnt how to use the new law. During the 1980s, the rate rose gradually by about 35% and then decreased by 11% from 1990 to 1992.

The increase in the abortion rate during the 1980s can largely be explained by the rise in the birth rate that peaked in 1962 [29,30]. Women born during the 'baby boom' reached sexual maturity during the 1980s. As a result, the proportion of women under 30 years of age (a group that has far more births and abortions than older women) increased during the 1980s and, without any change in the age-specific abortion rates, this by itself was expected to increase the number of terminations by 14% between 1972 and 1989 [31]. Additional factors that probably played a role in the rising rate from 1976 until 1990, and the fall since then, are changes in attitudes to marriage and single motherhood. Between 1973 and 1990, the proportion of married women in the '20–24' age group fell from 50 to 27%; similar, albeit less dramatic, falls occurred in the older age groups. Overall, amongst women aged 15–44 years the proportion marrying fell from 68 to 53%. This had a significant influence on the abortion rate as the average rate for married women during that period was only about 8.5 per 1000 compared to 27 per 1000 for unmarried women.

Effect of abortion on fertility rate

In the demographic transition, induced abortion is an essential element, although its importance as a determinant of fertility rate varies depending on the stage of the demographic transition process. Generally, as couples begin to feel motivated to limit the size of their family and the fertility rate starts to decline, the abortion rate frequently rises initially because the provision of contraceptives is often still low and couples are poorly informed about their use. At this point in the demographic transition the effect of abortion on the fertility rate is highest. Subsequently, when contraceptive use becomes sufficiently widespread and smaller families are achieved, the resort to abortion (legal or clandestine) diminishes, but many developing countries have not yet reached this point [12].

Demographic and social influences

Age, marital status, parity, ethnicity, prevalence of contraceptive use and level of education all influence use of abortion. However, detailed information about many of these factors is often not available to permit comprehensive analysis. Moreover, as discussed earlier, the information that is available cannot always be fully relied upon due to under-reporting and the possibility that certain factors, such as age and socioeconomic status, may influence access to abortion. Consequently, the findings described below, being based on a relatively small number of countries thought to have fairly reliable statistics (many of the European countries, the USA and Canada), are probably not representative of the global situation.

Within any given population the two subgroups that most often utilize abortion are young unmarried women wishing to delay the birth of their first child and married women with children who want to space additional children or end childbearing [11].

Age

The proportional distribution of abortions and the abortion rate and ratio, by age, for a selection of representative countries with reasonably reliable statistics are shown in Fig. 1.4.

In most of the English-speaking developed countries (Australia, Canada, England and Wales, New Zealand, Scotland and the USA) in which contraception has been available for many years and sterilization is

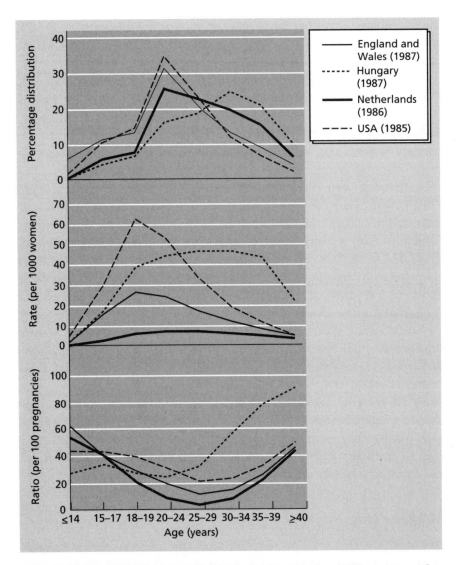

Fig. 1.4 Percentage distribution of abortions, abortion rate (per 1000 women aged 15–44 years) and abortion ratio (per 100 known pregnancies), by age, in selected countries. From Van Look and von Hertzen [14].

well accepted, nearly half or more of all abortions are done in women under 25 years of age.

In contrast, in countries in which availability and use of modern contraceptive methods including sterilization are low, such as the Central and Eastern European countries, of which Hungary is an example, the majority of abortions are done in women aged 35 years or older. In these countries, unmarried women who become pregnant generally marry and continue the pregnancy, but to older married couples abortion is often the only means available for spacing or preventing childbirth. A similar situation exists in Japan where the pill has not been approved for contraceptive use and sterilization is not common.

In several Western European countries such as the Netherlands and the Scandinavian countries the proportional distribution by age is intermediate between that in England and Wales and that in Hungary. This can be explained by a greater utilization of contraceptives by younger women and a lower reliance on sterilization at older ages in these countries compared to English-speaking developed countries.

In keeping with the above, the age-specific abortion rates peak at 18–19 years in most developed countries. The exceptions are Central and Eastern Europe and Japan in which rates do not show a distinctive maximum but remain elevated well into the older age groups. As illustrated in Fig. 1.4, abortion rates of teenagers vary greatly; amongst countries with reliable statistics the rate is highest in the USA at 45.7 abortions per 1000 women aged ≤ 19 years, while the rate of the Netherlands is the lowest at 4.2.

The abortion ratio (which is a measure of the proportion of known pregnancies that are aborted) is typically high amongst teenagers, declines to a minimum between the ages of 25–34 years and then increases again (Fig. 1.4). In Western Europe, North America and Australia between one-third and half of teenage pregnancies are terminated by legal abortion [32]. In Central and Eastern European countries with reliable data, such as Bulgaria and Hungary, ratios are particularly high in the older age groups, reflecting the fact that women in these countries have to rely on abortion to limit their family size.

Marital status

As can be expected from the distribution of abortions by age, the majority of women having abortions in English-speaking developed countries and in several Western European countries (France, Germany, the Netherlands and Scandinavia) are unmarried. In contrast, in the remaining countries for which data are available, more than two-thirds of the women who obtain abortions are married [12]. In most countries, amongst women having abortions, the proportion married has been decreasing during the last decade. Changes in marital status of the population resulting from delayed marriage and childbearing, lower marriage rates and higher divorce rates are probably responsible for this trend.

Data for developing countries are sparse but, where available, as for India and Singapore, women having an abortion are usually married; the same situation probably prevails in most of the other Asian countries. In both Africa and Latin America the distribution is thought to be intermediate between that in Asia and that in Europe: the proportion of abortions in unmarried women in Africa and Latin America is higher than in Asia, although probably still less than half [33].

In all populations for which data exist, the abortion ratio is substantially greater amongst unmarried women, including never-married and previously married women, than amongst married women. Data from England and Wales illustrate this point (Fig. 1.5). The abortion ratio for married women has remained constant since 1972 at about eight abortions per 100 births. In contrast, the ratio in unmarried women increased sharply from 53 in 1972 to 68 in 1976, remained more or less level until 1981 and has steadily declined since then to a value of 52 in 1991. The decline could be interpreted as evidence that unmarried couples used contraception more effectively in the last decade, but the relative increase in the proportion of older cohabiting couples was probably of greater importance. Older couples are likely to be more effective with contraception and may choose to continue unplanned pregnancies more often than those who are younger (D. Paintin, unpublished data).

Parity

Because age, marital status and parity are interrelated, the distribution pattern of abortions according to parity is linked to the patterns of the other two variables. Thus, in countries in which the majority of abortions are in young (unmarried) rather than older (married) women, those having abortions tend to have few or no children. For example, in English-speaking and Western European countries (except for Italy), around 50% of the women having an abortion are childless. In contrast,

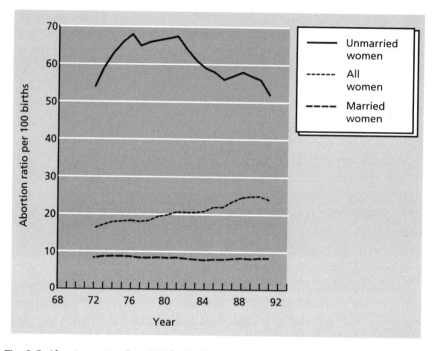

Fig. 1.5 Abortion ratios (per 100 births) by marital status for women aged 15–44 years resident in England and Wales. Based on Office of Population Censuses and Surveys data [29,30].

in Central and Eastern European countries, less than 20% of the women have no children. Marked changes in this pattern have been observed in some countries in the last 10–20 years. In Singapore, for instance, from 1970 to 1987, the percentage of women with no children having an abortion increased from < 1 to 41%, while those having an abortion with at least five children dropped from 53 to 2% [12].

Socioeconomic status

Few studies have examined the effect of socioeconomic status on abortion rates in countries that have non-restrictive laws and adequate, easily accessible services, because the relevant data are not collected systematically. In the USA, an inverse relationship has been reported between abortion rate and income [10]. Similarly, in Tayside (Scotland), the majority of legal abortions were performed amongst teenagers from deprived homes [34].

Abortion rates amongst urban women are usually higher than those of rural populations. The reasons for these differences are probably complex and may include the higher cost of childrearing in the city, the greater motivation of the usually better-educated urban women to balance childbearing against career development and the higher concentration of services, both legal and illegal, in the cities. Women may also find it easier to seek an abortion in the relative anonymity of the city [11].

Ethnicity

Few studies have been able to compare abortion rates between different racial and ethnic groups either because the required data are not collected or because of the difficulty in controlling for important variables such as socioeconomic status, educational attainment, access to family planning and abortion services, etc. In the USA, in 1987, the abortion rate among non-white women was 2.7 times higher than that of white women [35]. Unintended pregnancies are relatively more common amongst women of minority groups and they lead to both more abortions and more unplanned births. The higher rate of unplanned pregnancies among minorities is due in part to a lower prevalence of contraceptive use and in part to higher contraceptive failure rates. In the Netherlands, the abortion rates among resident immigrants are far higher than that of native Dutch women [11], which can be attributed, at least in part, to the lower prevalence of contraceptive use amongst the immigrant groups [7].

Length of gestation

The length of pregnancy at the time of abortion is dependent on the availability of adequate and accessible services and also on the provisions of the abortion law. In virtually all countries where 'liberalization' of the law was accompanied by easy access to well-functioning services there has been a shift toward earlier abortion. For England and Wales the proportion of abortions performed after the end of the first trimester (i.e. later than 12 weeks after the onset of the last menstrual period) declined from 34% in 1969 to 14% in 1987 [20]. This last figure is still markedly higher, however, than in most other European countries. For example, in all Scandinavian countries, the percentage of second-trimester abortions is well below 5%. Second-trimester abortions were also rare in former Czechoslovakia and Yugoslavia as well as in Hungary and other Eastern

European countries where they are generally authorized on medical indications only [11].

The stage of gestation when women present for abortion is important since it determines the type of procedure and the risk of morbidity and mortality (see Chapter 6). More widespread use of medical methods for inducing abortion such as the combination regimen of an antiprogestogen followed by a prostaglandin may further favour the shift towards abortion at earlier durations of gestation since these medical methods are sufficiently efficacious only when used within the first 8–9 weeks [36].

Unsafe abortion—the silent tragedy

Unsafe abortion has been defined by the WHO as a procedure for terminating an unwanted pregnancy either by persons lacking the necessary skills, or in an environment lacking the minimal medical standards or both [2].

Unsafe abortion may be induced in unhygienic conditions by the woman herself, by a non-medical person or by a health worker. It may be provoked by insertion of a solid object (usually a root, twig or catheter) into the uterus, an improperly performed dilatation and curettage procedure, ingestion of harmful substances or exertion of external force. The mortality and morbidity risks depend on the facilities and skill of the provider, the method used and certain characteristics of the woman herself (for example, her general health, age, parity, presence of genital tract infection, etc.). The risks are also dependent on the availability, utilization and quality of treatment facilities when complications occur [2].

For the reasons described above, the number of unsafe abortions and the risks associated with them can only be estimated indirectly. A summary of the WHO's most recent global and regional estimates on incidence of, and mortality from, unsafe abortions is given in Table 1.3. Worldwide, some 20 million unsafe abortions take place each year; this represents nearly one in 10 pregnancies, or a ratio of one unsafe abortion to seven births. Almost 90% of unsafe abortions occur in developing countries [2].

An estimated 70 000 women die each year due to complications from unsafe abortions. Inevitably, this estimate has a large margin of error and the number could be as low as 50 000 or as high as 100 000. The figures in Table 1.4 indicate that, in 1990, the risk of dying from an unsafe abortion was at least 15 times greater in developing countries than in industrialized countries and as much as 40–50 times greater in some

Table 1.3 Global and regional estimates on incidence of, and mortality from, unsafe abortions (figures may not add to totals due to rounding)*. From World Health Organization data [2]

Region	No. of unsafe abortions (1000s)	Unsafe abortions per 1000 women of 15–49 years	No. of deaths from unsafe abortion	Mortality from unsafe abortion per 100 000 live births	Per cent of maternal deaths
World total	20 000	15	70 000	49	13
'More' developed countries	2 340	8	600	4	14
'Less' developed countries	17 620	17	69 000	55	13
Africa	3 740	26	23 000	83	13
Asia†	9 240	12	40 000	47	12
Europe	260	2	100	2	10
Latin America	4 620	41	6 000	48	24
Oceania†	20	17	< 100	29	5
Former USSR	2 080	30	500	10	23

* For Northern America where the incidence of unsafe abortion is negligible, no estimate has been made.
† Australia, Japan and New Zealand have been excluded from the regional estimates, but are included in the total for developed countries.

regions of the world. In the USA, for example, the case fatality rate of legal induced abortion is now 0.6 per 100 000 procedures, making it as safe as an injection of penicillin [37].

As is evident from Table 1.3, there are large differences in incidence of, and mortality from, unsafe abortion between regions. Among developing regions, Asia has the lowest abortion rate at 12 per 1000 women of reproductive age, but the largest absolute number of unsafe abortions because it has the largest population of women in the reproductive age group. Nearly half of the world's unsafe abortions, and more than half of the worldwide total of deaths due to unsafe abortion, occur in Asia. In Latin America, the unsafe abortion rate of 40 per 1000 women of reproductive age corresponds to more than one unsafe abortion for every three births, and the abortion mortality ratio of 48 per 100 000 live births represents nearly a quarter of all maternal deaths. In Africa, the abortion mortality ratio is over 80 per 100 000 live births, and the absolute number of deaths represents one-third of the worldwide total. Like in Asia, abortion-related deaths in Africa account for some 12–13% of all

Table 1.4 Global and regional estimated risk of death from unsafe abortion (figures may not add to totals due to rounding). From World Health Organization data [2]

Region	No. of unsafe abortions (1000s)	No. of deaths from unsafe abortion
World total	20 000	70 000
More developed countries*	2 340	600
Less developed countries	17 620	69 000
Africa	3 740	23 000
Asia*	9 240	40 000
Europe	260	100
Latin America	4 620	6 000
Oceania*	20	< 100
Former USSR	2 080	500

* Australia, Japan and New Zealand have been excluded from the regional estimates, but are included in the total for developed countries.

maternal deaths; this percentage is relatively low due to the fact that overall maternal mortality in these two regions is high. Although induced abortion is legal in the countries of the former USSR, services are inadequate and their quality is often poor, resulting in a high unsafe abortion rate of 30 per 1000 women of reproductive age, the world's second highest after Latin America. Almost 25% of maternal deaths in this region are related to unsafe abortion.

The 70 000 women who die each year from botched abortions are a tragic illustration that neither restrictive abortion laws nor lack of access to professional care stop women from seeking abortion. Many of the unintended pregnancies can be avoided by increasing access to acceptable and affordable methods of family planning, including emergency contraception. However, neither the methods that are presently available nor the people who use them are perfect, and it would be unrealistic to believe that the recourse to abortion can be totally eliminated. The mere recognition of this fact would go a long way towards finding appropriate solutions for the public health problems due to unsafe abortion, 'one of the great neglected problems of health care in developing countries' [1].

Acknowledgement

We are grateful to Dr D. Paintin for permission to use some of his unpublished material including Figs 1.3 and 1.5.

References

1 Fathalla MF. Reproductive health in the world: two decades of progress and the challenge ahead. In: Khanna J, Van Look PFA, Griffin PD, eds. *Reproductive Health: a Key to a Brighter Future*. Geneva: World Health Organization, 1992: 3–31.
2 Maternal Health and Safe Motherhood Programme. *Abortion. A Tabulation of Available Data on the Frequency and Mortality of Unsafe Abortion*, 2nd edn. Geneva: World Health Organization Division of Family Health, 1993.
3 World Health Organization. *Official Records* 1967; 160: 25.
4 *Report of the International Conference on Population, 1984*. Mexico City, 6–14 August 1984. New York: United Nations, 1984.
5 *Report of the International Conference on Population and Development, 1994*. Cairo, 5–13 September 1994. New York: United Nations, 1994.
6 Jacobson JL. *The Global Politics of Abortion*. Worldwatch paper no. 97. Washington: Worldwatch Institute, 1990.
7 Rademakers J. *Abortus in Nederland 1989/1990*. Jaarverslag van de landelijke abortusregistratie. Utrecht: Stimezo-Onderzoek, 1992.
8 Bromham DR, Cartmill RSV. Knowledge and use of secondary contraception among patients requesting termination of pregnancy. *Br Med J* 1993; 306: 556–557.
9 Van Look PFA, von Hertzen H. Emergency contraception. *Br Med Bull* 1993; 49: 158–170.
10 Segal SJ, LaGuardia KD. Termination of pregnancy—a global view. *Baillières Clin Obstet Gynaecol* 1990; 4: 235–247.
11 Tietze C, Henshaw SK. *Induced Abortion. A World Review 1986*, 6th edn. New York: Alan Guttmacher Institute, 1986.
12 Henshaw SK. Induced abortion: a world review, 1990. *Fam Plann Perspect* 1990; 22: 76–89.
13 Sundström K. *Abortion: a Reproductive Health Issue*. Washington: World Bank, Department of Population, Health and Nutrition, 1993.
14 Van Look PFA, von Hertzen H. Demographic aspects of induced abortion. *Curr Obstet Gynaecol* 1993; 3: 2–10.
15 Dunstan GR. *The Human Embryo: Aristotle and the Arabic and European Traditions*. Exeter: University of Exeter Press, 1990.
16 Department of Economic and Social Development. *Abortion Policies: a Global Review*. Volume 1. *Afghanistan to France*. New York: United Nations, 1992.
17 Department for Economic and Social Information and Policy Analysis. *Abortion Policies: a Global Review*. Volume 2. *Gabon to Norway*. New York: United Nations, 1993.
18 Department for Economic and Social Information and Policy Analysis. *Abortion Policies: a Global Review*. Volume 3. *Oman to Zimbabwe*. United Nations: New York, 1995.
19 Potts M, Diggory P, Peel J. *Abortion*. Cambridge: Cambridge University Press, 1977.
20 Munday D, Francome C, Savage W. Twenty one years of legal abortion. *Br Med J* 1989; 298: 1231–1234.
21 David HP. Abortion in Europe, 1920–91: a public health perspective. *Stud Fam Plann* 1992; 23: 1–22.
22 David HP. Abortion legislation in Europe, 1991–1993. *Entre Nous* (The European

Family Planning Magazine). Copenhagen: WHO Regional Office for Europe, 1994; 25: 13.

23 Cook RJ. Clandestine abortions are not necessarily illegal. *Fam Plann Perspect* 1991; 23: 283.

24 Paxman JM, Rizo A, Brown L, Benson J. The clandestine epidemic: the practice of unsafe abortion in Latin America. *Stud Fam Plann* 1993; 24: 205–226.

25 Barreto T, Campbell OM, Davies JL *et al.* Investigating induced abortion in developing countries: methods and problems. *Stud Fam Plann* 1992; 23: 159–170.

26 World Health Organization. *Spontaneous and Induced Abortion.* Report of a WHO Scientific Group. Geneva: World Health Organization, 1970 (WHO Technical Report Series, no. 461).

27 Office of Population Censuses and Surveys. *Abortion Statistics 1991.* Series AB, no. 18. London: HMSO, 1993.

28 Office of Population Censuses and Surveys. *Population Trends.* No. 74. London: HMSO, 1993.

29 Office of Population Censuses and Surveys. *Birth Statistics 1837–1983.* Series FM1, no. 13. London: HMSO, 1987.

30 Office of Population Censuses and Surveys. *Birth Statistics 1992.* Series FM1, no. 21. London: HMSO, 1994.

31 Baird DT. Abortion rates still rising. *Br Med J* 1991; 303: 579.

32 Henshaw SK, Morrow E. *Induced Abortion: a World Review. 1990 Supplement.* New York: Alan Guttmacher Institute, 1990.

33 Liskin L. Complications of abortion in developing countries. *Pop Rep* (F) 1980; 105–155.

34 Smith T. Influence of socioeconomic factors on attaining targets for reducing teenage pregnancies. *Br Med J* 1993; 306: 1232–1235.

35 Henshaw SK, Koonin LM, Smith JC. Characteristics of US women having abortions, 1987. *Fam Plann Perspect* 1991; 23: 75–81.

36 Van Look PFA, von Hertzen H. Clinical uses of antiprogestogens. *Hum Reprod Update* 1995; 1: 19–34.

37 Gold RB. *Abortion and Women's Health. A Turning Point for America.* New York and Washington: Alan Guttmacher Institute, 1990.

2   Overview of Abortion Techniques

David T. Baird

Introduction

The establishment and maintenance of pregnancy depends on a carefully coordinated sequence of events involving ovulation, fertilization of the ovum, implantation of the embryo in the endometrium and subsequent nourishment of the growing embryo and fetus. Throughout pregnancy, the uterus is kept in a quiescent state due mainly to the action of progesterone on the myometrium. The uterus is intrinsically a contractile organ which, in the absence of suppression, exhibits a pattern of spontaneous contractions which result in expulsion of its contents. Consequently, inhibition of this propensity to contraction is absolutely essential for the maintenance of pregnancy. In addition, the cervix of the uterus remains closed during pregnancy and any softening and dilation is likely to lead to abortion. Thus, any substance or technique which could reverse these physiological changes that occur in pregnancy could potentially be used as a method of abortion.

This chapter outlines what is known about the physiological mechanisms responsible for the establishment and maintenance of pregnancy and indicates potential ways of interrupting these processes for the induction of abortion.

Establishment of pregnancy

Ovarian steroids are essential for the establishment of pregnancy. Oestradiol secreted by the developing follicle stimulates proliferation of the endometrium which, following ovulation, is converted into a secretory endometrium under the influence of progesterone produced by the corpus luteum. Although the corpus luteum also secretes oestradiol, it appears that in the non-human primate and in women, only progesterone is essential to induce the changes in the endometrium which are necessary for successful implantation of the blastocyst [1,2]. Pregnancy has occurred in rhesus monkeys that are treated with progesterone alone following oophorectomy in the early luteal phase [3,4]. In agonadal women and castrate monkeys, successful pregnancies have been reported following embryo transfer after treatment with exogenous steroids involving oestrogen before transfer followed by progesterone alone after transfer [2]. The changes induced by progesterone in the endometrium include increased tortuosity of the glands, the appearance of secretory material both within the cytoplasm of the glandular cells and in the lumen of the glands, as well as stromal oedema [5]. Receptors for both oestradiol and progesterone are progressively lost from the glandular cells with a corresponding increase in concentration of progesterone receptors in the stroma [6]. These latter cells undergo morphological and functional changes collectively known as decidualization, a process that occurs even in the non-pregnant cycle during the late luteal phase. Coincidental with this change in morphology, the decidualized endometrium secretes a range of progesterone-dependent proteins including PP14, PP12, relaxin, prolactin, and so on [7]. The function of these proteins is not entirely clear, although it has been suggested that PP14 may have immuno-suppressive properties. PP12 is now known to be identical to insulin-like growth factor binding protein I (IGFBP-I), a protein which appears to be a modulator of the action of insulin-like growth factor (IGF) in many tissues. For example, IGFBP-I influences the mitogenic effect of IGF on endo-metrial cells by inhibiting the binding of IGF to its membrane receptors [8].

Implantation in women involves, in the first instance, apposition of the blastocyst at the embryonic pole to the endometrium on about the sixth to eighth day of the luteal phase. Although the data in women are scant, evidence from animal experiments suggest that a series of interactions between the trophectoderm and the decidua are important in this early process. Invasion of the decidua involves digestion of the extracellular matrix of the surface epithelium followed by migration of the cytotrophoblast cells within the decidua [5]. The alterations of integrin molecules allow invasion of the trophoblast cells to occur which eventually leads to establishment of the chorionic villi of the placenta. Extravillous cytotrophoblast cells invade the stroma and the maternal blood vessels, the muscular walls of which are replaced. This invasion of maternal vessels reduces the resistance to flow and is thought to ensure a constant and generous blood supply to the placental bed.

As soon as the blastocyst attaches to the endometrium, the mother is exposed to embryonic proteins which are potentially antigenic [9]. All mammals have devised mechanisms, which are not fully understood, to prevent rejection by the mother of the embryo or fetus [10]. In women, the extravillous trophoblast expresses an unusual type of class I histocompatibility locus antigen (HLA) which is different from that found in somatic cells [11]. It is mainly intracellular, slightly smaller and non-pleiomorphic, i.e. it does not differ between individuals. It has been suggested that this unique type of HLA antigen is recognized by a special type of lymphocyte (the large granular lymphocyte, LGL) found in abundance in late secretory endometrium and decidua. LGLs have a unique phenotype and are only found in the uterus. Although they possess natural killer activity, their function may be to recognize the unique class of HLA antigen present in extravillous trophoblast and, in doing so, inhibit immunological rejection.

In addition to the progesterone-dependent proteins mentioned above, it is likely that trophoblast, uterine stroma and epithelial cells as well as lymphohaemopoietic cells such as macrophages and leucocytes play important roles during implantation [12,13]. Proliferation of endometrial stroma cells, decidualization, growth of the conceptus and trophoblast and formation of new blood vessels (angiogenesis) are all subject to control by locally produced growth factors and cytokines as well as systemic hormones. Indeed, there is considerable evidence that such factors are involved in the mechanism by which steroid hormones affect uterine function. For example, epidermal growth factor (EGF) is a small polypeptide that stimulates proliferation and differentiation of a range of cells in the body including those in the endometrium [14]; mRNAs for EGF and the proteins are present in the uterus and EGF receptors have been demonstrated in the human uterus. Oestrogen stimulates the production of both EGF and its receptor in uterine epithelial cells and myometrium. Thus, EGF and transforming growth factor-α (TGF-α), which binds to the same receptor, are likely candidates for paracrine and autocrine factors which may be important during the interaction that occurs between trophoblast and maternal decidua at the time of implantation.

Recently, there has been considerable interest in the report that one such substance—leukaemia-inhibiting factor (LIF)—is essential for implantation in the mouse [15,16]. Implantation does not occur in transgenic mice that are deficient in LIF due to site-directed mutagenesis. Blastocysts from LIF-deficient mice implant normally when transferred to the uterus of normal mice, thus establishing that the defect is in the maternal decidual response. These findings, therefore, raise the possibility of devising new methods of contraception and/or abortion by interfering with LIF or other local factors that are essential for implantation to occur.

Maintenance of pregnancy

Although all the factors necessary for implantation have not yet been identified, decidual transformation is induced by progesterone, the continuous secretion of which is essential for the establishment and maintenance of pregnancy. As soon as the embryo attaches to the decidua on day 6–8 of the luteal phase, human chorionic gonadotrophin (hCG) is secreted by the trophectoderm and can be detected in the peripheral blood by day 8–9 [17,18]. hCG binds to the luteinizing hormone (LH) receptor on the corpus luteum and stimulates the continued secretion of progesterone. The secretion of progesterone by the corpus luteum is essential for the maintenance of pregnancy in the first 5 weeks (7 weeks of amenorrhoea) until adequate amounts are produced by the placenta [19]. If the corpus luteum is enucleated in early pregnancy, there is a drastic fall in the concentration of progesterone and abortion occurs in association with an increase in uterine contractility.

The way by which hCG maintains the structure and function of the corpus luteum is not entirely understood. In the non-pregnant cycle, progesterone production declines at about day 12 of the luteal phase and menstruation ensues within 2 or 3 days. Although the secretion of pituitary LH declines during the luteal phase, luteal regression is not due solely to deficiency of LH because it occurs even if the levels of LH are maintained by injection of exogenous gonadotrophin-releasing hormone (GnRH)[20]. It may be that the very high levels of hCG which are found in the luteal phase of the pregnancy cycle have a luteotrophic effect that is difficult to mimic with the shorter acting LH. Whatever the mechanism, hCG is essential for the maintenance of the corpus luteum, and neutralization of chorionic gonadotrophin (CG) in monkeys by anti-hCG antibodies results in abortion [18]. This observation is the basis of current clinical trials involving active immunization against hCG as a contraceptive [21,22].

Progesterone has effects on the myometrium and cervix as well as the endometrium. The luteal phase of the cycle is characterized by uterine contractions of very low amplitude and the basal intrauterine pressure is relatively low [23]. At luteal regression there is an increase in high-amplitude coordinated contractions, characteristic of menstruation. Thus, changes in contractility are a consequence of the fall in the concentration of progesterone because they can be reproduced by the administration of antagonists of progesterone such as mifepristone [23]. Mifepristone induces a similar increase in contractility when given to pregnant women [24]. The increase in uterine contractility produced by the withdrawal of progesterone is probably mediated at the level of both the myometrium and the decidua. Progesterone induces hyperpolarization of the membrane of the myometrial cells, thus rendering a greater change in electrical potential necessary before contraction can occur [25]. In addition, progesterone inhibits the conversion of these action potentials to contractions by preventing the increase of intracellular calcium ions. Uterine contractions require the coordination of many myometrial cells which are coupled by connections called gap-junctions. Gap-junctions are intercellular channels that link cells to their neighbours by allowing the passage of inorganic ions and small molecules. The connections consist of small pores that are composed of proteins, named connexins, the synthesis of which is suppressed in the uterus by progesterone. Thus, during pregnancy, coordinated uterine contractions are rare due to a relative insensitivity of the uterus to electrical excitability as well as to the lack of propagation of any stimulus. Prior to the onset of labour, or following the administration of antiprogestins, there is an increase in the number of gap-junctions between myometrial cells.

The uterus is a rich source of potential uterotonic agents such as prostaglandins and endothelium [26,27]. During the menstrual cycle, under the influence of oestradiol and progesterone, the endometrium acquires an increased capacity for the synthesis of prostaglandins. While the levels of progesterone remain high during the luteal phase, this biosynthetic capacity is suppressed and, hence, the uterus remains relatively quiescent [28]. When the levels of progesterone fall during luteal regression, the stromal and epithelial cells of the endometrium release large amounts of prostaglandins which are thought to be involved in vascular changes associated with menstruation as well as with the increased myometrial activity [26]. The inhibition of prostaglandin dehydrogenase that occurs in association with a fall of progesterone concentration at luteal regression, further increases the effective local concentration of any prostaglandin that is synthesized by the uterus [29,30].

In early pregnancy, the concentration of progesterone is maintained due to persistence of the corpus luteum and, hence, the release of prostaglandins by the endometrium/decidua is prevented. In addition, the biosynthetic capacity of the decidua to produce prostaglandins is suppressed [31]. The mechanism by which the ability of decidua to synthesize prostaglandins is markedly impaired in early pregnancy is not fully understood. It may involve the release by the embryo of some inhibiting substance analogous to ovine trophoblastic protein (oTP), a protein similar to interferon-α which is released by the sheep embryo early in pregnancy, at about the time of expected luteal regression [32].

Spontaneous abortion

In comparison with other mammals, human beings have a seemingly very inefficient reproductive system. For a normal healthy woman, the chances of becoming pregnant in any one cycle following unprotected intercourse with a fertile man around the time of ovulation, are probably not more than 25% [33,34]. The fertilization rate is probably higher because many very early embryos are lost before or around the time of implantation and, hence, these conceptions are unrecognized because menstruation occurs at the expected time. Analysis of pre-implantation embryos obtained following *in vitro* fertilization (IVF) has demonstrated that about 30% have an abnormality of their karyotype, many of which are incompatible with further development [35]. Thus, one of the reasons for the apparently low fecundity of human beings is a high incidence of abnormal embryos [36].

Further evidence to support this explanation comes from the chromosomal analysis of spontaneous abortions. About 10–15% of recognized pregnancies end in abortion, with the majority occurring in the first 10 weeks [37,38]. Over 50% of embryos from spontaneous abortions have abnormal karyotypes and it is presumed that the abortion is secondary to failure of normal fetal development [39]. By using banding techniques to identify the origin of the individual chromosomes, it has been shown that the majority of chromosome anomalies are maternal in origin and, hence, must occur during meiosis of the egg [40,41]. It is possible that the relatively high incidence of errors of meiosis is related to damage incurred over a woman's lifetime due to cumulative environmental insults. Whatever the reason, the majority of early spontaneous abortions are associated with abnormal embryos and their rejection is an important mechanism to allow rapid return to fertile cycles.

The incidence of recognizable fetal abnormalities in spontaneous abortions declines as gestation advances [42]. Abortion may be associated with maternal disease such as lupus, malaria, and so on. Local infection arising systemically or transcervically is also a cause of spontaneous abortion. Although the mechanism by which these factors result in abortion is not understood, it is likely that there is a final common pathway involving leucocyte infiltration, release of cytokines and prostaglandins [43]. Indeed, it has been proposed that menstruation, spontaneous abortion and parturition can all be regarded as inflammatory processes that involve many of the same cellular mechanisms as inflammation which occurs in response to bacterial infection [44,45]. They are all characterized by hyperaemia, transmigration of leucocytes into the extravascular compartment of the tissue and the release of prostaglandins and cytokines from stromal and epithelial cells as well as cells of the lymphohaemopoietic system.

A small proportion of women (probably about 1%) have early spontaneous abortion repeatedly [37]. This group of women with recurrent spontaneous abortion represents a considerable clinical problem for which little if any effective treatment is known [46]. The proportion of embryos that are karyotypically abnormal is lower in this group of women than in sporadic abortions and, hence, it is presumed that in the majority there is some other aetiology. In women with recurrent miscarriage, a relatively low number of small granular lymphocytes is associated with failure of the trophoblast to invade the spiral arterioles and convert them into low-resistance vessels [47]. There is some evidence that there may be a breakdown in the normal mechanisms by which the fetal allograft is tolerated, but clinical trials of treatment involving attempts to induce immunological recognition have been inconclusive [46].

The changes that occur in the uterus and cervix during abortion induced by antiprogestins may provide a model for spontaneous abortion. Within 12 h of the administration of mifepristone there is an increase in uterine contractility which reaches a maximum by about 36 h [24]. The increase in contractility is probably due, in part, to an increase in the production of prostaglandins by the decidua [48]. As mentioned above, there is a striking reduction in the activity of prostaglandin dehydrogenase, particularly in the perivascular tissue, which leads to an increase in the concentration of prostaglandins F and E (PGF and PGE) [49,50]. PGE is known to induce hyperaemia and extravasation of blood into the extracapillary space [51,52]. Moreover, experiments *in vivo* and *in vitro* have demonstrated that blockage of the action of progesterone by mifepristone is followed by the release of interleukin 8 (IL-8)—a potent chemotactic cytokine for leucocytes [53]. Thus, following mifepristone, a positive feedback loop is established which leads to hyperaemia, leucocyte infiltration and release of prostaglandins and cytokines within the decidua and cervix. Attraction of leucocytes to the cervix may be important in the softening process because they are a rich source of lytic enzymes such as collagenase and proteases, the release of which is essential in the remodelling of the cervical ground substance [54].

Methods of inducing abortion

In spite of the complex interactions that are required for implantation, it is surprisingly difficult to dislodge an embryo or fetus once implantation has been completed. Spontaneous abortion occurs at a varying time interval following the death of the fetus and is associated with necrosis and bleeding from the decidua, softening and dilatation of the cervix, and uterine contractions which expel the fetus and placenta [19]. These events usually occur over several days or weeks and are associated with changes in the hormonal environment. The placenta secretes decreasing amounts of hCG which results in a fall in the secretion of progesterone by the corpus luteum. This, together with the reduction in the production of progesterone by the placenta, leads to a decrease in the level of progesterone in peripheral blood with consequent changes in myometrial contractility and prostaglandin production by the decidua and cervix. Prostaglandins are thought to play a role in the changes in ground substance and connective tissue that cause cervical softening. This softening process becomes progressively more important as the length of gestation increases. After 8–10 weeks, significant dilatation of the cervix is required before the uterine contents can be expelled.

A wide variety of methods to induce abortion have been tried since the beginning of recorded history. The methods have been based either on mechanical dilatation of the cervix and removal of the uterine contents (surgical) or ingestion of substances that will promote the process of abortion (medical). The effectiveness of methods that involve the insertion of tubes or substances into the uterus, e.g. Utus paste or bark of slippery elm, probably rely on their ability to induce an inflammatory response in association with infection. As mentioned above, menstruation, spontaneous abortion and parturition all involve mechanisms very similar to those that occur during bacterial infection. It would, therefore, not be surprising to find that intrauterine infection is usually followed by abortion.

Mechanical or surgical methods

Pregnancy can be safely terminated by vacuum aspiration or dilatation and evacuation (D & E) up to 20 weeks gestation, as reviewed in Chapters 3–5. Although dilatation of the cervix can be performed mechanically, it is now recognized that some prior preparation of the cervix is preferable in order to reduce the risk of damage during the dilatation process. Current methods involve prostaglandin pessaries applied locally for up to 6 h or insertion of cervical dilators made of seaweed or other hygroscopic substances. Recent data suggest that softening of the cervix can be achieved at any stage of pregnancy following the administration of antiprogestogens [55,56]. The changes induced by antiprogestogens probably simulate more accurately those which occur during spontaneous abortion. However, the existing data suggest that it is necessary to wait at least 24 h after giving mifepristone to obtain optimal effect on the cervix [57]. This relatively long interval may make the use of antiprogestogens for this purpose difficult for logistic reasons. As we understand more about the molecular mechanisms involved in cervical ripening it may be possible to devise more effective and selective agents to prepare the cervix prior to surgical abortion.

Medical methods

Of the many methods for the medical induction of abortion that have been tried over the centuries, the most promising development has been the combination of antiprogestins and prostaglandins [58]. Withdrawal of progesterone support can be achieved either by inhibiting the synthesis of progesterone, e.g. with epostane, or by blocking the progesterone receptors with antagonists such as mifepristone. Both approaches result in an increase in myometrial contractions and uterine bleeding and have been shown in clinical trials to induce abortion of pregnancies up to 20 weeks gestation [59–65]. However, the incidence of complete abortion varies from 85% at 6 weeks of amenorrhoea to about 50% at gestations over 9 weeks. In order to increase the rate of complete abortion it is necessary to combine the antiprogestin with a prostaglandin such as gemeprost given 36–48 h later. It is possible to induce abortion with prostaglandins alone [59]. However, the dose required is associated with troublesome side effects such as diarrhoea and vomiting in many women. Because antiprogestins sensitize the uterus to prostaglandins and induce softening and dilatation of the cervix, the dose of prostaglandin required to complete the abortion is reduced fivefold and, hence, side effects are much less frequent.

Another potential method of reducing the level of progesterone in early pregnancy is by inducing regression of the corpus luteum. The classical experiments of Csapo and Pulkkinen demonstrated that the corpus luteum is necessary for the maintenance of early pregnancy and its enucleation in the first 7 weeks leads to abortion [19]. As mentioned earlier, in monkeys, injection of antibodies to hCG results in abortion [21]. While immunization is unlikely to be practical in women, analogues of hCG that bind to the receptors but do not stimulate progesterone secretion, could be an effective alternative strategy. However, whether or not it would be possible to inject sufficient antagonist to neutralize the very large amounts of hCG secreted even in the early stages of pregnancy, is not known.

The trophoblast is a very actively dividing tissue and, as such, is very sensitive to cytotoxic drugs like methotrexate, which forms the basis of the highly successful treatment of trophoblastic tumours such as hydatidiform mole and choriocarcinoma. It has been known for over 30 years that cytotoxic drugs will kill the fetus and result in abortion [66]. However, because such drugs are potentially teratogenic, it is unlikely that they will provide a useful alternative medical method of inducing abortion as there would be a risk of developing an abnormal fetus should the pregnancy continue [67].

In the past, a number of methods for inducing abortion have been used that involved the injection of substances into the uterus, either into the amniotic sac, e.g. hypertonic saline, urea or glucose, or extra-amniotically through the cervical canal, e.g. Utus paste [68]. It is not clear how these methods worked but there is usually some delay between the injection and the onset of uterine contractions. Hypertonic solutions cause damage to the amnion and decidua, and often fetal death. It is likely that these changes result in release of endogenous prostaglandins and other substances and, hence, the cascade of events that occurs during spontaneous abortion is initiated [19]. If these mechanisms were better understood it may become possible to devise more effective and specific methods of interrupting pregnancy.

References

1 de Ziegler D, Bergeron C, Cornel C et al. Effects of luteal estradiol on the secretory transformation of the human endometrium and plasma gonadotropins. *J Clin Endocrinol Metab* 1992; 74: 322–331.
2 Asch RH. Egg and embryo donation: implantation aspects. In: Templeton AA, Drife JO, eds. *Infertility. Proceedings of RCOG Study Group—Active Management of Infertility.* London: Springer-Verlag, 1992: 277–289.

3 Bosu WT, Johansson EDB. Implantation and maintenance of pregnancy in mated rhesus monkeys following bilateral oophorectomy or lutectomy with and without progesterone replacement. *Acta Endocrinol* 1975; 79: 598–609.

4 Ghosh D, De P, Sengupta J. Luteal phase ovarian oestrogen is not essential for implantation and maintenance of pregnancy from surrogate embryo transfer in the rhesus monkey. *Hum Reprod* 1994; 9: 629–637.

5 Johannisson E. Morphological and histochemical factors related to implantation. *Baillières Clin Obstet Gynaecol* 1991; 5: 191–209.

6 Bouchard P, Marraoui J, Massai MR et al. Immunocytochemical localization of oestradiol and progesterone receptors in human endometrium: a tool to assess endometrial maturation. *Baillières Clin Obstet Gynaecol* 1991; 5: 107–115.

7 Seppälä M, Angervo M, Koistinen R, Riittinen L, Julkunen M. Human endometrial protein secretion relative to implantation. *Baillières Clin Obstet Gynaecol* 1991; 5: 61–72.

8 Rutanen EM, Pekonen F, Mäkinen T. Soluble 34K binding protein inhibits binding of insulin-like growth factor I to its cell receptors in human secretory phase endometrium: evidence for autocrine/paracrine regulation of growth factor action. *J Clin Endocrinol Metab* 1988; 66: 173–180.

9 Loke YW, King A. Recent developments in the human maternal–fetal immune interaction. *Curr Opin Immunol* 1991; 3: 762–766.

10 Medawar PB. Some immunological and endocrinological problems raised by the evolution of vivi parity in vertebrates. *Symp Soc Exp Biol* 1953; 7: 320–338.

11 King A, Loke YW. On the nature and function of human uterine granular lymphocytes. *Immunol Today* 1991; 12: 432–435.

12 Lea RG, Clark DA. Macrophages and migratory cells in endometrium relevant to implantation. *Baillières Clin Obstet Gynaecol* 1991; 5: 25–59.

13 Clark DA. Cytokines, decidua and early pregnancy. *Oxf Rev Reprod Biol* 1993; 15: 83–111.

14 Pollard JW. Regulation of polypeptide growth factor synthesis and growth factor-related gene expression in the rat and mouse uterus before and after implantation. *J Reprod Fertil* 1990; 88: 721–731.

15 Stewart CL, Kaspar P, Brunet LJ et al. Blastocyst implantation depends on maternal expression of leukaemia inhibitory factor. *Nature* 1992; 359: 76–79.

16 Kurzrock R, Estrov Z, Wetzler M, Gutterman JV, Talpaz M. LIF: not just a leukemia inhibitory factor. *Endocr Rev* 1991; 12: 208–217.

17 Lenton EA, Woodward AJ. The endocrinology of conception cycles and implantation in women. *J Reprod Fertil* 1988; 36 (Suppl.): 1–15.

18 Hearn JP, Webley GE, Gidley-Baird AA. Chorionic gonadotrophin and embryo–maternal recognition during the peri-implantation period in primates. *J Reprod Fertil* 1991; 92: 497–509.

19 Csapo AI, Pulkkinen MO. Indispensability of the human corpus luteum in the maintenance of early pregnancy. *Obstet Gynecol Surv* 1978; 33: 69–81.

20 Leyendecker G, Wildt L. Induction of ovulation with chronic intermittent (pulsatile) administration of Gn-RH in women with hypothalamic amenorrhoea. *J Reprod Fertil* 1983; 69: 397–409.

21 Griffin PD. A fertility regulating vaccine based on the carboxyl-terminal peptide of the β subunit of human chorionic gonadotrophin. In: Talwar GP, ed. *Immunological Approaches to Contraception and Promotion of Fertility*. New York: Plenum Press, 1986: 43–60.

22 Talwar GP, Singh O, Pal R *et al*. A vaccine that prevents pregnancy in women. *Proc Natl Acad Sci USA* 1994; 91: 8532–8536.

23 Gemzell K, Swahn ML, Bygdeman M. Regulation of non-pregnant human uterine contractility. Effect of antihormones. *Contraception* 1990; 42: 323–335.

24 Swahn ML, Bygdeman M. The effect of the antiprogestin RU 486 on uterine contractility and sensitivity to prostaglandin and oxytocin. *Br J Obstet Gynaecol* 1988; 95: 126–134.

25 Garfield RE, Blennerhassett MG, Miller SM. Control of myometrial contractility: role and regulation of gap junctions. *Oxf Rev Reprod Biol* 1988; 10: 436–490.

26 Smith SK. The role of prostaglandins in implantation. *Baillières Clin Obstet Gynaecol* 1991; 5: 73–93.

27 Cameron IT, Davenport AP, van Papendorp CL *et al*. Endothelin-like immunoreactivity in human endometrium. *J Reprod Fertil* 1992; 95: 623–628.

28 Abel MH, Baird DT. The effect of 17β estradiol and progesterone on prostaglandin production by human endometrium maintained in organ culture. *Endocrinology* 1980; 106: 1599–1606.

29 Casey ML, Hemsell DL, MacDonald PC, Johnston JM. NAD$^+$-dependent 15-hydroxyprostaglandin dehydrogenase activity in human endometrium. *Prostaglandins* 1980; 19: 115–122.

30 Abel MH, Kelly RW. Metabolism of prostaglandins by the nonpregnant human uterus. *J Clin Endocrinol Metab* 1983; 56: 678–685.

31 Abel MH, Smith SK, Baird DT. Suppression of concentration of endometrial prostaglandin in early intra-uterine and ectopic pregnancy in women. *J Endocrinol* 1980; 85: 379–386.

32 Bazer FW, Thatcher WW, Hansen PJ, Mirando MA, Ott TL, Plante C. Physiological mechanisms of pregnancy recognition in ruminants. *J Reprod Fertil* 1991; 43 (Suppl.): 39–47.

33 Short RV. When a conception fails to become a pregnancy. In: *Maternal Recognition of Pregnancy*. Amsterdam: Excerpta Medica, 1979: 377–387.

34 Chard T. Frequency of implantation and early pregnancy loss in natural cycles. *Baillières Clin Obstet Gynaecol* 1991; 5: 179–189.

35 Angell RR, Hillier, SG, West JD, Glasier AF, Rodger MW, Baird DT. Chromosome anomalies in early human embryos. *J Reprod Fertil* 1988; 36 (Suppl.): 73–81.

36 Edwards RG. Causes of early embryonic loss in human pregnancy. *Hum Reprod* 1986; 1: 185–198.

37 Cooke ID. Failure of implantation and its relevance to subfertility. *J Reprod Fertil* 1988; 36 (Suppl.): 155–159.

38 Regan L. Recurrent early pregnancy failure. *Curr Opin Obstet Gynecol* 1992; 4: 220–228, 497.

39 Boue J, Boue A, Lazar P. Retrospective and prospective epidemiological studies of 1500 karyotyped spontaneous abortions. *Teratology* 1975; 12: 11–26.

40 Sherman SL, Takaesu N, Freeman SB *et al*. Trisomy 21: association between reduced recombination and non-disjunction. *Am J Hum Genet* 1991; 49: 608–620.

41 Jacobs PA. The chromosome complement of human gametes. *Oxf Rev Reprod Biol* 1992; 14: 47–72.

42 Jacobs PA, Hassold TJ. Chromosome abnormalities: origin and etiology in abortions and live births. *Hum Genet* 1987; 77: 233–244.

43 Clark DA, Lea RG, Podor T, Daya S, Banwatt D, Harley C. Cytokines determining the success or failure of pregnancy. *Ann NY Acad Sci* 1991; 262: 524–536.

44 Liggins GC. Cervical ripening as an inflammatory reaction. In: Ellwood DA, Anderson ABM, eds. *The Cervix in Pregnancy and Labour: Clinical and Biochemical Investigations*. Edinburgh: Churchill Livingstone, 1981: 1–9.

45 Kelly RW. Pregnancy maintenance and parturition: the role of prostaglandin in manipulating the inflammatory response. *Endocr Rev* 1994; 15: 684–706.

46 Clark DA, Daya S. Trials and tribulation in the treatment of recurrent spontaneous abortion. *Am J Reprod Immunol* 1991; 25: 18–24.

47 Michel MZ, Khong TY, Clark DA, Beard RW. A morphological and immunological study of human placental bed biopsies in miscarriage. *Br J Obstet Gynaecol* 1990; 97: 984–988.

48 Norman JE, Kelly RW, Baird DT. Uterine activity and decidual prostaglandin production in women in early pregnancy in response to mifepristone with or without indomethacin *in vivo*. *Hum Reprod* 1991; 6: 740–744.

49 Cheng L, Kelly RW, Thong KJ, Hume R, Baird DT. The effects of mifepristone (RU 486) on prostaglandin dehydrogenase in decidual and chorionic tissue in early pregnancy. *Hum Reprod* 1993; 8: 705–709.

50 Cheng L, Kelly RW, Thong KJ, Hume R, Baird DT. The effect of mifepristone (RU 486) on immunohistochemical distribution of prostaglandin E and its metabolite in decidual and chorionic tissue in early pregnancy. *J Clin Endocrinol Metab* 1993; 77: 873–877.

51 Williams TJ, Morley J. Prostaglandins as potentiators of increased vascular permeability in inflammation. *Nature* 1973; 246: 215–217.

52 Williams TJ, Peck MJ. Role of prostaglandin-mediated vasodilatation in inflammation. *Nature* 1977; 270: 530–532.

53 Kelly RW, Leask R, Calder AA. Choriodecidual production of interleukin-8 and mechanism of parturition. *Lancet* 1992; 339: 776–777.

54 Rådestad A, Thyberg J, Christensen NJ. Cervical ripening with mifepristone (RU 486) in first trimester abortion. An electron microscope study. *Hum Reprod* 1993; 8: 1136–1142.

55 Rådestad A, Gréen K, Bygdeman M. Induced cervical ripening with mifepristone (RU 486) and bioconversion of arachidonic acid in human uterine cervix in first trimester abortion. *Contraception* 1990; 41: 283–292.

56 Baird DT, Norman JE. Antifertility effects of antigestogens. *Reprod Med* 1993; 2: 95–108.

57 Bygdeman M, Van Look PFA. Anti-progesterones for the interruption of pregnancy. *Baillières Clin Obstet Gynaecol* 1988; 2: 617–630.

58 Van Look PFA, Bygdeman M. Antiprogestational steroids: a new dimension in human fertility regulation. *Oxf Rev Reprod Biol* 1989; 11: 1–60.

59 Bygdeman M. Menstrual regulation. In: Hillier K, ed. *Eicosanoids and Reproduction*. Lancaster: MTP Press, 1987: 63–72.

60 Bygdeman M, Swahn ML. Progesterone receptor blockage. Effect on uterine contractility and early pregnancy. *Contraception* 1985; 32: 45–51.

61 Cameron IT, Michie AF, Baird DT. Therapeutic abortion in early pregnancy with antiprogestogen RU 486 alone or in combination with prostaglandin analogue (gemeprost). *Contraception* 1986; 34: 459–468.

62 Selinger M, Mackenzie IZ, Gillmer MD, Phipps SL, Ferguson J. Progesterone inhibition in mid-trimester termination of pregnancy: physiological and clinical effects. *Br J Obstet Gynaecol* 1987; 94: 1218–1222.

63 Birgerson L, Odlind V. Early pregnancy termination with antiprogestins: a

comparative clinical study of RU 486 given in two dose regimens and epostane. *Fertil Steril* 1987; 48: 565–570.

64 Urquhart DR, Templeton AA. The use of mifepristone prior to prostaglandin-induced midtrimester abortion. *Hum Reprod* 1990; 5: 883–886.

65 Rodger MW, Baird DT. Pretreatment with mifepristone (RU 486) reduces interval between prostaglandin administration and expulsion in second trimester abortion. *Br J Obstet Gynaecol* 1990; 97: 41–45.

66 Creinin MD, Vittinghoff E. Methotrexate and misoprostol vs misoprostol alone for early abortion. A randomized controlled trial. *JAMA* 1994; 272: 1190–1195.

67 Darab DJ, Minkoff R, Sciote J, Sulik KK. Pathogenesis of median facial clefts in mice treated with methotrexate. *Teratology* 1987; 36: 77–86.

68 Toppozada M, Ismail A. Intrauterine administration of drugs for termination of pregnancy in the second trimester. *Baillières Clin Obstet Gynaecol* 1990; 4: 327–349.

3   Termination of Pregnancy up to 8 or 9 Weeks

Marc Bygdeman

Introduction

Unwanted pregnancies occur as a consequence of the difficulties many couples have in planning their sexual activity and in using contraceptives. The decision to terminate a pregnancy is difficult to make, but is for many women the only possible solution since the continuation of the pregnancy would have serious effects on her future life. For most people it is obvious that in this situation, women have the right to have the abortion performed by methods that are both effective and safe and take into consideration the needs of the woman.

For many years the surgical procedure of vacuum aspiration has been the method of choice for termination of early pregnancy. The development of prostaglandins and antiprogestogens, which interact with progesterone at the receptor level, has created new possibilities for improvement of present abortion technology. Some data are also available for compounds that act as competitive inhibitors of the 3β-hydroxysteroid dehydrogenase enzyme system. Inhibition of this enzyme will block conversion of dehydroepiandrosterone to androstenedione as well as that of pregnenolone to progesterone. Among these compounds, epostane is the one tested for pregnancy termination since it preferentially inhibits ovarian/placental steroidogenesis [1]. Since the compound was withdrawn from clinical use early in its development by the pharmaceutical company, the amount of clinical data is limited.

The aim of this chapter is to summarize the present stage of development using antiprogestogen and/or prostaglandin for termination of early pregnancy and to compare available data with those of vacuum aspiration. Since RU 486 (mifepristone; Roussel Uclaf, Paris, France) is the only antiprogestogen that has been used clinically alone or in combination with prostaglandin to any extent, this review will be limited mainly to this compound.

Termination of early pregnancy: mifepristone versus epostane

Efficacy of mifepristone

Clinical evidence that it is possible to interrupt early human pregnancy with mifepristone was first provided in 1982 by Herrmann *et al.* [2] and was confirmed shortly afterwards in a dose-finding study conducted under the auspices of the World Health Organization (WHO)[3]. Although carried out in a relatively small number of women, these two studies permitted several tentative conclusions that were subsequently proven in further trials. Undoubtedly, the most disconcerting finding was the relatively low rate of complete abortion (73 and 61%, respectively), and the absence of a clear dose–response relationship. Efforts to improve the therapeutic efficacy were made by various investigators and focused on changing the daily dose and the duration of treatment (for references see [4]). From these studies, two conclusions could be drawn: (i) the frequency of complete abortion decreased with advancing pregnancy; and (ii) there was no relationship between the success rate and the treatment regimen employed for women at the same stage of gestation. For pregnancies up to 8 weeks, the frequency of complete abortion was generally between 60 and 70%. A somewhat higher success rate could be achieved if treatment was given within the first 10–14 days after the missed menstrual period. For example, Couzinet *et al.* [5] reported a complete abortion rate of 85% following treatment with up to 800 mg mifepristone for 2–4 days in women who were within 10 days of missed menses. Even if administered at the time of expected menstruation, the failure rate is around 10–15% [6–9].

Efficacy of epostane

Following epostane alone a success rate during early pregnancy of between 75 and 84% has been reported [10–12]. The dose used was 200 mg four times daily for 7 days. If the dose was reduced from 200 mg four times daily to three times daily during the same time, the frequency of complete abortion decreased from 75 to 57% [12]. In a small randomized study, 25 and 50 mg mifepristone given twice daily for 7 days was found equally effective as 200 mg epostane four times daily during the same period of time [13].

Epostane has been demonstrated to increase the sensitivity of the myometrium to prostaglandin. In a preliminary study the combination of epostane and prostaglandin E_2 (PGE$_2$) pessaries was found to be more effective than epostane alone in terminating early pregnancy [14].

Bleeding patterns

Most of the patients started to bleed following epostane therapy. The women who aborted as a result of treatment usually started to bleed on day 3–4 which was significantly later than if mifepristone was used [13]. The duration of bleeding ranged from 5 to 21 days with a geometric mean ($\pm$ SD) of 10.7 ± 3 days. In most instances patients reported heavy bleeding for 2–4 days followed by bleeding that was scantier than a normal menstruation for the following days. None of the 56 patients experienced heavy bleeding resulting from treatment [10].

Side effects

Among side effects reported by the patients nausea, sometimes associated with vomiting, was dominant. This was also the reported reason for discontinuation of therapy in five out of 56 women treated with 200 mg epostane four times daily for 7 days [10]. This side effect was more common following epostane than after mifepristone in the randomized study reported above. Other side effects such as uterine pain did not differ between the two compounds [13].

Termination of early pregnancy with prostaglandin alone

Efficacy

Initially, the naturally occurring prostaglandins PGF$_{2\alpha}$ and PGE$_2$ were used [15], but their widespread action, especially after systemic administration, resulted in a high incidence of side effects. Intrauterine instillation of PGF$_{2\alpha}$ or PGE$_2$ will induce abortion with acceptable side effects. However, the medical skill required and the risk of introducing infection into the uterine cavity has limited the clinical usefulness of these procedures [16]. The situation has changed to some extent since the introduction of prostaglandin analogues, especially those belonging to the PGE series. Their slower inactivation in the circulation facilitates the route of administration as they are stable enough for intravaginal or intramuscular administration. They also seem to exert a more selective

Table 3.1 Termination of early pregnancy by gemeprost (1 mg five times with 3-h interval), meteneprost (75 or 60 mg plus 30 or 45 mg 6 h later) or sulprostone (0.5 mg three times at 3-h intervals) and vacuum aspiration

	Comparative study [18]			Randomized study [19]	
	Sulprostone	Gemeprost	Meteneprost	Sulprostone	Vacuum aspiration
Complete abortion	94	92	93	91.1	94.0
Incomplete abortion	3	5	7	7.4	2.8
Pregnancy continuation	3	3	0	1.5	3.2

effect on the myometrium, thus reducing systemic adverse reactions substantially. The PGE analogues mainly used for termination of early pregnancy are sulprostone (Schering AG, Berlin, Germany), gemeprost (May and Baker, Dagenham, UK) and meteneprost (Upjohn Co., Kalamazoo, Michigan, USA). The first is given via intramuscular injection and the latter two are available for vaginal use. A number of studies have shown that repeated administration of these compounds will result in a frequency of complete abortion ranging from 90 to 100% (for references see [17]) (Table 3.1).

Bleeding pattern

Following prostaglandin treatment, the patient will start to bleed within 3–6 h. The duration of bleeding is generally between 1 and 2 weeks, although, in a few patients, occasional spotting will continue until the first menstrual period. The bleeding is generally characterized as comparable to a heavy menstrual period. The mean blood loss has been objectively measured to be 62 ml [18]. Heavy bleeding is a very rare phenomenon after prostaglandin therapy. In a WHO study [19] using sulprostone and comprising 216 patients, blood transfusion was never required.

Side effects

The most common side effects with prostaglandin alone are vomiting, diarrhoea and uterine pain. In the WHO study [19] almost 30% expressed occasional episodes of vomiting during treatment with sulprostone. The corresponding figures for diarrhoea were 21% and for analgesic injections to alleviate pain 12%. In a Swedish study in which the three PGE analogues were used, between 50 and 60% of patients experienced no side effects whereas 30–40% of patients had occasional episodes of vomiting and diarrhoea. However, more than four episodes occurred only in 2–6% of patients. In this study, between 32 and 56% of the women required morphine analgesics for alleviation of uterine pain [18].

Mifepristone in combination with prostaglandin

Efficacy

If mifepristone is combined with prostaglandin, the outcome of treatment is quite different from that of mifepristone alone. In the first study with the combined therapy, 25 mg mifepristone was given twice daily for 3–6 days. On the last day, 0.25 mg sulprostone was injected intramuscularly [20]. The overall frequency of complete abortion was 94%. Success rates of between 95 and 100% were also reported in other pilot studies where mifepristone was combined with vaginal administration of 0.5–1 mg gemeprost [21,22].

Mifepristone is available for routine clinical use in France, the UK, China and Sweden. The dose schedule recommended by the pharmaceutical company (Roussel Uclaf, Paris, France) is a single dose of 600 mg mifepristone followed 36–48 h later by 1 mg gemeprost. Sulprostone, which was mainly used initially, is no longer available since the intramuscular preparation has been withdrawn from the market. In Sweden and the UK, the procedure is used through the ninth week of pregnancy (63 days of amenorrhoea), while in France the upper limit is 49 days of amenorrhoea. The clinical outcome of the treatment has been evaluated in two large multicentre clinical studies from France and the UK [23,24]. Mifepristone, followed by either vaginal gemeprost or intramuscular injection of sulprostone, was shown to be highly effective in terminating early pregnancy. The frequency of complete abortion was around 95% and failures in terms of continuing pregnancy occurred in between 0.4 and 0.8% of patients (Table 3.2).

The ideal dose of mifepristone and prostaglandin remains to be established. Studies in both pregnant and non-pregnant women have shown that the pharmacokinetics of mifepristone are non-linear and that oral administration of the drug in single doses bigger than 100 mg results

Table 3.2 Termination of early pregnancy by 600 mg mifepristone and vaginal administration of 1 mg gemeprost, 0.25 mg sulprostone intramuscularly or 0.4 mg misoprostol orally. From UK Multicentre Trial [23]; Ulmann *et al.* [24]; Silvestre *et al.* [25]

| | French multicentre studies (< 49 days) | | | UK multicentre study (< 63 days) |
	Gemeprost	Sulprostone	Misoprostol	Gemeprost
Complete abortion	96.5	95.4	95.4	94.0
Incomplete abortion	2.3	2.8	2.8	5.0
Ongoing pregnancy	0.9	0.6	1.5	
Haemostatic surgical procedure	0.8	0.4	0.3	1.0

in serum concentrations that differ only minimally or not at all [4,26]. A multicentre study conducted under the auspices of WHO has shown that similar effectiveness as seen with 600 mg mifepristone (94%) could be achieved with repeated small doses of mifepristone (five doses of 25 mg given at 12-h intervals) followed by an intramuscular injection of 0.25 mg sulprostone [27]. In another more recent WHO study, it was shown that single doses of 200, 400 or 600 mg mifepristone followed 48 h later by one vaginal pessary of 1 mg gemeprost resulted in a 95.5% frequency of complete abortion with no differences between the different doses. Furthermore, the frequencies of incomplete abortion, 3.6–3.8%, and continuing live pregnancy, 0.3–0.5%, were the same [28].

Bleeding pattern

Following combined treatment with mifepristone and prostaglandin, patients start to bleed 2–3 days after the initiation of therapy. Approximately 50% of patients have started to bleed at the time of prostaglandin administration and almost all within 4 h thereafter [23]. In the French multicentre study [24], the frequency of non-responders was 0.3%. The mean duration of bleeding was 8 days and in 89.7% the bleeding lasted for 12 days or less. In the WHO study [28], the median value for duration of bleeding was 12 days but the range was wide: between 4 and 72 days. In general, patients report the bleeding to be more than the normal menstrual type. However, excessive bleeding requiring therapy is a rare event. A haemostatic surgical procedure was performed in between 0.4 and 1% of patients. The frequency of blood transfusion varied between 0.1% in the French study and 0.9% in the UK study. In the latter study, there was little or no change in the haemoglobin value (up to 10 g/l) pretreatment and 7 days after gemeprost administration, while in 1% of patients there was a decrease of 20–40 g/l. In the WHO study, there was a significant decrease from approximately 125 g/l pretreatment to approximately 122 g/l 1 week post-treatment. Haemoglobin values returned to their initial levels 6 weeks post-treatment. The overall mean blood loss has been objectively measured to be 81 ml [21].

Side effects

Uterine pain is the most common side effect and occurs especially during the first few hours following prostaglandin treatment. In the UK multicentre study, 21% required opiate analgesia. The corresponding figure in the WHO multicentre study was between 11.4 and 14.5%. Complications in terms of infection occurred rarely. In the French multicentre study, the frequency was 0.7% and in the WHO study 1.5%. In the latter study, vomiting and dizziness were unchanged by mifepristone treatment but increased slightly after gemeprost administration.

In the French study, which included more than 16 000 women, serious cardiovascular side effects were reported in four cases after sulprostone injection, consisting of one acute myocardial infarction attributed to a coronary spasm, and marked hypotension in the other three women. Since the drug has been marketed and used in more than 60 000 cases in France, two additional myocardial infarctions have occurred, one of them fatal. Thus, the frequency of severe cardiac complications after sulprostone administration is approximately one in 20 000 cases. As a consequence, relative contraindications to the method include smoking more than 10 cigarettes/day, age over 35 years and any suspicion of cardiovascular disease. It is noteworthy that so far, no myocardial infarction has occurred if gemeprost has been used, and most likely smaller doses of prostaglandin may still be sufficient and associated with a lower frequency of this type of complication.

Termination of early pregnancy by mifepristone and orally active prostaglandins

Efficacy

Oral administration of the prostaglandin may be an advantage. The analogue 9-methylene PGE_2 is orally active and has, in combination with mifepristone, been reported to terminate 95% of early pregnancies [29]. Another alternative is misoprostol. Misoprostol is licensed for sale in many countries for the treatment of gastric and duodenal ulceration. It is active orally, inexpensive and stable at room temperature. If administered alone during early pregnancy, doses ranging from 200 to 600 µg induce significant uterine pressure. However, only two of the 40 women given misoprostol alone aborted. When misoprostol was administered after mifepristone, there was a significant increase in both the amplitude and frequency of uterine contractions; complete abortion took place in 18 out of 21 women [30]. Aubény and Baulieu [31] treated 100 women undergoing legal abortion at gestations of up to 49 days with 600 mg mifepristone followed 2 days later by 400 µg oral misoprostol. Complete abortion was found in 95 women, four women had an incomplete abortion and in one woman the pregnancy continued despite the treatment.

Recently, an extended study from France has been published [32]. It includes 25 centres and 895 women with amenorrhoea of less than 50 days. The majority of women ($n = 505$) were treated with 600 mg mifepristone and 48 h later, if the abortion had not occurred, with 400 µg misoprostol (trial 1). In the remaining 390 women, a second dose of 200 µg misoprostol was given 4 h later if the patient had not aborted. This was necessary in approximately 25% of patients (trial 2). In the first trial using a fixed dose of misoprostol, the success rate (complete abortion) was 96.9%. This rate is similar to that previously observed for mifepristone followed by sulprostone or gemeprost. In the second study, in which an extra dose of misoprostol was added if necessary, the success rate increased to 98.7%.

The latest summary of the French experience with the combination of mifepristone and misoprostol for termination of early pregnancy was reported at the recent VIIIth World Congress in Human Reproduction [25]. The report included 1288 early pregnant women (duration of amenorrhoea < 50 days) who received 600 mg mifepristone followed 2 days later by a fixed dose of misoprostol (400 µg). The efficacy of the treatment was evaluated 2 weeks after the treatment by clinical examination, β-human chorionic gonadotrophin (β-hCG) and/or ultrasound scan. The success rate, defined as complete expulsion of the conceptus with no need for additional surgical procedure, was 95.4%. Of the remaining patients, 2.8% experienced an incomplete abortion, in 1.5% the pregnancy continued and in 0.3% a haemostatic vacuum aspiration was performed (Table 3.2). Expulsion of the conceptus occurred within

Table 3.3 Suggested differences between mifepristone in combination with either gemeprost or misoprostol. From McKinley *et al.* [33]

Efficacy	
50 days	The same
50–63 days	Probably higher for gemeprost
Complications	The same
Side effects, mainly uterine pain	Probably less for misoprostol
Cost	Considerably less for misoprostol

4 h of administration of misoprostol in 59% and within 24 h in 82% of the women.

If treatment with mifepristone in combination with gemeprost or misoprostol is compared, available data indicate that both treatments are equally effective at least up to 49 days of amenorrhoea. After 49 days of amenorrhoea the efficacy of mifepristone in combination with oral misoprostol seems to decrease significantly [33] (Table 3.3).

Bleeding pattern and side effects

In the two French studies cited above almost all women responded with uterine bleeding. The mean duration of bleeding was 9 days and the mean drop in haemoglobin value was 7 g/l. Excessive bleeding necessitating blood transfusion was reported to occur in only one woman, corresponding to a frequency of only 0.1%.

The majority of women felt uterine cramps, 20% required a non-opiate analgesic and narcotic analgesic was given to only one woman (0.1%). Although the degree of pain and need for analgesic treatment varies considerably between different studies, it seems that the replacement of gemeprost by misoprostol in the doses used will result in a less painful treatment (Table 3.3).

Comparison between medical methods and vacuum aspiration to terminate early pregnancy

Comparative studies

There are very few studies comparing medical methods and vacuum aspiration for termination of early pregnancy. Such studies are essential, since the definition of success and side effects varies considerably. In the earliest study, intrauterine administration of 5 mg $PGF_{2\alpha}$ was used in

pregnancies which are < 56 days [16]. In two studies, vaginal administration of PGE analogues were used [34,35]. The most extensive study
was performed by WHO [19] in women with amenorrhoea of < 50 days.
In this study, 0.5 mg sulprostone was administered intramuscularly three
times at 3-h intervals. Cameron and Baird [36] compared gemeprost (in a
dose of 1 mg five times with 3-h intervals), mifepristone (150 mg daily for
4 days) and the same dose of mifepristone followed by 1 mg gemeprost in
pregnancies < 56 days. All these studies conclude that prostaglandin
treatment was as effective as vacuum aspiration for termination of early
pregnancy. Mifepristone in combination with gemeprost was also equally
effective as gemeprost alone and vacuum aspiration, whereas mifepristone alone was significantly less effective (60%).

The mean duration of bleeding was significantly longer after prostaglandin or mifepristone in combination with gemeprost: in all studies
this was 9–14 days after the medical treatment, compared with approximately 5 days for vacuum aspiration. The prolonged bleeding associated
with medical abortion could constitute an increased risk for infection.
However, in all the above-mentioned studies the incidence of pelvic
infection was low; between 1 and 3% for both the surgical and
prostaglandin-induced abortions. Gastrointestinal side effects were consistently more common following prostaglandin treatment than after
vacuum aspiration, and also higher than following mifepristone alone or
in combination with prostaglandin. Strong uterine pain was also less
common following the combined treatment than after prostaglandin
alone. However, it is noteworthy that in the studies where patients were
treated with prostaglandin at home [35], only 6% needed opiate analgesics compared to 40% of those treated in hospital. These drawbacks and
side effects may decrease the tolerance for medical abortion considerably.
In only one study has the acceptance of the prostaglandin therapy and
vacuum aspiration been compared [35]. Sixty patients, pregnant for < 56
days, were randomly allocated to either medical treatment by vaginal
pessaries containing meteneprost at home or in hospital, or to vacuum
aspiration. Their attitudes and preferences were gathered via interview
and rating scales on three separate occasions, i.e. before, immediately
after and 2 weeks after the abortion. The investigation revealed that those
treated with prostaglandin remained very positive after the abortion. The
majority intended to use the same method in case of repeated abortion
and would also recommend the treatment to other women.

In view of the low incidence of pain and gastrointestinal side effects
generally reported for the combined treatment of antiprogestin and
prostaglandin, it is probable that this method should be at least equally

acceptable. The attitudes of women towards vacuum aspiration and antiprogestin in combination with prostaglandin was evaluated via interviews performed 2 weeks post-treatment. Although women undergoing a medical abortion reported more bleeding and slightly more pain than the women treated surgically, they also felt relief at being spared a surgical procedure. Women treated with antiprogestin also mention moral considerations more often than other women. Taking the tablets had made them think twice: they terminated the pregnancy themselves with no one to perform the abortion for them [37]. Henshaw et al. [38], in a partly randomized study, concluded that both the procedures were highly acceptable to those who had made the choice of procedure themselves. In women who had been randomly allocated to either the medical or surgical procedure, there was no difference in acceptability if the treatment was performed at < 50 days of amenorrhoea. If the treatment was given later (between 50 and 63 days of amenorrhoea), vacuum aspiration was found significantly more acceptable.

Non-comparative studies

The comparative studies include only a limited number of patients while large clinical studies normally describe the outcome of only one procedure. Cates and Grimes [39] reviewed the data from over 210 000 vacuum aspirations. The frequency of complications reported was excessive bleeding (0.05–4.9%), pelvic infection (0.1–2.2%), cervical injury (0.01–1.6%) and uterine perforation (0.02–0.7%) in pregnancies up to 12 weeks gestation. In pregnancies of up to 8 weeks, the complication rates were 1.1, 0.9, 0 and 0.2%, respectively [40]. In the study by Ulmann et al. [24], which included 16 369 women in whom pregnancy was terminated with mifepristone and prostaglandin, the corresponding figures were excessive bleeding necessitating surgical treatment 0.8%, blood transfusion 0.1% and pelvic infection 0.7%. Obviously, no cases of cervical injury and uterine perforation occurred in this study. Although these figures are not strictly comparable, they suggest that even in large comparative studies it is rather unlikely that the medical procedure would be shown to be associated with a higher frequency of complications in terms of excessive bleeding and infection than the surgical one.

Service facilities

Both the medical facilities necessary for performing abortion and the cost of these procedures are important factors for society as a whole. The medical treatment includes four visits to the clinic. The woman is seen by the physician at the initial visit and 2 weeks after the start of treatment to evaluate the outcome of therapy. The nurse supervises the intake of mifepristone and the woman during the 4–6 h observation period at the out-patient clinic following prostaglandin therapy. The second visit, at which mifepristone is administered, is not medically necessary and could equally well be performed by the woman herself at home. However, in some countries like Sweden and the UK, the conditions of the licence insist that the drug be administered in licensed premises or hospital. Three visits are also recommended for vacuum aspiration. It is important not to perform vacuum aspiration at the first visit but to give the woman a few days to consider the information given. For both methods, a return visit to follow-up on contraceptive use approximately 3 months later is recommended. Since treatment with antiprogestin in combination with prostaglandin and vacuum aspiration seem to be equally effective, and the frequency of complications of the medical method is not higher than with the surgical one, the former will be cheaper since surgical facilities are not necessary. Vacuum aspiration, although often regarded as a simple procedure, needs surgical skill and experience in order to minimize the rate of complications. For the medical method, good knowledge of the procedure is an important factor, but the treatment itself is certainly less complicated. However, the need for medical back-up in case of pregnancy continuation, incomplete abortion, recurettage and heavy bleeding is equally necessary for both procedures.

Conclusion

Both mifepristone, which competes with progesterone at the receptor level, and epostane, which inhibits the 3β-hydroxysteroid dehydro-genase enzyme system are able to terminate early pregnancy. However, if used alone the efficacy rate of 60–80% is not sufficient to be clinically useful.

Suitable doses of either of the three prostaglandin analogues (sulpro-stone, gemeprost and meteneprost), and mifepristone in combination with gemeprost are equally as effective as vacuum aspiration to terminate early first-trimester pregnancy. The medical methods are associated with longer duration of bleeding, a higher incidence of uterine pain and gastrointestinal side effects. The obvious advantages of the medical methods are the avoidance of surgical and anaesthetic complications associated with vacuum aspiration. The risks of heavy bleeding, blood transfusion, recurettage and infection are not any higher following medical than surgical abortion.

If prostaglandin alone is compared with mifepristone in combination with gemeprost, the latter method is preferable with regard to need for analgesic treatment and frequency of gastrointestinal side effects. Recent data indicate that these side effects may be further reduced if the prostaglandin analogue misoprostol, given orally or vaginally [41,42], is used instead of gemeprost.

Acceptability studies indicate that both vacuum aspiration and the medical methods are well accepted by patients, especially if the women are allowed to choose the method they prefer.

Acknowledgements

The studies included in this article were performed at the Department of Obstetrics and Gynaecology, Karolinska Hospital, Stockholm, and kindly supported by the World Health Organization, Special Programme of Research, Development and Research Training in Human Reproduction, Geneva, and the Swedish Medical Research Council (Project 05696). The author is also grateful to Ms Astrid Häggblad for typing the manuscript.

References

1 Creange JE, Anzalone AJ, Potts GO, Schane HP. WIN 32.729: a new potent interceptive agent in rats and rhesus monkeys. *Contraception* 1981; 24: 289–299.

2 Herrmann W, Wyss R, Riondel A *et al.* Effet d'un steroide anti-progestine chez la femme interruption du cycle et de la grossesse au début. *CR Acad Sci* (Paris) 1982; 294: 933–938.

3 Kovacs L, Sas M, Resch B *et al.* Termination of very early pregnancy by RU 486—an antiprogestational compound. *Contraception* 1984; 29: 399–410.

4 Van Look PFA, Bygdeman M. Antiprogestational steroids: a new dimension in human fertility regulation. *Oxf Rev Reprod Biol* 1989; 11: 1–60.

5 Couzinet B, Le Strat N, Ulmann A, Baulieu EE, Schaison G. Termination of early pregnancy by the progesterone antagonist RU 486 (mifepristone). *N Engl J Med* 1986; 315: 1565–1570.

6 Ulmann A. Uses of RU 486 for contragestion: an update. *Contraception* 1987; 36 (Suppl.): 27–31.

7 Van Santen MR, Haspels AA. Interception. Part III. Postcoital luteal contragestion by an antiprogestin (mifepristone, RU 486) in 62 women. *Contraception* 1987; 35: 423–431.

8 Dubois C, Ulmann A, Baulieu EE. Contragestion with late luteal administration of RU 486 (mifepristone). *Fertil Steril* 1988; 50: 593–596.

9 Lähteenmäki P, Rapeli T, Kääriäinen M, Alfthan H, Ylikorkala O. Late postcoital:

treatment against pregnancy with antiprogesterone RU 486. *Fertil Steril* 1989; 50: 38–42.

10 Birgerson L, Ölund A, Odlind V, Somell C. Termination of early human pregnancy with epostane. *Contraception* 1987; 35: 111–120.

11 Crooij MJ, de Nooyer CCA, Rao BR, Berends GT, Gooren LGJ, Janssens J. Termination of early pregnancy by the 3β-hydroxysteroid dehydrogenase inhibitor epostane. *N Engl J Med* 1988; 319: 813–817.

12 Webster MA, Gillmer MD. Induction of abortion in early first trimester human pregnancy using epostane. *Br J Obstet Gynaecol* 1989; 96: 963–968.

13 Birgerson L, Odlind V. Early pregnancy termination with antiprogestins: a comparative clinical study of RU 486 given in two dose regimens and epostane. *Fertil Steril* 1987; 48: 565–570.

14 Webster MA, Phipps SL, Gillmer MD. Interruption of first trimester human pregnancy following epostane therapy. Effect of prostaglandin E_2 pessaries. *Br J Obstet Gynaecol* 1985; 92: 963–968.

15 Mocsary P, Csapo AI. Menstrual induction with $PGF_{2\alpha}$ and PGE_2. *Prostaglandins* 1973; 10: 545–547.

16 Ragab MJ, Edelman DA. Early termination of pregnancy: a comparative study of intrauterine prostaglandin $F_{2\alpha}$ and vacuum aspiration. *Prostaglandins* 1976; 11: 275–283.

17 Swahn ML, Bygdeman M. Medical methods to terminate pregnancy. In: Bygdeman M, ed. *Medical Induction of Abortion. Volume 4. Baillière's Clinical Obstetrics and Gynaecology.* London: Baillière Tindall, 1990: 293–306.

18 Bygdeman M, Christensen NJ, Gréen K, Cheng S, Lundström V. Termination of early pregnancy—future development. *Acta Obstet Gynecol Scand* 1983; 113 (Suppl.): 125–129.

19 World Health Organization. Menstrual regulation by intramuscular injection of 16-phenoxy-tetranor PGE_2 methyl sulfonylamide or vacuum aspiration. A randomized multicentre study. *Br J Obstet Gynaecol* 1987; 94: 949–956.

20 Bygdeman M, Swahn ML. Progesterone receptor blockage. Effect on uterine contractility in early pregnancy. *Contraception* 1985; 32: 45–51.

21 Cameron IT, Michie AF, Baird DT. Therapeutic abortion in early pregnancy with antiprogestogen RU 486 alone or in combination with a prostaglandin analogue (gemeprost). *Contraception* 1986; 34: 459–468.

22 Dubois C, Ulmann A, Aubény E *et al.* Contragestion par le RU 486: intérêt de l'association à un dérivé prostaglandine. *CR Acad Sci* (Paris) 1988; 306: 51–61.

23 UK Multicentre Trial. The efficacy and tolerance of mifepristone and prostaglandin in first trimester termination of pregnancy. *Br J Obstet Gynaecol* 1990; 97: 480–486.

24 Ulmann A, Silvestre L, Chemama L *et al.* Medical termination of early pregnancy with mifepristone (RU 486) followed by a prostaglandin analogue. *Acta Obstet Gynecol Scand* 1992; 71: 278–283.

25 Silvestre L, Peyron R, Ulmann A. Sequential treatment with an antiprogestin (mifepristone, RU 486) and a prostaglandin analogue for termination of early pregnancy. *VIIIth World Congress in Human Reproduction.* Bali, 4–9 April 1993, 43 (Abstract).

26 Puri CP, Van Look PFA. Newly developed competitive progesterone antagonists for fertility control. In: Agarwal MK, ed. *Antihormones in Health and Disease. Volume 19. Frontiers of Hormone Research.* Basel: Karger, 1991: 127–167.

27 World Health Organization. Pregnancy termination with mifepristone and gemeprost: a multicenter comparison between repeated doses and a single dose of mifepristone. *Fertil Steril* 1991; 56: 32–40.
28 World Health Organization. Termination of pregnancy with reduced doses of mifepristone. *Br Med J* 1993; 307: 532–537.
29 Swahn ML, Gottlieb C, Gréen K, Bygdeman M. Oral administration of RU 486 and 9-methylene PGE$_2$ for termination of early pregnancy. *Contraception* 1990; 41: 461–473.
30 Norman JE, Thong KJ, Baird DT. Uterine contractility and induction of abortion in early pregnancy by misoprostol and mifepristone. *Lancet* 1991; 338: 1233–1236.
31 Aubény E, Baulieu EE. Activité contragestive de l'association au RU 486 d'une prostaglandin active par voie orale. *CR Acad Sci* (Paris) 1991; 312: 539–545.
32 Peyron R, Aubény E, Targosz V et al. Early pregnancy interruption with RU 486 (mifepristone) and misoprostol, an orally active prostaglandin analogue. *N Engl J Med* 1993; 328: 1509–1513.
33 McKinley C, Thong KJ, Baird DT. The effect of dose of mifepristone and gestation on efficacy of medical abortion with mifepristone and misoprostol. *Hum Reprod* 1993; 8: 1502–1505.
34 Lundström V, Bygdeman M, Fotiou S, Gréen K, Kinoshita K. Abortion in early pregnancy by vaginal administration of 16, 16-dimethyl PGE$_2$ in comparison with vacuum aspiration. *Contraception* 1977; 16: 167–173.
35 Rosén AS, von Knorring K, Bygdeman M, Christensen NJ. Randomized comparison of prostaglandin treatment in hospital or at home with vacuum aspiration for termination of early pregnancy. *Contraception* 1984; 29: 423–435.
36 Cameron IT, Baird DT. Early pregnancy termination: a comparison between vacuum aspiration and medical abortion using prostaglandin (16, 16-dimethyl-trans-Δ^2 PGE$_1$ methyl ester) or the antiprogestogen RU 486. *Br J Obstet Gynaecol* 1988; 95: 271–276.
37 Holmgren K. Women's evaluation of three early abortion methods. *Acta Obstet Gynecol Scand* 1992; 71: 616–623.
38 Henshaw RC, Naji SA, Russell IT, Templeton AA. Comparison of medical abortion with surgical vacuum aspiration: women's preferences and acceptability of treatment. *Br Med J* 1993; 307: 714–717.
39 Cates W, Grimes DA. Morbidity and mortality of abortion in the United States. In: Hodgson JE, ed. *Abortion and Sterilization: Medical and Social Aspects.* London: Academic Press, 1981: 155–180.
40 Freedman MA, Jillson DA, Coffin RR, Novick LF. Comparison of complication rates in first trimester abortion performed by physician assistants and physicians. *Am J Public Health* 1980; 76: 550–554.
41 El-Refaey H, Templeton A. Early induction of abortion by a combination of mifepristone and misoprostol administered by the vaginal route. *Contraception* 1994; 49: 111–114.
42 El-Refaey H, Rajasekar D, Abdatta M, Calder L, Templeton A. Induction of abortion with mifepristone (RU 486) and oral or vaginal misoprostol. *N Engl J Med* 1995; 332: 983–987.

4   Termination of Pregnancy between 9 and 14 Weeks

Pak Chung Ho

Introduction

Medical abortion has been extensively studied in the last two decades [1,2]. However, most of the studies concentrate on women either in their early pregnancies (< 9 weeks gestation) or in their second trimester. The gestational age of 9–14 weeks is seldom studied and there is relatively little data on the efficacy and acceptability of the new methods of medical abortion at this gestational age. This chapter reviews the available data and compares the medical methods with the surgical methods of abortion.

Medical methods

One of the first groups of drugs used for medical abortion was the prostaglandins. Both natural prostaglandins and prostaglandin analogues have been evaluated. The results with the natural prostaglandins (PGF$_{2\alpha}$ and PGE$_2$) are disappointing [3–10]. Although serious complications are rare, the incidence of gastrointestinal side effects is high and the complete abortion rate in most series is less than 85%. The induction–abortion intervals ranged from 13 to 24 h. The results with synthetic prostaglandin analogues, where data for 9–14 weeks are available, are summarized in Table 4.1. The induction–abortion intervals with 15s, 15-methyl PGF$_{2\alpha}$ (intramuscular and vaginal) [10–14] were shorter (around 13 h), but the incidence of vomiting and diarrhoea was still high [11–14]. The use of gemeprost (16, 16-dimethyl-trans-Δ^2 PGE$_1$ methyl ester) was associated with a lower incidence of side effects and a shorter induction–abortion interval of around 8–14 h [10,15–17]. However, the complete abortion rate was only around 53–77%. Therefore, the efficacy of prostaglandins at this gestational age is lower than that in early pregnancy [2], while the incidence of side effects is high.

Mifepristone is a progesterone antagonist at the receptor level and its abortifacient effect was first demonstrated by Herrmann *et al.* [18]. When

54

Table 4.1 Abortion induced by prostaglandin analogues

Prostaglandin route/schedule	No. of subjects	Period of gestation (weeks)	Complete abortion (%)	Mean induction abortion interval (h)	Incidence of side effects			Reference
					V (%)	D (%)	F (%)	
15s, 15-methyl PGF$_{2a}$								
250 μg every 1.5–2.5 h (i.m.)	388	9–15	77	13	68	61	NA	[11]
250–500 μg every 2 h (i.m.)	15	10–16	NA	14	91	71	23	[12]
1 mg every 3 h × 6 to 1.5 mg every 3 h × 3 (v.)	61	10–12	58	NA	NA	NA	NA	[13]
1 mg every 3 h × 4 (v.)	58	8–12	52	12	7	9	NA	[14]
Gemeprost								
1 mg every 3 h (v.)	34	7–12	53	NA	6	42	4	[15]
1 mg every 3 h (v.)	13	9–14	54	8	4	0	0	[16]
1 mg every 3 h (v.)	24	12–15	45	10–13	15	15	15	[17]
1 mg every 3 h (v.)	57	12–16	77	14	19	12	77	[10]

D, diarrhoea; F, fever; i.m., intramuscular; NA, data not available; v., vaginal; V, vomiting.

used alone, it can induce complete abortion in only 61% [19] and the complete abortion rate was found to decrease with increase in gestational age [20–22]. At the gestational age of 8–10 weeks, the complete abortion rate was only 33% [21]. Therefore, most of the subsequent studies were conducted in pregnant women with gestational age ⩽ 9 weeks. Even after it had been shown that the sequential administration of mifepristone and a prostaglandin analogue could increase the complete abortion rate to 95% [23,24], almost all the studies recruited only women with gestational age ⩽ 9 weeks. The only study where data are available for gestational age beyond 9 weeks is the multicentre study conducted in the UK [25]. Among the 15 women with gestational age between 9 and 10 weeks treated with mifepristone and gemeprost, one of them (7%) required surgical evacuation. Recently, an orally active prostaglandin analogue, misoprostol, has also been used in combination with mifepristone for termination of pregnancy with a complete abortion rate of over 90–95% [26,27]. However, the rate was also found to decrease with increase in gestational age [28]. In women with gestational age ⩽ 49 days the complete abortion rate was 97.5%, which was significantly higher than that in women with gestational age of 50–63 days (89.1%). It is likely that the complete abortion rate is even lower beyond 9 weeks. In France, the mifepristone–prostaglandin combination can be used for termination of pregnancy only up to 7 weeks, while in the UK and Sweden, it can be used to terminate pregnancies only up to 9 weeks.

Surgical procedures

The classical method for termination of pregnancy in the first trimester is dilatation and curettage (D & C). In recent years, this method has been increasingly replaced by vacuum aspiration (VA). With VA, a catheter is inserted into the uterine cavity and the products of conception are removed by application of a negative pressure which can be generated either by an electric pump or manually by a syringe device. Cervical dilatation is usually necessary at the gestational age of 9–14 weeks before insertion of the suction catheter. The procedure can be performed under either local or general anaesthesia, often as an out-patient procedure or as part of a day-surgery programme. D & C and VA have recently been reviewed by Greenslade et al. [29]. Most of the available data show that in the first trimester of pregnancy, VA is simpler and quicker than D & C. The incidence of complications is also lower.

VA has been extensively evaluated in many countries and its efficacy and safety have been well proven. The results of some of the larger series [30–39] are summarized in Table 4.2. In most series, only women at the gestational age of 12 weeks or less are included, but in some series those at up to 14 weeks or beyond are included [31,35,38,39]. All the available data show that VA is a highly effective method of pregnancy termination at up to 14 weeks with a complete abortion rate of over 98%.

The most common complications arising from VA include incomplete or failed evacuation, uterine perforation, excessive haemorrhage, cervical injury and infection. On the whole, the incidence of complications is low in most series. Failed or incomplete abortion occurred in < 2% of cases. Uterine perforation is a serious complication which may lead to bowel injury and intraperitoneal bleeding. Fortunately, this is rare, with an incidence of < 0.2% in most series. The incidence of excessive haemorrhage, pelvic infection and cervical injury varied in these studies according to the criteria used to define the complication, but these complications are uncommon with an incidence of < 1% in most series. The incidence also varied according to the selection of patients. Patients with pre-existing disease and those undergoing sterilization procedures at the same time had a higher incidence of complications [31]. VA performed by experienced surgeons had a lower complication rate [36]. Adequate follow-up of patients would also reveal a higher complication rate [31]. Although the complication rate increases with the gestational age of the woman [31,35,36,38], it is still very low when VA is performed in women up to 14 weeks of pregnancy [31,35,39].

Preoperative cervical dilatation

Cervical dilatation is probably the most critical step in VA. The cervical dilator is the most common instrument responsible for uterine perforation in VA [30]. Cervical injuries may result from forceful dilatation. Failed cervical dilatation has been reported in some series. If there is inadequate cervical dilatation, the chance of incomplete evacuation may also be higher. Finally, while controversies exist, there is concern that forceful dilatation of the cervix may lead to permanent damage of the cervix especially if the cervix is dilated to beyond 12 mm [40], thus affecting subsequent reproductive performance [41]. Therefore, a number of methods have been developed for preoperative cervical dilatation before VA. The two methods which have been used most often are: (i) the intracervical tents [42]; and (ii) prostaglandins [2].

Table 4.2 Results of VA in termination of first-trimester pregnancy

No. of women	Period of gestation (weeks)	LA/GA	Incidence of complications					Reference
			Incomplete abortion (%)	Uterine perforation (%)	Excessive bleeding (%)	Pelvic infection (%)	Cervical injury (%)	
22 909	≤12	LA	1.3	0.04	3.4	0.3	NA	[30]
50 352	6–15	Both	0.2–1.1	0.2–0.6	0.8–2	0.6–1	0.9–1.2	[31]
26 000	≤12	LA	0.35	0.14	0.2	1.5	NA	[32]
20 248	≤12	LA	0.5	0.12	NA	0.2	0.004	[33]
23 290	≤12	LA	0.36	0.09	0.03	NA	NA	[34]
16 410	≤14	LA	0.5	0.2	0.3	0.1	0.13	[35]
10 890	≤13	LA	0.1	0.02	0.015	0.06	0.18	[36]
36 430	≤12	LA	0.64	0.13	0.32	0.95	0.59	[37]
17 725	≤12	GA	0.55	0.29	0.54	1.08	1.73	[37]
13 252	≤12	NA	0.05	0.007	0.07	0.06	0.12	[38]
525	13–16	NA	3.6	0.38	11.2	2.85	8.0	[38]
170 000	≤14	Both	0.38	0.01	0.01	0.48	0.01	[39]

GA, general anaesthesia; LA, local anaesthesia; NA, data not available.

Intracervical tents

The three types of tents that have been shown to be useful are the laminaria tents, Dilapan and Lamicel. Laminaria tents are made from the seaweeds *Laminaria japonica* or *L. digitata*. In a dried state, they become hygroscopic and will increase their mass three to five times when placed in a moist environment. Modern methods of sterilization like radiation and ethylene oxide have overcome the initial problem of sepsis [42]. A number of clinical studies [43–47] including some controlled trials [45,47] have confirmed their efficacy in dilating the cervix before VA for termination of pregnancy in both the first and second trimesters. It has also been demonstrated that a few weeks after the abortion, the cervical diameter in the group with the cervix dilated by laminaria tent was significantly smaller than that in the group with the cervix dilated by Hegar's dilators [45]. This suggests that the use of laminaria tents may protect the cervix from permanent damage. The maximal cervical dilatation effect is observed at about 24 h [43]. When inserted 1 day before the VA, over 96% of patients did not require further dilatation [43,44]. However, to incorporate it into a day-surgery programme, the tent is usually inserted about 3 h before the operation in most recent series. While it is still more effective than the control group [47], the percentage of patients who did not require further dilatation fell below 20% [48,49]. Complications of the laminaria tent include uterine perforation [42], displacement of the tent into the uterine cavity [42,50] and fragmentation of the tent [42], but these are rare.

Lamicel is a synthetic tent made from polyvinyl alcohol foam sponge impregnated with magnesium sulphate [51]. It is also effective in dilating the cervix before VA [46,51–54]. The main advantage of Lamicel is its rapid action. It reaches its maximal effect in about 4 h [53]. Its efficacy is probably similar to that of the laminaria tent [46]. The incidence of side effects is also similar to the laminaria tent except that the removal of Lamicel results in a significantly lower incidence of bleeding from the os [46].

Dilapan is a synthetic tent made of a hydrophilic polyacrylonitrile block polymer called Hypan [55]. When placed in water it rapidly expands increasing its diameter threefold within 1 h and it can dilate the cervix very rapidly and more effectively than the laminaria tent [47]. The disadvantage is that it tends to fragment and fracture leaving the distal portion within the uterine cavity [42]. The rapid dilatation of the cervix may cause pain to the patient. The removal of Dilapan is also more difficult and painful so that about 23% of patients required placement of a paracervical block before the removal of the tent [55].

Pharmacological methods

Both natural prostaglandins and prostaglandin analogues have been used for preoperative cervical dilatation before VA. In many studies the cervical diameter is taken as the size of the largest Hegar's dilator which can be passed through the cervix without resistance. There is a subjective element depending on the skill and sensation of the surgeon. Therefore, the efficacy of a prostaglandin can only be proven by conducting a double-blind placebo-controlled trial. While there are a lot of studies on the use of prostaglandins in preoperative cervical dilatation in termination of pregnancy in the first and second trimester [56–84], only a few are double-blind placebo-controlled trials [56–62]. The results of these trials are summarized in Table 4.3. They show that pretreatment with PGE_2, or prostaglandin analogues like 15s, 15-methyl PGE_2 methyl ester, 15s, 15-methyl $PGF_{2\alpha}$ or gemeprost is effective in dilating the cervix before VA. Any further dilatation can be performed easily. In most series, the amount of blood loss during operation was significantly reduced in the treatment group [57–62]; probably due to the stimulation of uterine contractions by the prostaglandins. The duration of vaginal bleeding after the abortion was also shorter in the prostaglandin-treated group [60]. The incidence of late complications in the prostaglandin-treated group including recurettage, readmission for abnormal bleeding and pelvic infection was also significantly lower than in the placebo group [60]. The incidence of gastrointestinal side effects like vomiting and diarrhoea is higher in the prostaglandin-treated group. About 5–20% of patients may also require analgesics for uterine cramps. These side effects are less common with gemeprost.

Significant cervical dilatation is possible when the prostaglandin is given 3 h before the VA. The effect is better when the prostaglandin is given 12 h before the VA [60], but this would lead to a higher incidence of side effects and some patients may abort before the VA. It is also difficult to incorporate a 12 h pretreatment regimen into a day-surgery programme. Therefore, unless a larger cervical dilatation is necessary, most centres administer the prostaglandin only about 3–4 h before the VA.

A number of studies have been conducted comparing the various prostaglandins with the intracervical tents in preoperative cervical dilatation. Christensen *et al.* [49] showed that the 15-methyl $PGF_{2\alpha}$,

Table 4.3 Summary of results of double-blind placebo-controlled trials on the use of the natural prostaglandins and their analogues in preoperative cervical dilatation

Prostaglandin regimen	No. of subjects	PG–VA interval (h)	Period of gestation (weeks)	Cervical diameter		Side effects			Blood loss (ml)	Reference
				Mean	% ≥ 8 mm	V	D	P		
PGF$_{2a}$										
10 mg	40	12	≤ 12	3.9	NA	0	0	NA	NA	[56]
Placebo	20	12	≤ 12	4.0	NA	0	0	NA	NA	[56]
PGE$_2$ 15 mg (v.)	65	1–6	≤ 13	7.4	39	30	12	7	123	[57]
PGE$_2$ 10 mg (v.)	169	1–6	≤ 13	6.7	28	15	3	1	123	[57]
PGE$_2$ 5 mg (v.)	65	1–6	≤ 13	5.8	11	8	0	0	123	[57]
Placebo	114	1–6	≤ 13	5.9	11	3	0	0	175	[57]
15s, 15-methyl PGE$_2$ methyl ester										
25 µg (e.a.)	25	20	≤ 14	9.7	88	24	12	16	NA	[58]
Placebo	25	20	≤ 14	3.7	0	0	0	0	NA	[58]
15s, 15-methyl PGF$_{2a}$ methyl ester										
1 mg (v.)	10	12	8–12	8.4	50	NA	NA	NA	108	[59]
Placebo	9	12	8–12	0.9	0	NA	NA	NA	192	[59]
1 mg (v.)	225	3	8–12	7.3	47	22	28	8	68	[60]
Placebo	219	3	8–12	5.0	9	1	1	4	90	[60]
1 mg (v.)	209	12	8–12	8.1	70	39	56	27	68	[60]
Placebo	219	12	8–12	5.3	11	1	1	4	90	[60]
Gemeprost										
1 mg (v.)	23	3	≤ 12	8.1	61	10	2	0	112	[61]
Placebo	23	3	≤ 12	6.7	26	2	0	0	158	[61]
1 mg (v.)	22	3	7–13	7.4	33	4	4	4	134	[62]
Placebo	17	3	7–13	5.8	0	4	0	0	219	[62]

D, diarrhoea; e.a., extra-amniotic; NA, data not available; P, abdominal pain requiring analgesics; PG–VA interval, interval between administration of prostaglandin and vacuum aspiration; v., vaginal; V, vomiting.

sulprostone, gemeprost and 9-methylene PGE_2 analogues were more effective than a medium-sized laminaria tent in dilating the cervix before VA and that the three E analogues were most effective. The blood loss at operation was also significantly lower in the group pretreated with prostaglandins. The incidence of gastrointestinal side effects and degree of uterine pain following 9-methylene PGE_2 and gemeprost was similar to that following laminaria tent insertion. In the World Health Organization (WHO) multicentre study [48], the cervical dilatation achieved with the three E analogues was also larger than that of the laminaria tent and the $PGF_{2\alpha}$ although the difference was not statistically significant. Gemeprost has also been shown to be more effective than Lamicel in preoperative cervical dilatation when inserted 3–4 h before VA [84]. Therefore, it appears that the prostaglandin E analogues are more effective than the intracervical tents when the pretreatment period is limited to 3 h. Moreover, the intracervical tents require insertion by medical personnel while the prostaglandins can be administered by paramedical staff. The use of prostaglandins has the additional benefit of reduction in blood loss. Therefore, in patients with no contraindication to prostaglandins, prostaglandin E analogues (except intramuscular sulprostone because the manufacturer has now advised against the intramuscular route for sulprostone), if available, are probably preferable to the intracervical tents.

After it had been shown that mifepristone is capable of inducing abortion, its effect on dilating the cervix before VA has also been evaluated [85–90]. All the double-blind placebo-controlled trials [85–88,90] showed that the cervical dilatation in the mifepristone group was significantly greater than in the placebo group and the cervix was softer and easier to dilate. The effect could be achieved by multiple doses [85,86,90] or a single dose [87–89]. The effect was evident with a single dose of mifepristone (100 mg) or more given orally 24 h before the VA, but the effect was more significant at 48 h [88]. The main advantage of mifepristone therapy is that it is not associated with any side effects except vaginal bleeding in some patients. In contrast to pretreatment with prostaglandins, there was no significant reduction in blood loss at operation [90]. The cervical dilatation achieved with mifepristone seemed to be less than that with prostaglandins [90], but there is as yet no prospective randomized study comparing the two methods of treatment. Another disadvantage of mifepristone is that it must be given 24–48 h prior to VA before it will be effective.

Comparison between VA and medical methods of abortion

There is as yet no prospective randomized study comparing VA and the medical methods of abortion at the gestational age of 9–14 weeks. From the available data, the main disadvantage of medical methods including the mifepristone–prostaglandin treatment regimen at this gestational age is that the incidence of incomplete abortion is likely to be more than 10%. This compares unfavourably with VA. The use of intracervical tents or pharmacological agents for preoperative cervical dilatation would make VA even more effective and safer. Serious complications are rare with either VA or medical abortion, but the abortion process with prostaglandins and mifepristone lasts for at least a few hours when the patients may experience side effects like vomiting, diarrhoea and uterine cramps which may require parenteral analgesics. VA is a much shorter process. Finally, the passage of products of gestation in medical abortion may lead to psychological distress.

The acceptability of abortion by prostaglandins and mifepristone has not been studied at this gestational age. In a prospective randomized study comparing D & C and intra-amniotic instillation of $PGF_{2\alpha}$ in abortion between 13 and 18 weeks gestation, Grimes et al. [91] found that women undergoing D & C had significantly better compliance with the assigned treatment and less delay prior to abortion. This study also found that some women were afraid of a long and painful abortion process. In a more recent study comparing women's preferences and acceptability of VA and medical abortion with mifepristone–prostaglandin, Henshaw et al. [92] found that the gestational age had a definite effect on acceptability in patients randomized to either form of treatment. At < 50 days there were no differences in acceptability of the two methods. Between 50 and 63 days, VA is significantly more acceptable. It was postulated that the more painful abortion process associated with a more advanced gestation was a possible factor making the medical abortion method less acceptable. Therefore, it is likely that VA may be a more acceptable method for many women at 9–14 weeks.

Conclusion

The limited data available indicate that medical abortion with prostaglandins and mifepristone at the gestational age of 9–14 weeks is associated with a higher incidence of incomplete abortion than in early pregnancy.

The method is also less acceptable than in early pregnancy. Conversely, VA has been shown to be a safe, effective and acceptable method for abortion at this gestational age. The safety and efficacy of VA can be further enhanced by the use of intracervical tents or pharmacological agents like prostaglandins or mifepristone to dilate the cervix before VA. Therefore, for many doctors and patients, VA with preoperative cervical dilatation is probably the preferred method of abortion at this gestational age.

References

1 Baird DT, Norman JE. Antifertility effects of antigestogens. *Reprod Med Rev* 1993; 2: 95–108.

2 Lauersen NH. Induced abortion. In: Bygdeman M, Berger GS, Keith G, eds. *Prostaglandins and their Inhibitors in Clinical Obstetrics and Gynaecology.* Lancaster: MTP Press, 1986: 271–314.

3 Wiqvist N, Bygdeman M, Toppozada M. Induction of abortion by the intravenous administration of prostaglandin $F_{2\alpha}$. *Acta Obstet Gynecol Scand* 1971; 50: 381–389.

4 Gillett PG, Kinch RAH, Wolfe LS, Pace-Asciak C. Therapeutic abortion with the use of prostaglandin $F_{2\alpha}$. *Am J Obstet Gynecol* 1972; 112: 330–338.

5 Lauersen NH, Wilson KH. Continuous extraovular administration of prostaglandin $F_{2\alpha}$ for midtrimester abortion. *Am J Obstet Gynecol* 1974; 120: 273–280.

6 Lange AP, Secher NJ, Pedersen GT. Comparison of extra-amniotic administration of $PGF_{2\alpha}$, 0.9% saline, and 20% saline followed by oxytocin for therapeutic abortion. *Acta Obstet Gynecol Scand* 1975; 37 (Suppl.): 61–66.

7 Nyberg R. Intra-amniotic administration of prostaglandin $F_{2\alpha}$ for therapeutic abortion. *Acta Obstet Gynecol Scand* 1975; 37 (Suppl.): 41–46.

8 Karim SMM, Filshie GM. The use of prostaglandin E_2 for therapeutic abortion. *J Obstet Gynaecol Br Commonw* 1972; 79: 1–13.

9 Lauersen NH, Secher NJ, Wilson KH. Mid-trimester abortion induced by intra-vaginal administration of prostaglandin E_2 suppositories. *Am J Obstet Gynecol* 1975; 122: 947–954.

10 Cameron IT, Baird DT. The use of 16, 16-dimethyl-trans Δ^2 prostaglandin E_1 methyl ester (gemeprost) vaginal pessaries for the termination of pregnancy in the early second trimester. A comparison with extra-amniotic prostaglandin E_2. *Br J Obstet Gynaecol* 1984; 91: 1136–1140.

11 Schwallie PC, Lamborn KR. Induction of abortion by intramuscular administration of 15s, 15-methyl $PGF_{2\alpha}$. *J Reprod Med* 1979; 23: 289–293.

12 Lauersen NH, Wilson KH. Midtrimester abortion induced by serial intramuscular injections of 15s, 15-methyl-prostaglandin $F_{2\alpha}$. *Am J Obstet Gynecol* 1975; 121: 273-276.

13 Leader A, Bygdeman M, Eneroth P, Lundström V, Martin JN Jr. Induced abortion in the 8–9th week of pregnancy with vaginally administered 15-methyl $PGF_{2\alpha}$ methyl ester. *Prostaglandins* 1976; 12: 631–637.

14 Borell U, Bygdeman M, Leader A, Lundström V, Martin JN Jr. Successful first trimester abortion with 15s, 15-methyl-prostaglandin $F_{2\alpha}$-methyl ester vaginal suppositories. *Contraception* 1976; 13: 87-94.

15 Wagatsuma T, Tabuchi T, Tabei T, Kaku R. Interruption of pregnancy with vaginal suppositories containing 16, 16-dimethyl-trans-Δ^2-prostaglandin E_1. *Contraception* 1979; 19: 591–597.

16 Nakano R, Hata H, Sasaki K, Yamoto M. The use of prostaglandin E_1 analogue pessaries in patients having first trimester induced abortions. *Br J Obstet Gynaecol* 1980; 87: 287–291.

17 Takagi S, Yoshida T, Ohya A et al. The abortifacient effect of 16, 16-dimethyl-trans-Δ^2-PGE_1 methyl ester, a new prostaglandin analogue, on mid-trimester pregnancies and long-term follow-up observations. *Prostaglandins* 1982; 23: 591–601.

18 Herrmann W, Wyss R, Riondel A et al. Effet d'un stéroide anti-progestérone chez la femme: interruption du cycle menstruel et de la grossesse au début. *CR Acad Sci Paris* 1982; 294: 933–938.

19 Kovacs L, Sas M, Resch BA et al. Termination of very early pregnancy by RU 486—an antiprogestational compound. *Contraception* 1984; 29: 399–410.

20 Couzinet B, Le Strat N, Ulmann A, Baulieu EE, Schaison G. Termination of early pregnancy by the progesterone antagonist RU 486 (mifepristone). *N Engl J Med* 1986; 315: 1565–1570.

21 Haspels AA. Interruption of early pregnancy by an anti-progestational compound, RU 486. *Europ J Obstet Gynecol Reprod Biol* 1985; 20: 169–175.

22 Grimes DA, Mishell DR Jr, Shoupe D, Lacarra M. Early abortion with a single dose of the antiprogestin RU 486. *Am J Obstet Gynecol* 1988;158:1307–1312.

23 Bygdeman M, Swahn M-L. Progesterone receptor blockage—effect on uterine contractility and early pregnancy. *Contraception* 1985; 32: 45–51.

24 Silvestre L, Dubois C, Renault M et al. Voluntary interruption of pregnancy with mifepristone (RU 486) and a prostaglandin analogue. A large-scale French experience. *N Engl J Med* 1990; 322: 645–648.

25 UK Multicentre Trial. The efficacy and tolerance of mifepristone and prostaglandin in first trimester termination of pregnancy. *Br J Obstet Gynaecol* 1990; 97: 480–486.

26 Norman J, Thong KJ, Baird DT. Increase in uterine contractility and induction of abortion in early pregnancy by misoprostol and mifepristone. *Lancet* 1991; 338: 1233–1236.

27 Peyron R, Aubény E, Targosz V et al. Early termination of pregnancy with mifepristone (RU 486) and the orally active prostaglandin misoprostol. *N Engl J Med* 1993; 328: 1509–1513.

28 McKinley C, Thong KJ, Baird DT. The effect of dose of mifepristone and gestation on the efficacy of medical abortion with mifepristone and misoprostol. *Hum Reprod* 1993; 8: 1502–1505.

29 Greenslade FC, Leonard AH, Benson J, Winkler J, Henderson VL. Manual vacuum aspiration: a summary of clinical and programmatic experience worldwide. *USA IPAS* 1993.

30 Beric BM, Kupresanin M. Vacuum aspiration, using pericervical block, for legal abortion as an outpatient procedure up to the 12th week of pregnancy. *Lancet* 1971; ii: 619–621.

31 Tietze C, Lewit S. Joint Program for the Study of Abortion (JPSA): early medical complications of legal abortion. *Stud Fam Plann* 1972; 3: 97–122.

32 Nathanson BN. Ambulatory abortion: experience with 26 000 cases (1 July 1970 to 1 August 1971). *N Engl J Med* 1972; 286: 403–407.

33 Hodgson JE. Major complications of 20 248 consecutive first trimester abortions: problems of fragmented care. *Adv Plan Parenthood* 1975; 9: 52–59.

34 Schonberg LA. Complications of outpatient abortion. *Adv Plann Parenthood* 1975; 10: 45–48.

35 Wulff GJL Jr, Freiman M. Elective abortion. Complications seen in a free-standing clinic. *Obstet Gynecol* 1977; 49: 351–357.

36 Bozorgi N. Statistical analysis of first-trimester pregnancy terminations in an ambulatory surgical center. *Am J Obstet Gynecol* 1977; 127: 763–768.

37 Grimes DA, Schulz KF, Cates W Jr, Tyler CW Jr. Local versus general anesthesia: which is safer for performing suction curettage abortions? *Am J Obstet Gynecol* 1979; 135: 1030–1035.

38 Smith RG, Palmore JA, Steinhoff PG. The potential reduction of medical complications from induced abortion. *Int J Gynaecol Obstet* 1978; 15: 337–346.

39 Hakim-Elahi E, Tovell HMM, Burnhill MS. Complications of first-trimester abortion: a report of 170 000 cases. *Obstet Gynecol* 1990; 76: 129–135.

40 Johnstone FD, Beard RJ, Boyd IE, McCarthy TG. Cervical diameter after suction termination of pregnancy. *Br Med J* 1976; 1: 68–69.

41 Wright CSW, Campbell S, Beazley J. Second trimester abortion after vaginal termination of pregnancy. *Lancet* 1972; 1: 1278–1279.

42 Johnson N. Intracervical tents: usage and mode of action. *Obstet Gynecol Surv* 1989; 44: 410–420.

43 Eaton CJ, Cohn F, Bollinger CC. Laminaria tent as a cervical dilator prior to aspiration-type therapeutic abortion. *Obstet Gynecol* 1972; 39: 533–537.

44 Newton BW. Laminaria tent: relic of the past or modern medical device? *Am J Obstet Gynecol* 1972; 113: 442–448.

45 Caspi E, Schneider D, Sadovsky G, Weinraub Z, Bukovsky I. Diameter of cervical internal os after induction of early abortion by laminaria or rigid dilatation. *Am J Obstet Gynecol* 1983; 146: 106–108.

46 Grimes DA, Ray IG, Middleton CJ. Lamicel versus laminaria for cervical dilation before early second-trimester abortion: a randomized clinical trial. *Obstet Gynecol* 1987; 69: 887–890.

47 Darney PD, Dorward K. Cervical dilation before first-trimester elective abortion: a controlled comparison of meteneprost, laminaria and Hypan. *Obstet Gynecol* 1987; 70: 397–400.

48 World Health Organization Task Force on Prostaglandins for Fertility Regulation. Randomized comparison of different prostaglandin analogues and laminaria tent for preoperative cervical dilatation. *Contraception* 1986; 34: 237–251.

49 Christensen NJ, Bygdeman M, Gréen K. Comparison of different prostaglandin analogues and laminaria for preoperative dilatation of the cervix in late first trimester abortion. *Contraception* 1983; 27: 51–61.

50 Liang ST, Woo JSK, Tang GWK. Ultrasonic localization of a displaced laminaria tent. *Am J Obstet Gynecol* 1983; 146: 988–989.

51 Brenner WE, Zuspan K. Synthetic laminaria for cervical dilatation prior to vacuum aspiration in midtrimester pregnancy. *Am J Obstet Gynecol* 1982; 143: 475–477.

52 Welch CC, Macpherson M, Johnson IR, Nicolaides K, Filshie GM. Preoperative dilatation of the first-trimester cervix: a comparison between Lamicel and 16, 16-dimethyl-trans Δ^2 prostaglandin E_1 methyl ester pessaries. *Am J Obstet Gynecol* 1984; 149: 400–402.

53 Norström A, Bryman I, Hansson HA. Cervical dilatation by lamicel before first trimester abortion: a clinical and experimental study. *Br J Obstet Gynaecol* 1988; 95: 372–376.

54 Rådestad A, Christensen NJ. Magnesium sulphate and cervical ripening. *Contraception* 1989; 39: 253–263.

55 Chvapil M, Droegemueller W, Meyer T, Macsalka R, Stoy V, Suciu T. New synthetic laminaria. *Obstet Gynecol* 1982; 60: 729–733.

56 Quinn MA, Jalland M, Wein R, Kloss M. Vaginal prostaglandin $F_{2\alpha}$ gel before first trimester termination of pregnancy. *Aust NZ J Obstet Gynaecol* 1981; 21: 93–95.

57 Mackenzie IZ, Fry A. Prostaglandin E_2 pessaries to facilitate first trimester aspiration termination. *Br J Obstet Gynaecol* 1981; 88: 1033–1037.

58 Cheng MCE, Karim SMM, Ratnam SS. Preoperative cervical dilatation with 15s, 15-methyl prostaglandin E_2 methyl ester in first trimester nulliparae—a double-blind study. *Contraception* 1975; 12: 59–67.

59 Lauersen NH, Seidman S, Wilson KH. Cervical priming prior to first-trimester suction abortion with a single 15-methyl-prostaglandin $F_{2\alpha}$ vaginal suppository. *Am J Obstet Gynecol* 1979; 135: 1116–1118.

60 World Health Organization Task Force on Prostaglandins for Fertility Regulation. Vaginal administration of 15-methyl-$PGF_{2\alpha}$ methyl ester for preoperative cervical dilatation. *Contraception* 1981; 23: 251–257.

61 Ho PC, Liang ST, Tang GWK, Ma HK. Preoperative cervical dilatation in termination of first trimester pregnancies using 16, 16-dimethyl-trans-Δ^2 PGE_1 methyl ester vaginal pessaries. *Contraception* 1983; 27: 339–346.

62 Chen JK, Elder MG. Preoperative cervical dilatation by vaginal pessaries containing prostaglandin E_1 analogue. *Obstet Gynecol* 1983; 62: 339–342.

63 Dingfelder JR, Brenner WE, Hendricks CH, Staurovsky LG. Reduction of cervical resistance by prostaglandin suppositories prior to dilatation for induced abortion. *Am J Obstet Gynecol* 1975; 122: 25–30.

64 Brenner WE, Dingfelder JR, Staurovsky LG, Hendricks CH. Vaginally administered $PGF_{2\alpha}$ for cervical dilatation in nulliparas prior to suction curettage. *Prostaglandins* 1973; 4: 819–836.

65 Craft IL, Evans DV, Richfield LB. Facilitation of suction termination using extra-amniotic prostaglandins in gel. *Prostaglandins* 1979; 18: 143–152.

66 Rath W, Kühnle H, Theobald P, Kuhn W. Objective demonstration of cervical softening with a prostaglandin $F_{2\alpha}$ gel during first trimester abortion. *Int J Gynaecol Obstet* 1982; 20: 195–199.

67 Chatterjee TK, Grech ES, Niles L. Preoperative cervical dilatation with 15s, 15-methyl $PGF_{2\alpha}$ methyl ester pessaries. *Int J Gynaecol Obstet* 1978; 15: 423–427.

68 Frankman O, Bygdeman M, Gréen K, Moberg P, Sandberg C-G. Dilatation of the cervix prior to vacuum aspiration by single vaginal administration of 15-methyl-$PGF_{2\alpha}$ methyl ester. *Contraception* 1980; 21: 571–576.

69 Ganguli AC, Gréen K, Bygdeman M. Preoperative dilatation of the cervix by single vaginal administration of 15-methyl-$PGF_{2\alpha}$-methyl ester. *Prostaglandins* 1977; 14: 779–784.

70 Fayemi A, Schulman H, Mitchell J, Fleischer A. Internal and external cervical os dilatation with vaginal 15-methyl prostaglandin $F_{2\alpha}$. *Am J Obstet Gynecol* 1983; 146: 219–220.

71 Niloff JM, Stubblefield PG. Low-dose vaginal 15-methyl prostaglandin $F_{2\alpha}$ for

cervical dilatation prior to vacuum curettage abortion. *Am J Obstet Gynecol* 1982; 142: 596–597.

72 Fehrmann H, Praetorius B. The cervix-ripening effect of the prostaglandin E analogue sulprostone, before vacuum aspiration in first trimester pregnancy. *Acta Obstet Gynecol Scand* 1983; 113 (Suppl.): 141–144.

73 Borten M, Dileo LA, Friedman EA. Low-dose prostaglandin E_2 analogue for cervical dilatation prior to pregnancy termination. *Am J Obstet Gynecol* 1984; 150: 561–565.

74 Sidhu MS, Kent DR. Effects of prostaglandin E_2 analogue suppository on blood loss in suction abortion. *Obstet Gynecol* 1984; 64: 128–130.

75 Moberg PJ, Bygdeman M, Carnsjö L-G, Frankman O, Gréen K. Pre-abortion treatment with a single vaginal suppository containing 9-deoxo-16, 16-dimethyl-9-methylene PGE_2 in late first and early second trimester pregnancies. *Acta Obstet Gynecol Scand* 1983; 113: 137–140.

76 Karim SMM, Ratnam SS, Selvadural V, Wun W, Prasad RNV. Cervical dilatation with 16, 16 dimethyl PGE_2 *p*-benzaldehyde semicarbazone ester prior to vacuum aspiration in first trimester nulliparae. *Prostaglandins* 1977; 13: 333–338.

77 Welch C, Elder MG. Cervical dilatation with 16, 16-dimethyl-trans-Δ^2 PGE_1 methyl ester vaginal pessaries before surgical termination of first trimester pregnancies. *Br J Obstet Gynaecol* 1982; 89: 849–852.

78 Leader A, Bygdeman M, Gréen K, Martin JN Jr, Wiqvist N. Vaginally administered 16, 16-dimethyl-prostaglandin E_2 as an agent for pre-operative cervical dilatation. *Prostaglandins* 1975; 10: 357–364.

79 Karim SMM, Ratnam SS, Prasad RNV, Wong YM. Vaginal administration of a single dose of 16, 16-dimethyl prostaglandin E_2 *p*-benzaldehyde semicarbazone ester for preoperative cervical dilatation in first trimester nulliparae. *Br J Obstet Gynaecol* 1977; 84: 269–271.

80 Prasad RNV, Lim C, Wong YC, Karim SMM, Ratnam SS. Vaginal administration of 16, 16 dimethyl trans-Δ^2 PGE_1, methyl ester (Ono 802) for preoperative cervical dilatation in first trimester nulliparous pregnancy. *Singapore J Obstet Gynaecol* 1978; 9: 69–71.

81 Bygdeman M, Bremme K, Christensen N, Lundström V, Gréen K. A comparison of two stable prostaglandin E analogues for termination of early pregnancy and for cervical dilatation. *Contraception* 1980; 22: 471–483.

82 Lauersen NH, Den T, Iliescu C, Wilson KH, Graves ZR. Cervical priming prior to dilatation and evacuation: a comparison of methods. *Am J Obstet Gynecol* 1982; 144: 890–894.

83 Lauersen NH, Graves ZR. Preabortion cervical dilatation with a low-dose prostaglandin suppository. *J Reprod Med* 1984; 29: 133–135.

84 Helm CW, Davies N, Beard RJ. A comparison of gemeprost (cervagem) pessaries and Lamicel tents for cervical preparation for abortion by dilatation and suction. *Br J Obstet Gynaecol* 1988; 95: 911–915.

85 Durlot F, Dubois C, Brunerie J, Frydman R. Efficacy of progesterone antagonist RU 486 (mifepristone) for preoperative cervical dilatation during first trimester abortion. *Hum Reprod* 1988; 3: 583–584.

86 Rádestad A, Christensen NJ, Strömberg L. Induced cervical ripening with mifepristone in first trimester abortion. *Contraception* 1988; 38: 301–312.

87 Gupta JK, Johnson N. Effect of mifepristone on dilatation of the pregnant and non-pregnant cervix. *Lancet* 1990; 335: 1238–1240.

88 Lefebvre Y, Proulx L, Elie R, Poulin O, Lanza E. The effects of RU 38486 on cervical ripening. *Am J Obstet Gynecol* 1990; 162: 61–65.

89 Johnson N, Bryce FC. Could antiprogesterones be used as alternative cervical ripening agents? *Am J Obstet Gynecol* 1990; 162: 688–690.

90 World Health Organization Task Force on Post-ovulatory Methods for Fertility Regulation. The use of mifepristone (RU 486) for cervical preparation in first trimester pregnancy termination by vacuum aspiration. *Br J Obstet Gynaecol* 1990; 97: 260–266.

91 Grimes DA, Hulka JF, McCutchen ME. Midtrimester abortion by dilatation and evacuation versus intra-amniotic instillation of prostaglandin $F_{2\alpha}$: a randomized clinical trial. *Am J Obstet Gynecol* 1980; 137: 785–790.

92 Henshaw RC, Naji SA, Russell IT, Templeton AA. Comparison of medical abortion with surgical vacuum aspiration: women's preferences and acceptability of treatment. *Br Med J* 1993; 307: 714–717.

5   Termination of Pregnancy after 14 Weeks

Mokhtar Toppozada

Introduction

Induction of abortion after 14 weeks of gestation (i.e. up to viability) is attended by a progressive and sharp rise in the rate of complications and costs. Despite the fact that they constitute only 10–20% of all induced abortions, they cause two-thirds of major complications and half of related maternal mortalities [1]. Induced abortion after 14 weeks should be limited to a minimum with proper counselling prior to the decision to end the pregnancy.

Medically induced abortion after 14 weeks involves three phases constituting a mini-labour: (i) cervical dilatation; (ii) fetal expulsion; and (iii) placental expulsion. Methods available include the following.

1   Medical methods. There are three types of medical method:
   (a) invasive (intrauterine drug administration);
   (b) non-invasive (systemic and vaginal drug administration);
   (c) combined.
2   Surgical methods, including:
   (a) vaginal approach such as dilatation and evacuation (D & E);
   (b) abdominal hysterotomy.
3   Combined methods. Preoperative cervical dilatation by antiprogestins, prostaglandins or slow mechanical dilators followed by surgical evacuation.

The intrauterine route of administration delivers active agents to the site of action (target organ), thus reducing both the dose and any side effects. This route also reduces the induction–abortion time. Methods with limited reported experience, or those involving agents associated with increased risk or which have become obsolete will not be discussed. This includes intra- or extra-amniotic administration of hypertonic glucose, magnesium or sodium phosphate, potassium chloride, mannitol, formalin, alcohol, iodine, Utus paste, soaps, creams, Pargyline, hydrochloride and bougies.

70

Methods used for clandestine second-trimester terminations in areas where restrictive abortion laws exist involve inadequate techniques and unhygienic conditions, and are necessarily performed in a hostile environment [2]. These will not be discussed here.

Methods of dilating and reducing resistance in the cervix

Medically induced late abortions (i.e. those up to 14 weeks) involve dealing with the opposition between one driving force represented by uterine power or myometrial activity and another represented by obstructive cervical resistance at the isthmic level (Fig. 5.1). The main obstacle to medical termination after 14 weeks is the resistance offered by the cervix. To overcome this via myometrial contractions alone entails

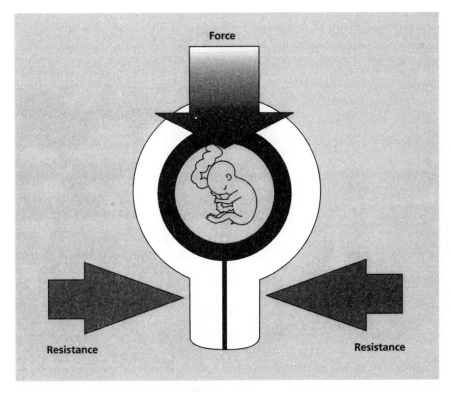

Fig. 5.1 A schematic representation of the challenge between uterine stimulation and cervico-isthmic resistance opposing expulsion in second-trimester induced abortion.

Table 5.1 The outcome of induced abortion trials as a function of the balance between myometrial contractions and the cervico–isthmic resistance

Force	Resistance	Outcome
Weak	Marked	Failed induction
Excessive	Marked	Cervical rupture or failed induction
Moderate or excessive	Reduced	Success in short time, low dose and side effects
Weak	Reduced	Failed induction or success in a long time

hyperstimulation with high drug doses. This process is lengthy and involves increased levels of risk and complications (Table 5.1). For instance, increased pain can result if the obstruction is not reduced leading to possible failure of the procedure or bursting of the cervix. Recent techniques favour a dual approach to facilitate the termination by both reducing cervical resistance and using a lower drug dose to provoke uterine contractions. Pretreatment or simultaneous therapy to reduce cervical resistance leads to increased success rates, reduced cervical injury and future cervical incompetence and reduced side effects. It also causes shorter induction–abortion times and a reduction in the required dose of uterine stimulant. Methods for dilating the cervix follow.

1 Slow cervical dilators:
   (a) *Laminaria japonica* tent (Mizotani Co., Nagoya, Japan);
   (b) osmotic cervical dilator (Lamicel, Merocel Corporation, Mystic, Conneticut, USA);
   (c) synthetic hygroscopic dilator (Dilapan, Gyneotech Inc., Lebanon, New Jersey, USA);
   (d) double-balloon catheter (Atad Migada Medical Equipment, Israel).
2 Pharmaceutical agents:
   (a) antiprogestins (oral);
   (b) prostaglandin E_2 (PGE_2)—vaginal, extra-amniotic or cervical;
   (c) intracervical oestradiol;
   (d) combinations (mechanical and pharmacological or two drugs).

Slow mechanical dilators

The use of laminaria tents (*L. japonica* or *digitata*) prior to or concomitant with medically induced second-trimester abortions has recently been revived. They are derived from seaweed which is dried and compressed into rods about 5 cm long with variable widths. A thread is present at one end to aid extraction. The tents swell slowly in the presence of moisture (hygroscopic), increasing within 4–12 h to about three to five times the original diameter, enhancing the softening of the cervix. Between one and five are inserted either manually or by a special tent introducer, passing beyond the internal os. Usually, this procedure requires no anaesthetic or the need to dilate the cervix. Laminaria dilatation can be performed in stages, first inserting one tent for 12 h and then replacing it with new dry ones. Uncommon complications include patient inconvenience, infection and local problems such as migration into the uterine cavity or impaction and breakage in the cervix.

Two synthetic slow dilators are commercially available, Lamicel and Dilapan. Lamicel is made of polyvinyl alcohol polymer sponge impregnated with approximately 200 mg of magnesium sulphate to form a cylindrical tent with a diameter of 3–5 mm and a length of 75 mm. This osmotic dilator swells to about four times its dry size by absorption of water from neighbouring cervical tissues. It stimulates collagenolytic activity in the cervix and increases the sensitivity of cervical tissues to PGE_2 [3]. The insertion of two osmotic dilators into the cervical canal past the internal os compares favourably with laminaria in terms of reducing both the induction time and cervical ruptures [4].

Dilapan is a hydrophilic polymer made of polyacrylonitrile. It swells more rapidly and dilates more effectively than other slow dilators as it opens the cervix 8–12 mm within 2–4 h [5]. It acts mainly via mechanical forces, while enzymatic and local humoral factors inducing cervical softening appear to be minimally involved. Thus, its removal is more difficult due to impaction in the cervix particularly if left *in situ* for > 4 h. Forceful attempts to remove the Dilapan rods in these circumstances may be attended with fragmentation and breaking down of the rods.

A double-balloon catheter, the Atad ripener, has been tested for dilating the cervix in 32 women up to 15 weeks gestation [6]. One uterine balloon is placed just inside the internal os while the other is located at the external os by pulling the catheter after inflating the inner balloon. Each balloon is filled with 60–80 ml saline. The device induced a very good degree of cervical dilatation (10–18 mm), but the study involved many variables such as different parities, use of PGE_2 extra-ovular drip in some cases (250 µg/h) and inconsistent duration between application and evacuation.

Pharmacological agents

Progesterone antagonists

Two groups of progesterone antagonists are available for pregnancy termination. The first involves progesterone synthesis inhibitors such as epostane (Sterling-Winthrop, Guildford, UK), which is a potent inhibitor of 3β-hydroxysteroid dehydrogenase, thus blocking the conversion of pregnenolone to progesterone [7]. The second group includes antagonists which act by binding strongly to progesterone receptors and, thus, blocking the action of progesterone through competitive inhibition. The former group has only been evaluated clinically in few limited trials while the receptor blockers have been more extensively tested and are available in some countries.

Of the blockers, RU 486 or mifepristone (Roussel Uclaf, Romainville, France) is the only one available, while others such as ZK 98.299 (onapristone) or ZK 98.734 (lilopristone) (Schering AG, Berlin) have not been used in clinical trials [8]. Mifepristone is a 19-norsteroid derived from norethisterone with strong antiprogesterone activity as well as antigluco-corticoid activity. After oral intake, a peak blood level is achieved in 1–3 h while its half-life ranges between 26 and 48 h [9]. Single or multiple doses of mifepristone (25–1000 mg) have been used clinically. The effect of reducing cervical stiffness was dose-related in the range of 25–100 mg but higher doses did not seem to improve the effect [10]. However, doses in common use range between 200 and 600 mg. A single administration is preferable due to better patient compliance. The time-lag between mife-pristone intake and the second procedure of stimulating uterine activity ranged between 12 and 48 h, although 24–36 h appears to be optimal [11].

As a preparatory agent prior to active second-trimester terminations, mifepristone does not seem to induce side effects except the uncommon occurrence of mild lower abdominal cramps and occasional minor vaginal bleeding. It softens and dilates the cervix by: (i) releasing the myometrium from progesterone suppression and increasing its sensitivity to prostaglandins or ergot derivatives (not oxytocin); and (ii) exerting a direct effect on the cervix [12]. Changes in the cervix occur prior to the establishment of significant uterine activity at about 36 h after progest-erone blockade. This indicates that the observed changes are mainly induced by a direct effect.

The local mechanism of action of mifepristone on the cervix is unclear

[13]. It has been suggested that it acts through an increase in prostanoid synthesis, but such an assumption could not be confirmed by analytical methods. Moreover, the effect was not reduced by the prostaglandin synthesis inhibitor naproxen [10,12,13]. Accordingly, it has been suggested that mifepristone softens the cervix by increasing the cervical concentration of PGE receptors together with an inhibition of prostaglandin dehydrogenase activity, leading to a decreased prostaglandin catabolism not reflected in the peripheral circulation [12–14].

The future prospects for the use of mifepristone as a preparatory step in medical methods of induced second-trimester abortions are very promising and the combination with prostaglandins offers many attractive clinical potentials. Moreover, the combination would allow an out-patient phase of mifepristone effect (24–36 h) followed by a day-case prostaglandin termination of mid-trimester pregnancy [11,12]. Also, the combined administration of the antiprogestins mifepristone and epostane may prove to be a valuable method and a logical approach to the block of both the synthesis and actions of progesterone.

PGE_2

Prostaglandins were identified more than 20 years ago as useful agents for dilating the cervix prior to termination of pregnancy in the first trimester as well as in the early stages of the second trimester [15]. Initially, natural prostaglandins (PGE_2 and $PGF_{2\alpha}$) were used systemically or locally, but with the introduction of the new analogues, intramuscular and vaginal applications were preferred because they are non-invasive and simple to use [16]. The World Health Organization (WHO) conducted several studies with intramuscular and vaginal prostaglandins to dilate the cervix preoperatively [16,17]. Three PGE analogues were found to be equally effective as one medium-sized laminaria tent inserted into the cervix. Cervical preparation by prostaglandins can reduce early and remote complications liable to result from subsequent intervention whether surgical (D & E) or pharmacological (saline or prostaglandins). Intracervical PGE_2 gel is a medical primer of the cervix and is just as effective as a laminaria tent in preparing the cervix [18].

Intracervical oestradiol

Overnight preliminary treatment with intracervical 17β-oestradiol gel (50 mg) significantly improved the cervical score (compared to the placebo-treated group) and reduced the induction–abortion time subsequently induced by gemeprost vaginal pessaries (May and Baker, Dagenham, UK) [19].

Medical methods

Invasive intrauterine administration of drugs

Invasive approaches are accompanied by particular problems and risks such as faulty injection (maternal tissue damage, bloody tap), the introduction of infection and the rupture of membranes. Rapid access of the drug to the maternal systemic circulation and the inability to withdraw the injected agent in cases of serious complication or toxicity represent major drawbacks. Moreover, intrauterine instillation requires a certain degree of skill and involves local manipulations inducing patient discomfort.

Intra-amniotic administration

Hypertonic saline

This method was first described in 1934 by Aburel, in Bucharest [20]. Many maternal deaths were reported in connection with this method but were mostly attributed to faulty technique or use of concentrations over 20% [21]. Proper insertion and positioning of the intra-amniotic needle and initial slow instillation of saline over 10 min are important safeguards that contributed to the lack of mortalities in 5000 consecutive terminations [22].

Amniocentesis is usually performed with an 18 gauge needle inserted in the suprapubic region at a point previously infiltrated with a local anaesthetic. Ultrasound scanning is a valuable guide for this purpose. The usual technique involves a slow instillation of 200 ml of 20% sodium chloride. This allows early detection of adverse manifestations that would necessitate the immediate cessation of administration. When used alone, intra-amniotic hypertonic saline is associated with a relatively long latent period prior to the onset of uterine contractions, which is the reason why only 20% would be expected to abort in the first 24 h. In the following 24 h, approximately 85% will abort and by 72 h from salt instillation almost 95–97% will have aborted [23]. Augmentation with intravenous oxytocin infusion within 12 h after the salt administration reduces abortion time to a mean of 24 h, but may slightly increase the risk of coagulopathies and uterine injury. The concomitant use of cervical dilators such as *L. japonica* further improves the clinical outcome of the induction.

The complications of intra-amniotic hypertonic saline instillation occur as follows [24].

1 Immediately after administration characterized by:
   (a) bloody tap;
   (b) acute abdominal pain;
   (c) rapid pulse, hypotension, irritability and agitation due to rapid access into the vascular compartment.
2 Slightly delayed or late after administration:
   (a) ascites due to leakage into the peritoneal cavity;
   (b) premature rupture of the membranes;
   (c) prolonged latent period;
   (d) fever;
   (e) abortion complications;
   (f) coagulopathies and hypernatraemia—these are the most serious risks.

Clinically significant hypofibrinogenaemia occurs in about 0.1% of cases (more frequently when oxytocin is administered). Hypernatraemia leads to a complex group of symptoms ranging from thirst to cardiac arrest. While lethal hypernatraemia is quite rare (approximately one in 50 000 abortions), symptomatic hypernatraemia occurs in about one in 200 cases [25].

Prostaglandins

Acting as a reservoir, the amniotic sac slowly releases the intra-amniotic prostaglandin to stimulate the myometrium. This route of administration was introduced by Bygdeman *et al.* [26] and Karim and Sharma [27]. It proved to be highly successful and associated with few side effects [28].

From a large number of investigations, the optimal intra-amniotic $PGF_{2\alpha}$ dose seems to be either 25 mg repeated after 6 h (and occasionally a third dose after 24 h) or 40–50 mg as a single dose [29,30]. PGE_2 in single doses (5–20 mg) or repeated installations (3–10 mg) were also very successful but less popular [31].

The most common analogue used via this route was 15-methyl $PGF_{2\alpha}$ (Prostin, 15 M = Carboprost) which is approximately 20 times more potent than its parent compound (Table 5.2) [32]. It was evaluated in two large multicentre studies (2406 subjects) comparing a single 2.5 mg dose with either 40 or 50 mg $PGF_{2\alpha}$ [29,33]. The analogue was significantly more effective (95 versus 81–89%). The mean induction–abortion interval was 18–20 h and side effects were clinically acceptable. Cervical injuries were similar with both compounds in the WHO study but more common with $PGF_{2\alpha}$ in the Indian study. Thus, a single intra-amniotic dose of 2.5 mg of 15-methyl $PGF_{2\alpha}$ appears to be an effective and acceptable method for late mid-trimester induced abortions [34].

Hyperosmolar urea

Intra-amniotic instillation of 80 g urea in 5% dextrose is favoured by some American institutions for the induction of late second-trimester abortions. Administration is simple and urea crosses cell membranes and acts as an osmotic diuretic. Thus, in contrast to hypertonic saline, the method is relatively harmless if the active agent gains rapid access to the systemic circulation. When used alone, urea has a low efficacy and a long induction–abortion interval. For this reason, the method is usually combined with a high intravenous infusion of oxytocin or intra-amniotic $PGF_{2\alpha}$ (5–10 mg) or PGE_2 (2.5–10 mg) [35]. This raises the success rate to 95% within 24 h. Advantages include: (i) urea is available at a relatively low cost; (ii) a shorter hospital stay; (iii) reduced electrolyte abnormalities; and (iv) fetal death usually occurs soon after the injection. General complications related to the abortion remain but these are common to most methods. Cervical injuries could be significantly reduced by the concomitant intracervical insertion of laminaria tents.

Extra-amniotic (extra-ovular) administration

Hypertonic saline

This is usually carried out transcervically using a Nelaton or Foley catheter with its balloon located at the internal os. It is introduced for about 15 cm, followed by a slow injection of 80–150 ml of 20% saline. This method is unpopular, usually being reserved for the early stages of the second trimester. Intrauterine instillation of hypertonic saline is believed to exert its clinical effects mainly by stimulating the endogenous release of prostaglandins.

Table 5.2 Available prostaglandin analogues for clinical use to terminate pregnancies beyond 14 weeks. Pretreatment with cervical laminaria (12–48 h), Dilapan or Lamicel (4–6 h) or oral mifepristone (24–48 h) prior to prostaglandin administration markedly improves the clinical outcome

Analogue	Route of administration	Proprietary name and company	Schedule (mg/h)
15s, 15-methyl PGF$_{2\alpha}$-THAM salt	Intra-amniotic Extra-amniotic Intramuscular*	Prostin/15 M (Carboprost), Upjohn Co.	2.5 (single dose) 0.9–1 (single dose) 0.2–0.3 every 3 h
15s, 15-methyl PGF$_{2\alpha}$ methyl ester	Vaginal	In China	1–1.5 every 3 h
15-deoxy-16-hydroxy-16-methyl PGE$_1$	Oral	Misoprostol (Cytotec), G.D. Searle	0.4 every 3 h
16-phenoxy-ω-tetranor-17, 18, 19, 20-PGE$_2$-methyl sulphonylamide	Intramuscular† Intravenous infusion	Sulprostone (Nalador), Pfizer-Schering	0.5–1 every 4–8 h 1.5 every 6 h
16,16-dimethyl-trans-Δ^2 PGE$_1$ methyl ester	Vaginal	Gemeprost (Cervagem pessaries), Ono Pharmaceuticals and May and Baker	1 every 3 h
9-deoxy-16, 16-dimethyl-9-methylene PGE$_2$ (potassium salt)	Vaginal	Meteneprost gel (in India)	5 every 4 h

* Useful to finalize failed or arrested induction by other approaches.
† Not recommended at present due to possible cardiovascular complications.

Rivanol (ethacridine lactate)

(Also called Acrinol, Acridol, Rimaon, Vucine, Acrolactine, Ethodin, Metifex or Emcredil.) This is a weak base belonging to the acridine dye group with weak antiseptic properties. Having a German–Japanese origin, its use as a second-trimester abortifacient began in the West in the late 1960s. Despite reassuring human data on safety issues in clinical practice, the WHO toxicology review panel denied permission for clinical trials in view of significant acute toxicity data in animals.

The compound is used as a 0.1% solution injected in the extra-ovular compartment by a Nelaton or Foley catheter passed through the cervix. The injected volume should be in the range of 10 ml/week of gestation up to a maximum of 150 ml. Addition of an intravenous oxytocin drip 50 µl/min is commonly used and achieves a success rate of 90% in 72 h and a mean induction time of 24 h [36]. The incidence of cervical injuries compares favourably with hypertonic saline (one in 1000) or prostaglandin-induced abortions (one in 100) [37]. Moreover, coagulopathies have not been observed with rivanol abortions. Intra-amniotic rivanol instillation plus oxytocin infusion has been tried in a limited trial to terminate pregnancies after 14 weeks [38]. The mean injection–abortion time was long (37.2 h), but no complications were reported.

Prostaglandins

This method was first reported in 1970 by Wiqvist and Bygdeman [39]. The prostaglandin compounds are administered transcervically by a Nelaton or Foley catheter by repeated instillations, via continuous extra-amniotic infusion or as a single injection.

Repeated extra-amniotic instillations of $PGF_{2\alpha}$ or PGE_2 require an initial test dose of 250 µg $PGF_{2\alpha}$ or 50 µg PGE_2 followed by 750 µg $PGF_{2\alpha}$ or 200 µg PGE_2 every 2 h up to 36 h. A schedule like this would be expected to end the pregnancy (80–90% success rate) within 20–24 h [40]. Extra-ovular infusions of PGE_2 or $PGF_{2\alpha}$ have been used by several investigators in the second trimester of pregnancy with various success rates (up to 98%), but the conclusion was that it is a slow and painful although safe and effective procedure [41,42]. The inconvenience of having an indwelling catheter which may increase the risk of infection has been avoided by using longer acting analogues or mixing the active drug with a viscous solution to make a single administration sufficient to achieve the clinical goal. High single doses of natural prostaglandins (PGE_2 and PGF_2) induced an unacceptable rate of side effects [43]. When the dose was mixed in a slow-release gel or viscous solution (e.g. methyl cellulose) the side effects were reduced but an additional dose was sometimes necessary. A dose of 0.92–1 mg of 15-methyl $PGF_{2\alpha}$ mixed in viscous dextran 70 solution was evaluated in two large multicenter studies (2300 subjects pregnant between 10 and 20 weeks) (see Table 5.2). This form of treatment was successful in 80% of cases within 36 h and the incidence of side effects and cervical lacerations was acceptable [33,44]. Compared with intra-amniotic administration, the extra-ovular route is slightly less effective and may need repeated local manipulations. However, it requires lower doses, has a rapid onset of effects, causes less cervical lacerations and can be used in situations not suitable for intra-amniotic instillation, e.g. ruptured membranes, molar pregnancy, fibroid uterus and the early weeks of second trimester.

Present status of intrauterine administration of prostaglandins

Intra-amniotic and extra-amniotic (extra-ovular) injection of prostaglandins have been introduced to avoid the systemic side effects of vomiting and diarrhoea caused by parenteral or vaginal administration of $PGF_{2\alpha}$ and PGE_2. Local invasive administration provides advantages in terms of lower dosage and shorter induction interval. Local complications such as infection or bloody tap plus the introduction of new analogues with favourable properties has shifted the clinical attitude towards systemic and vaginal therapy. The two natural prostaglandins, PGE_2 and $PGF_{2\alpha}$, and one analogue, 15-methyl $PGF_{2\alpha}$ (Prostin/15 M or Carboprost, Upjohn, Kalamazoo, Michigan, USA), have been widely investigated for second-trimester induced abortions by the intrauterine route. Transabdominal intramyometrial PGF administration and intracervical PGE_2 (into the substance of the cervix or as a gel into the cervical canal) have been tried but never gained popularity as they offered no major advantages [45].

Non-invasive (systemic or vaginal) routes of drug administration

Oral administration

Either prostaglandins or antiprogestins (progesterone antagonists) are suitable to use via this route. In view of the unacceptable rate of gastrointestinal side effects and the need for relatively high doses due to low bioavailability, oral prostaglandins have not proved clinically attractive. Misoprostol (Cytotec, GD Searle, High Wycombe, UK) is a synthetic analogue of PGE_1, used in 72 countries for the treatment of gastric and duodenal ulcers [46]. Like any other prostaglandin, it also has a uterine-stimulating effect and is particularly useful because it is orally active (see Table 5.2). The drug is relatively inexpensive, effective as an abortifacient and is particularly convenient to use, especially at home. The pills can be taken orally or inserted vaginally (after crushing and mixing with a cream) and reported doses ranged from four to 16 tablets. Combination with mifepristone (RU 486) raised its success rate to 85–95% in early pregnancy [47,48]. In the second trimester, up to 20 weeks, misoprostol (400 mg at three-hourly doses up to three times) supplemented later by cervagem gemeprost, (1 mg three-hourly, twice) proved equally effective (90%) to gemeprost (three-hourly, five doses) when either regimen was given 36–48 h after oral mifepristone [49].

The available clinical data indicate that oral intake of the progesterone antagonist, mifepristone, if used alone is capable of inducing complete abortion in early pregnancy but the success rate is too low (approximately 60%) to be clinically acceptable [50]. The development of sequential treatment with a prostaglandin greatly improved clinical performance and achieved major advantages, both in first- and second-trimester terminations.

Intravenous administration

Two drugs are used via this route; oxytocin is only used as an accessory to other methods of terminating pregnancy, the other agent is a prostaglandin. Initially, PGE_2 and $PGF_{2\alpha}$ were used but because of an unacceptable rate of side effects, most prostaglandin infusions have been abandoned. The only prostaglandin compound used at present as the primary agent for induction of abortion via the intravenous route is the PGE_2 analogue sulprostone (Schering AG, Berlin) (see Table 5.2). The evaluated doses ranged between 1000 and 2000 µg in normal saline administered at a rate of 100–500 µg/h over a period of time from 4 to 15 h [51,52], the recommended optimal dose being 1500 µg/4–6 h. When used alone, the treatment is successful in about 80% within 12–24 h, with few side effects due to its uterine selective properties.

Intramuscular administration of prostaglandins

Only two prostaglandins are available for intramuscular administration to terminate second-trimester pregnancies, 15-methyl $PGF_{2\alpha}$ tromethamine (THAM: Prostin/15 M, Carboprost) and 16-phenoxy-ω-tetranor PGE_2 methyl sulphonylamide (Sulprostone, Nalador) (see Table 5.2).

Many trials were conducted using variable intramuscular doses and time intervals of 15-methyl $PGF_{2\alpha}$; a fixed dose of 0.2–0.3 mg every 2–3 h or an increasing dose from 0.1 up to 0.75 mg (every 1–2 h) [53–55]. Medical opinion favours a fixed dose of 0.25 mg administered every 3 h. Such a schedule achieved success in 80–90% of cases within 36 h but the incidence of gastrointestinal side effects was too high. It was therefore concluded that intramuscular carboprost, when used alone, is of limited clinical value but very useful as a supplement for other methods that initiated but failed to complete the abortion process [34].

Sulprostone (Nalador) is the second prostaglandin analogue suitable for intramuscular use to induce second-trimester abortion. It possesses what has been described as 'reproductive-specific properties'. It is equally effective as intramuscular carboprost (80–90% success rate in 30 h) but gastrointestinal side effects are much less [56]. The usually prescribed dose is 0.5 mg to be repeated every 4 h for a maximum period of 30–36 h but other schedules have also been tested such as 1 mg every 6–8 h [34,56].

Vaginal administration of prostaglandins

Although the vaginal route is not a truly systemic form of administration, the systemic absorption of the prostaglandin, and the simple non-invasive nature of intake makes it a useful non-invasive approach. Local effects on the cervix and uterus are possible additional actions. The development of clinically useful vaginal prostaglandin formulations is a valuable milestone and one of the most significant advances in the field of clinical prostaglandin research.

Initially, $PGF_{2\alpha}$ (50 mg) or PGE_2 (20 mg) were developed for vaginal administration but they induced substantial gastrointestinal side effects. At present, three analogues have been evaluated in clinical trials: (i) 15-methyl $PGF_{2\alpha}$ methyl ester (1.5–3 mg); (ii) 16, 16 dimethyl-trans-Δ^2 PGE_1 methyl ester (gemeprost, 1 mg); and (iii) 9-deoxo-16, 16-dimethyl-9-methylene PGE_2 (meteneprost). The latter was originally made in a lipid base of Witepsol (75 mg), but more recently a stable hydrophilic gel replaced the lipid base which markedly increased the drug bioavailability and reduced the dose to 4.5–5 mg [57]. Moreover, the gel consistency did not vary with temperature changes [58].

In a WHO multicentre study, repeated vaginal administration of 15-methyl $PGF_{2\alpha}$ methyl ester (1.5 mg) every 3 h up to 30 h was successful in 91.9% of 310 women between weeks 13 and 20 of gestation with a mean time of 14.2 h [59]. This performance was similar to that of the same drug administered intramuscularly. The development of long-acting suppositories (3 mg) or slow-release silastic devices (10 mg) has made a single insertion sufficient to terminate pregnancy in the second trimester [60]. This formulation has not gained popularity because of the high incidence of side effects, initial stability problems and relatively high failure rate (necessitating additional intramuscular carboprost) in one-fifth of subjects.

Meteneprost is a very stable prostaglandin compound dispensed in a stable hydrophilic gel containing 4.5 mg. This formulation is administered at 4 h intervals and appears to be highly effective (> 90%) in the second trimester with reduced incidence of side effects, particularly if combined with the insertion of laminaria tents.

Gemeprost (Cervagem) is one of the newest vaginal PGE_1 analogues for late second-trimester induced abortions (see Table 5.2). It has been developed by Ono Pharmaceuticals, Japan and licensed for use abroad to May and Baker, UK [61–65]. The recommended dose of this analogue is a vaginal pessary (1 mg) every 3 h up to five times in the first 24 h to be repeated if necessary. Addition of oxytocin drip was recommended at 36 h from the onset of the trial. Such a regimen was successful in 95% of 932 women pregnant between 12 and 27 weeks and the median induction–abortion time was 16.9 h. Few gastrointestinal side effects occurred but no cervical injuries were reported. However, 80% of women required parenteral opiates to alleviate pain [64]. Increasing the interval between the vaginal pessaries to 6 h did not seem to affect the clinical outcome by the end of 24 h (88 versus 82% in the 3- and 6-h interval groups), but more women failed to abort by the end of 48 h [65]. Thus, it can be tentatively concluded that there are several non-invasive, safe, effective and simple options for late induced abortions, although some drawbacks still exist such as some side effects, particularly pain, and an induction time that could not be reduced below 12–15 h by prostaglandins alone.

Surgical methods

Vaginal approach

Cervical dilatation and surgical evacuation of uterine contents by suction, and instrumental methods (D & E) is a common practice and in some countries such as the USA, it is the most common technique for pregnancy termination up to 21 weeks of gestation. Advocates of this method even recommend its use for more advanced stages of gestation (up to 20 weeks) based on data indicating a relatively high degree of safety [66]. Moreover, some sources have suggested the use of D & E up to 25 weeks gestation but this is unorthodox [67].

Initially, the Joint Program for the Study of Abortion (JPSA) showed a progressive rise in complication rates associated with D & E up to 15 weeks [68]. However, when compared to hypertonic saline or prostaglandins, the data indicates that D & E may be safer, and a lot cheaper [69]. Furthermore, at each period of gestation the lowest rate of complications for saline abortions was two to three times higher than the highest rates for suction abortions. Most of the above data are from the USA and a few other countries; in contrast, the rest of the world rarely practice late abortions by vaginal surgery.

D & E beyond 14 weeks of gestation requires experienced surgeons, special instruments and preoperative slow cervical dilatation. Lack of any of these prerequisites, particularly the surgical skill and experience, makes the approach risky, contributing to frequent serious complications. For this reason some gynaecologists prefer to reserve D & E for first-trimester terminations only, and only with special precautions allowing it to be used up to 14 weeks gestation, when slow preoperative preparation of the cervix is performed.

Abdominal approach (abdominal hysterotomy)

This is a major abdominal operation with all the attendant surgical and anaesthetic risks. It is not a routine approach but reserved for selected cases requiring other interventions, particularly sterilization by tubal ligation or excision of an associated ovarian cyst. The incidence of morbidity and mortality with abdominal hysterotomy is higher than other methods in most studies and surveys. However, data from India [70] indicate the contrary since hysterotomy was associated with lower morbidity rates than other methods used at the same stage of pregnancy.

Combined methods

The use of more than one approach (sometimes three) to improve the clinical outcome is frequently used. A complementary or supplementary drug or modality can be used to augment or improve the performance of a method. A large number of combinations have been tested, but most of them were only evaluated in a few studies and involved relatively small numbers of patients. Any of the pre-induction cervical ripening and dilating agents or devices can be used with any of the uterine stimulating procedures or D & E. The agent or device can be given via the same or a different route of administration. Also, the time of therapy may be sequential with an interval of up to 3 days between the methods. Popular combinations include the following:

1   intravenous oxytocin infusions with intrauterine drug administration;
2   intra-amniotic prostaglandins with hypertonic saline or urea;
3   preparation of the cervix (softening and dilatation) prior to uterine stimulants or D & E.

A combined, rather promising, approach was described more than 10 years ago whereby one medium-sized laminaria tent was inserted into the cervix 8–18 h prior to intramuscular administration of prostaglandin analogues. Intramuscular carboprost injections (0.25 mg every 2 h), starting 18 h after laminaria insertion, were successful in 99% of 490 second-trimester terminations within 48 h, with a mean induction–abortion interval of 12.6 h [71]. Also, intramuscular sulprostone (0.5 mg every 4 h), after pretreatment with laminaria succeeded in 96–100% of 60 cases in a mean time of approximately 11 h [72]. Both intramuscular analogues (with laminaria pretreatment) were compared in a WHO multicentre study involving 529 patients. The treatment was successful in about 95% within 24 h but the F analogue induced significantly more side effects and three cases had cervical lacerations [73]. This regimen of combined laminaria and intramuscular prostaglandin appeared at the time of development as the most effective non-surgical method with the shortest induction time and reduced cervical injuries.

As discussed above, the first major breakthrough in the field of medical methods of inducing mid-trimester abortions came in the 1970s with the development of prostaglandins. This was followed by the second in the 1980s with the introduction of progesterone antagonists to pretreat subjects scheduled for pregnancy termination by prostaglandins. The oral intake of 150–600 mg mifepristone, 24–48 h prior to the induction of late second-trimester abortion by intramuscular sulprostone, vaginal gemeprost (Cervagem), meteneprost or extra-amniotic PGE_2, proved to be an excellent pretreatment as the success rate was almost 100% [18,74–76]. Present knowledge indicates that the optimal single oral dose of mifepristone is 200 mg taken at home 24–36 h prior to prostaglandin administration. Lower doses may prove to be equally effective but 24 h seems to be the minimal time needed to prepare the cervix sufficiently.

The significant advantage of the mifepristone–prostaglandin combination is the marked reduction in the prostaglandin–abortion interval from a mean of 14–20 to 4.5–8.5 h. It seems likely that this time span (which may turn the abortion into a day-care service) has reached its minimum and to reduce it further may increase the risks to the patient. Additional important advantages include the lower dose and cost, reduced side effects and pain, as well as the simplicity of this non-invasive procedure.

Vaginal pessaries of gemeprost used to finalize the abortion after mifepristone pretreatment contain 1 mg of the PGE_1 analogue and are administered every 3–6 h [75,77]. The longer interval (lower dose) may guard against the very rare cardiovascular complications and reduce other risks, side effects and costs. The incidence of diarrhoea (5%), which is more prostaglandin-related than vomiting, is considerably lower than that observed with abortions induced by gemeprost alone and complete abortions were two-thirds more than those reported earlier with prostaglandins alone.

Meteneprost is the other new vaginal PGE analogue with improved properties administered 24 h after the antiprogestin mifepristone was orally administered. Hydrophilic vaginal gel (5 mg) given every 4 h up to 24 h, was successful in all cases pregnant for more than 14 weeks. However, a similar group pretreated with intracervical 0.5 mg PGE_2 (Minprostin) was only successful in about 85% of inductions. It was therefore concluded that oral mifepristone is a better preparatory agent than PGE_2 gel for late second-trimester terminations. When both antiprogestin and intracervical PGE_2 were used together, the interval to abortion was reduced to 6.6 h [18].

The only intramuscular analogue used in conjunction with mifepristone is the E derivative sulprostone. A prospective randomized double-blind, placebo-controlled trial was conducted in 13 nulliparous women between 14 and 20 weeks. Placebo tablets or mifepristone (600 mg) were administered orally followed after 36 h by intramuscular sulprostone [76]. All subjects in the mifepristone preparation group aborted within 10 h from the first prostaglandin injection, while half the women in the placebo group failed to abort by 24 h. The median interval between onset of intramuscular sulprostone and abortion was significantly shorter in the mifepristone group (4.6 h) than the placebo group (20 h).

Comparative evaluation

None of the methods in current use for termination of pregnancy beyond 14 weeks are ideal and the search for safer and more acceptable methods is a priority. However, in recent years major advances in medical abortion methods have been achieved.

There are many unresolved issues in this complex area. Where unlimited combination methods exist, habit favours certain combinations over others. Whether pretreatment or augmentation is used or not, the variable intervals between procedures and differing attitudes towards the management of the abortion process makes comparison between trials difficult. Lack of skill and experience with certain techniques creates an obstacle to proper scientific comparative evaluation. The lack of working definitions and well-designed comparative, properly randomized prospective studies involving enough cases also makes comparison difficult. These factors restrict even tentative conclusions as to what the most favourable method might be. Furthermore, investigative trials may not always reflect real life clinical practice.

As discussed above, there are three main approaches used for late second-trimester terminations: (i) intrauterine instillation of drugs or solutions (intra- or extra-amniotic); (ii) systemic administration (including vaginal) of prostaglandins; and (iii) D & E. Of the intra-amniotic methods, prostaglandins (particularly $PGF_{2\alpha}$ or carboprost) appear to be the most effective since higher proportions of subjects abort following a single (or two at most) instillation within a shorter period of time. Intra-amniotic prostaglandins may be associated with a lower mortality rate than saline but may induce more complications and side effects [36]. Inadvertent injection with hypertonic saline (intravascular, intramyometrial or intraperitoneal) can cause much more harm than with prostaglandins. Intra-amniotic hyperosmolar urea becomes comparable to other intra-amniotic agents only if $PGF_{2\alpha}$ is added, but experience with this combination is somewhat limited. Extra-amniotic instillation (single, repeated or continuous) particularly of prostaglandins, is popular in some countries, such as the UK, even though it carries the risk of introducing infection.

The development of new prostaglandin analogues with improved therapeutic ratios and selective reproductive properties has made systemic and vaginal administration possible. The refined clinical performance and non-invasive method of administration allowed these formulations to replace natural prostaglandins. Intramuscular carboprost or prostin (15 M) is not recommended for use alone because of frequent side effects, but pretreatment (12–24 h) with laminaria tents would improve clinical outcome. Slow mechanical dilators, however, require trained personnel, their insertion is inconvenient for patients, they need several hours to exert the desired effect and may have local complications. Due to these drawbacks, the use of mifepristone pretreatment prior to non-invasive prostaglandin administration seems to be the simplest non-surgical approach to recommend. This method involves minimal side effects and pain. It is also extremely efficient, markedly reduces prostaglandin–abortion time and involves less cost. It is also possible to give the prostaglandin on a day-care basis following a 24–36 h phase of the antiprogestin effect at home.

The practice and safety of D & E in pregnancies beyond 14 weeks is a matter of controversy, though some advocates consider it the safest, quickest and most cost-effective method of second-trimester pregnancy termination. However, there are no randomized trials between D & E and medical methods of inducing abortion, and contemporary series reported from the USA date from 15 to 20 years ago before antiprogestins and the newer generation of prostaglandins became available. The crucial issues here are that the only source of data for comparison is from the USA and then it only comes from certain selected centres with few individuals highly experienced in this sort of surgery. Continued surveillance by controlled prospective studies is necessary to determine the relative safety of D & E. The important factor remains that the long-term risks of mechanical dilatation on future reproductive performance may be more than after mifepristone and prostaglandins.

A recent retrospective study from Canada reported a 5-year experience with late (> 15 weeks) second-trimester abortions performed by general practitioners using D & E and compared the results with 5–15-week terminations using suction curettage [78]. The significantly lower complication rate occurring in later gestations was a surprising observation attributable to a combination of factors. However, to depend on such a highly promising result for the recommendation of D & E for late abortions without proper training and experience may be misleading and dangerous.

Two conclusions can be drawn from these complex issues.

1   Pre-induction cervical ripening (softening and dilatation) is a vital step in late second-trimester terminations (prior to D & E or medical methods)

for a safer more rapid procedure with less side effects. Mifepristone appears to be the best agent at present.

2 The experience and skill of the surgeon must be maintained as these remain essential prerequisites if D & E is to continue as a viable safe method.

References

1 Tietze C. Second trimester abortion: a global view. In: Berger GS, Brenner WE, Keith LG, eds. *Second Trimester Abortion*. Boston: John Wright, 1981: 1–11.

2 Paxman JM, Rizo A, Brown L, Benson J. The clandestine epidemic: the practice of unsafe abortion in Latin America. *Stud Fam Plann* 1993; 24: 205–226.

3 Norström A, Bryman I, Hansson HA. Cervical dilatation by Lamicel before first trimester abortion: a clinical and experimental study. *Br J Obstet Gynaecol* 1988; 95: 372–376.

4 Atienza MF, Burkman RT, King TM. Use of osmotic dilators to facilitate induced mid-trimester abortion: clinical evaluations. *Contraception* 1984; 30: 215–223.

5 Wells EC, Hulka JF. Cervical dilatation: a comparison of Lamicel and Dilapan. *Am J Obstet Gynecol* 1989; 161: 1124–1126.

6 Atad J, Bornstein J, Kogan O, Calderon I, Ben-David Y, Abramovici H. Gradual cervical dilatation for termination of early second trimester pregnancy with a double-balloon device. *Obstet Gynecol* 1991; 78: 1142–1145.

7 Birgerson K, Odlind V. Early pregnancy termination with antiprogestins: a comparative clinical study of RU 486 given in two dose regimens and epostane. *Fertil Steril* 1987; 48: 565–570.

8 Van Look PFA, Bygdeman M. Antiprogestational steroids: a new dimension in human fertility regulation. In: Milligan SR, ed. *Human Fertility Regulation. Oxford Review of Reproductive Biology*. Volume 2. Oxford: Oxford University Press, 1989: 1–60.

9 Heikinheimo O. Summary of a doctoral thesis. Antiprogesterone steroid RU 486. Pharmacokinetics and receptor binding in humans. *Acta Obstet Gynecol Scand* 1990; 69: 357–358.

10 Rådestad A, Bygdeman M, Gréen K. Induced cervical ripening with mifepristone (RU 486) and bioconversion of arachidonic acid in human pregnant uterine cervix in the first trimester. A double-blind randomized biomechanical and biochemical study. *Contraception* 1990; 41: 283–292.

11 Urquhart DR, Templeton AA. Use of mifepristone prior to prostaglandin induced mid-trimester abortion. *Hum Reprod* 1990; 5: 883–886.

12 Hill NCW, Selinger M, Ferguson J, Lopez-Bernal A. The physiological and clinical effects of progesterone inhibition with mifepristone (RU 486) in the second trimester. *Br J Obstet Gynaecol* 1990; 97: 487–492.

13 Rådestad A. *Softening of the human uterine cervix in early pregnancy. A biochemical and morphological study with special reference to the progesterone antagonist mifepristone (RU 486)*. Doctoral thesis, Department of Obstetrics and Gynecology, Karolinska Hospital, Stockholm, Sweden, 1993.

14 Norman JE, Wu WX, Kelly RW, Glasier AF, McNeilly AS, Baird DT. Effects of mifepristone *in vivo* on decidual PG synthesis and metabolism. *Contraception* 1991; 44: 89–98.

15 Toppozada M, Bygdeman M, Papageorgiou C, Wiqvist N. Administration of 15-methyl PGF$_{2\alpha}$ as a preoperative means of cervical dilatation. *Prostaglandins* 1973; 4: 371–379.

16 World Health Organization Task Force on Prostaglandins. Randomized comparison of different prostaglandin analogues and laminaria tent for pre-operative cervical dilatation. *Contraception* 1986; 34: 237–251.

17 World Health Organization Task Force on Prostaglandins. Vaginal administration of 15-methyl-PGF$_{2\alpha}$ methyl ester for pre-operative cervical dilatation. *Contraception* 1981; 23: 251–257.

18 Gottlieb C, Bygdeman M. The use of antiprogestin (RU 486) for termination of second trimester pregnancy. *Acta Obstet Gynecol Scand* 1991; 70: 199–203.

19 Allen J, Uldbjerg N, Petersen LK, Secher NJ. Intracervical 17-β-estradiol before induction of second trimester abortion with a prostaglandin E$_2$ analogue. *Europ J Obstet Gynecol and Reprod Biol* 1989; 32: 123–127.

20 Aburel E. Communicare la Societatea Stuntelar Medicale. *Revista Medico-Chirurgicala a Societati de medici si Naturalisti din IASI*, 1934.Quoted by Toppozada M, Ismail AA. Intra-uterine administration of drugs for termination of second trimester pregnancy. *Baillière's Clin Obstet Gynaecol* 1990; 4: 327–349.

21 Wagatsuma T. Intra-amniotic injection of saline for therapeutic abortion. *Am J Obstet Gynecol* 1965; 93: 743–746.

22 Kerenyi T. Mid-trimester abortion. In: Osofsky HH, Osofsky JD, eds. *The Abortion Experience*. Hagerstown: Harper and Row, 1973: 383–399.

23 Mackenzie JM, Roufa A, Tovell HM. Mid-trimester abortion, clinical experience with amniocentesis and hypertonic saline instillation in 400 patients. *Clin Obstet Gynecol* 1971; 14: 107–123.

24 Kerenyi T. Outpatient intra-amniotic injection of hypertonic saline. *Clin Obstet Gynecol* 1971; 14: 124–140.

25 Berger G, Tietze C, Pakter J, Katze S. Maternal mortality associated with legal abortion in New York State—1 July 1970 to 30 June 1972. *Obstet Gynecol* 1974; 43: 315–326.

26 Bygdeman M, Wiqvist N, Toppozada M. Induction of mid-trimester abortion by intra-amniotic administration of PGF$_{2\alpha}$. *Acta Physiol Scand* 1971; 82: 415–416.

27 Karim SMM, Sharma SD. Second trimester abortion with single intra-amniotic injection of prostaglandin E$_2$ or F$_2$. *Lancet* 1971; ii: 47–48.

28 Toppozada M, Bygdeman M, Wiqvist N. Induction of abortion by intra-amniotic administration of PGF$_{2\alpha}$. *Contraception* 1971; 4: 293–301.

29 World Health Organization Task Force on Prostaglandins. Comparison of single intra-amniotic injection of 15-methyl PGF$_{2\alpha}$ and PGF$_{2\alpha}$ for termination of second trimester pregnancy. An international multicenter study. *Am J Obstet Gynecol* 1977; 129: 601–606.

30 Bygdeman M. Prostaglandins in fertility regulation. In: Fenn CC, Griffin D, eds. *Recent Advances in Fertility Regulation*. Geneva: Atar SA, 1981: 301–318.

31 Toppozada M, Ismail AAA. Intrauterine administration of drugs for termination of pregnancy in the second trimester. *Baillière's Clin Obstet Gynaecol* 1990; 4: 327–350.

32 Toppozada M, Beguin F, Bygdeman M, Wiqvist N. Response of the mid trimester pregnant uterus to systemic administration of 15s, 15 methyl PGF$_{2\alpha}$. *Prostaglandins* 1972; 2: 239–249.

33 Tejuja S, Chaudhury SD, Manchanda PK. Use of intra- and extra-amniotic PG for

termination of pregnancies. Report of multicentric trials in India. *Contraception* 1978; 18: 641–651.

34 Toppozada M. Prostaglandins in mid-trimester abortion. *Prostaglandin Perspectives* 1986; 2: 1–3.

35 Burkman RT, Dubin NH, King TM. The use of hyperosmolar urea for the elective abortion of mid-trimester pregnancy. In: Zatuchni GI, Sciarra JJ, Speidel JJ, eds. *Pregnancy Termination*. Hagerstown: Harper and Row, 1979: 261–267.

36 Ingemanson CA. The ethacridine catheter method in second trimester abortion. In: Zatuchni GI, Sciarra JJ, Spieder JJ, eds. *Pregnancy Termination*. Hagerstown: Harper and Row, 1979: 282–289.

37 Lowensohn R, Ballard CA. Cervico-vaginal fistula. An apparent increased incidence with prostaglandin $F_{2\alpha}$. *Am J Obstet Gynecol* 1974; 119: 1057–1059.

38 Gardo S, Nagy M. Induction of second trimester abortion by intra-amniotic instillation of Rivanol (ethacridine) combined with oxytocin infusion. *Arch Gynecol Obstet* 1990; 247: 39–41.

39 Wiqvist N, Bygdeman M. Therapeutic abortion by local administration of prostaglandin. *Lancet* 1970; ii: 716–717.

40 Toppozada M, Bygdeman M, Wiqvist N. Prostaglandin administration for induction of mid-trimester abortion in complicated pregnancies. *Lancet* 1972; ii: 1420–1421.

41 Midwinter A, Shepherd A, Bowen M. Continuous extra-amniotic prostaglandin E_2 for therapeutic termination and the effectiveness of various infusion rates and dosages. *J Obstet Gynaecol Br Commonw* 1973; 80: 371–373.

42 Peat B. Second trimester abortion by extra-amniotic $PGF_{2\alpha}$ infusion: experience of 178 cases. *Aust NZ J Obstet Gynaecol* 1991; 31: 47–51.

43 Brenner WE. The current status of prostaglandins as abortifacients. *Am J Obstet Gynecol* 1975; 123: 306–328.

44 World Health Organization Task Force on Prostaglandins. Prostaglandins and abortion. II. Single extra-amniotic administration of 0.92 mg of 15-methyl $PGF_{2\alpha}$ in hyskon for termination of pregnancies in weeks 10–20 of gestation. An international multicenter study. *Am J Obstet Gynecol* 1977; 129: 597–600.

45 Morad M, Toppozada M. Induction of abortion by intra-uterine administration of prostaglandin via laparoscopy with concurrent sterilization. *Int J Gynaecol Obstet* 1977; 15: 256–257.

46 Barbosa RM, Arilha M. The Brazilian experience with cytotec. *Stud Fam Plann* 1993; 24: 236–240.

47 Norman JE, Thong KJ, Baird DT. Uterine contractility and induction of abortion in early pregnancy by misoprostol and mifepristone. *Lancet* 1991; 338: 1233–1236.

48 Aubeny E, Baulieu E. Activité contrageistive prostaglandine active pour voie orale. *CR Acad Sci (Paris)* 1991; 312: 539–546.

49 El-Refaey H, Henshaw K, Templeton A. The abortifacient effect of misoprostol in the second trimester. A randomized comparison with gemeprost in patients pretreated with mifepristone (RU 486). *Hum Reprod* 1993; 8: 1744–1746.

50 Bygdeman M, Van Look P. Antiprogesterones for the interruption of pregnancy. *Baillière's Clin Obstet Gynaecol* 1988; 2: 617–629.

51 Toppozada M, Warda A, Ramadan M, Attar AE. Termination of pregnancy for medical indications by systemic administration of sulprostone. In: Friebel K, Schneider A, Wurtel H, eds. *International Sulprostone Symposium, Vienna*. Berlin: Pfizer–Schering, 1978 (paper no. 22): 145–150.

52 Ulbrich I, Bartels H. Clinical results with sulprostone. In: Frieblel K, Schneider A, Wurtel H, eds. *Procedings of the International Sulprostone Symposium, Vienna*. Berlin: Pfizer–Schering, 1978: 40–51.

53 World Health Organization Task Force on Prostaglandins. Intramuscular administration of 15-methyl $PGF_{2\alpha}$ for induction of abortion in weeks 10–20 of pregnancy. *Am J Obstet Gynecol* 1977; 129: 593–600.

54 Lauersen NH, Wilson KH. Termination of mid-trimester pregnancy by serial intramuscular injections of 15,s 15-methyl $PGF_{2\alpha}$. *Am J Obstet Gynecol* 1976; 124: 169–176.

55 Karim SMM. Termination of second trimester pregnancy with prostaglandins. In: Karim SMM, ed. *Practical Applications of Prostaglandins and their Synthesis Inhibitor*. Lancaster: MTP Press, 1979: 375–410.

56 World Health Organization Task Force on Prostaglandins. Termination of second trimester pregnancy by intramuscular injection of 16-phenoxy-ω-17, 18, 19, 20 tetranor PGE_2 methyl sulphonylamide. *Int J Obstet Gynecol* 1982; 20: 383–386.

57 Gréen K, Bygdeman M, Swahn M-L, Vesterqvist O, Christensen NJ. Development of a vaginal gel containing 9-deoxo-16, 16-dimethyl-9-methylene PGE_2 for cervical dilatation and pregnancy termination. *Prostag Leukot Ess Fatty Acids* 1988; 32: 121–127.

58 Bygdeman M. Non-invasive methods for termination of second trimester pregnancy. *Baillière's Clin Obstet Gynaecol* 1990; 4: 351–359.

59 World Health Organization Task Force on Prostaglandins. Repeated vaginal administration of 15-methyl $PGF_{2\alpha}$ methyl ester for termination of pregnancy in the 13th to 20th week of gestation. *Contraception* 1977; 16: 175–181.

60 Bygdeman M, Gréen K, Lundström V, Ramadan M, Foutiou S, Bergström S. Induction of abortion by vaginal administration of 15s, 15-methyl $PGF_{2\alpha}$ methyl ester:a comparison of two delivery systems. *Prostaglandins* 1976; 12: 27–52.

61 Takagi S, Yoshida T, Ohya A. The abortifacient effect of 16, 16-dimethyl-trans Δ^2 PGE_1 methyl ester. A new prostaglandin analogue, on mid-trimester pregnancy and long-term follow-up observations. *Prostaglandins* 1982; 23: 591–601.

62 Cameron IT, Michie AF, Baird DT. Prostaglandin-induced pregnancy termination: further studies using gemeprost vaginal pessaries in the early second trimester. *Prostaglandins* 1987; 34: 111–117.

63 Thong KJ, Robertson AJ, Baird DT. A retrospective study of 932 second trimester terminations using gemeprost. *Prostaglandins* 1992; 44: 65–74.

64 Thong KJ, Baird DT. A study of gemeprost alone, dilapan or mifepristone in combination with gemeprost for the termination of second trimester pregnancy. *Contraception* 1992; 46: 11–17.

65 Thong KJ, Baird DT. An open study comparing two regimens of gemeprost for the termination of pregnancy in the second trimester. *Acta Obstet Gynecol Scand* 1992; 71: 191–196.

66 Grimes DA, Cates W Jr. Dilatation and evacuation. In: Berger GS, Brenner WE, Keith LG, eds. *Second Trimester Abortion*. Boston: John Wright–PSG Publishing, 1981: 119–133.

67 Hern WM. Serial multiple laminaria and adjunctive urea in late outpatient dilatation and evacuation abortion. *Obstet Gynecol* 1984; 63: 543–549.

68 Joint Program for the Study of Abortion (JPSA). Early medical complications of legal abortion. *Studies Fam Plann* 1972; 3: 97–124.

69 Gillett PG. Therapuetic abortion in the late second trimester: experience with

prostaglandins. In: Zatuchni GI, Sciarra JJ, Speidel JJ, eds. *Pregnancy Termination.* Hagerstown: Harper and Row, 1979: 268–276.

70 Indian Council of Medical Research. *Collaborative Study on Short-term Sequelae of Induced Abortion.* New Delhi: Cambridge Printing Works, 1981: 25–50.

71 Sharma SD, Steinmiller VM, Hale RW. Intramuscular administration of 15-methyl $PGF_{2\alpha}$ and laminaria for termination of mid-trimester pregnancy. In: Toppozada M, Bygdeman M, Hafez S, eds. *Prostaglandins and Fertility Regulation.* Lancaster: MTP Press, 1984: 119–128.

72 Karim SMM, Ratnam SS, Lim AI, Yeo KC, Choo HT. Termination of second trimester pregnancy with laminaria and intramuscular 16-phenoxy-ω-tetranor, 17, 18, 19, 20 PGE_2 methyl sulphonylamide. A randomized study. *Prostaglandins* 1982; 23: 257–263.

73 World Health Organization Task Force on Prostaglandins. Termination of second trimester pregnancy by intramuscular 15-methyl $PGF_{2\alpha}$ or 16-phenoxy-ω-17, 18, 19, 20 tetranor PGE_2 methyl sulphonylamide. A randomized multicenter study. *Int J Obstet Gynecol* 1988; 26: 129–135.

74 Urquhart DR, Templeton AA. Mifepristone (RU 486) and second trimester pregnancy. *Lancet* 1987; ii: 1405.

75 Rodger MW, Baird DT. Pretreatment with mifepristone (RU 486) reduces interval between PG administration and expulsion in second trimester abortion. *Br J Obstet Gynaecol* 1990; 97: 41–45.

76 Ho PC, Ma HK. Termination of second trimester pregnancy with sulprostone and mifepristone: a randomized double-blind placebo controlled trial. *Contraception* 1993; 47: 123–129.

77 Thong KJ, Baird DT. Induction of second trimester abortion with mifepristone and gemeprost. *Br J Obstet Gynaecol* 1993; 100: 758–761.

78 Jacot FRM, Poulin C, Bilodeau AP *et al.* A five year experience with second trimester induced abortion: no increase in complication rate as compared to the first trimester. *Am J Obstet Gynecol* 1993; 168: 633–637.

6   Sequelae of Abortion

David A. Grimes

Scope of the problem

Complications of abortion still persist in the 1990s as a major public health problem in much of the world. While most developed countries with a population of over 1 million persons have safe legal abortion, many developing countries do not. About 26–31 million abortions are performed legally each year, but an estimated 10–22 million more take place outside of the law [1]. As many as 125 000 deaths are caused annually by unsafe abortion [2].

Recent reports confirm the continuing morbidity and mortality from unsafe abortion in developing countries [3–6]. Commonly used methods include oral ingestion of drugs and intrauterine insertion of toxic solutions or foreign bodies. Infection, haemorrhage and uterine injury are important complications. In recent reports, case-fatality rates from unsafe abortion in developing countries have ranged from 400 [3] to 17 000 per 100 000 procedures [5].

This chapter reviews the sequelae of induced abortion. Most of the literature relates to surgical methods, but data on medical abortion are included when available. Since the abortion literature is vast, this review focuses on reports with large numbers of patients and those published since 1980. Studies involving large numbers of women offer the best assessment of infrequent complications and provide statistical stability for estimates of complication rates. The review outlines trends in morbidity and mortality, describes specific complications and summarizes strategies for their prevention.

Morbidity

Complications from abortion are infrequent where safe, legal abortion is accessible. National health statistics have shown conclusively that early abortions are safer than later procedures and that rates of complications have diminished in recent decades. Both first-trimester (Fig. 6.1) and

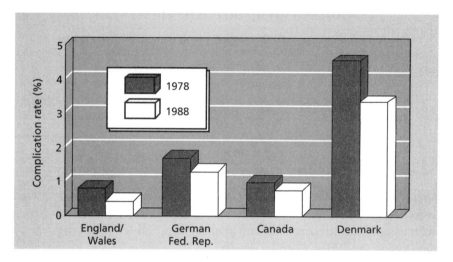

Fig. 6.1 First-trimester abortion morbidity rates in selected countries with centralized reporting, 1978 and 1988. From Henshaw [1].

second-trimester abortion (Fig. 6.2) have become progressively safer in countries where abortion morbidity is centrally monitored. Rates in different countries are not directly comparable because of a lack of uniform definitions and reporting requirements. The improved safety over time reflects a shift to earlier procedures, more skilled clinicians,

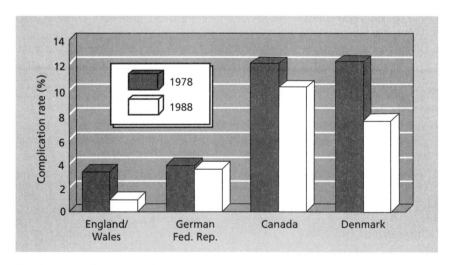

Fig. 6.2 Second-trimester abortion morbidity rates in selected countries with centralized reporting, 1978 and 1988. From Henshaw [1].

Table 6.1 Complication rates per 1000 procedures in selected large case-series reports

Reference	[12]	[11]	[10]	[8]
Country	USA	Sweden	Denmark	Canada
No. of patients	170 000	1000	5851	351 879
Gestational age (weeks)	⩽ 14	⩽ 14	⩽ 12	All
Dates	1971–87	1987	1980–85	1975–80
Complication				
infection	4.6	47	24	1.8
cervical laceration	0.1	NR	1	3.5
incomplete abortion	0.28	NR	NR	19.6
uterine perforation	0.09	0.0	4	1.3
haemorrhage	0.07	0.0	42	2.5
twin intra-/extrauterine pregnancy	0.02	NR	NR	NR
Hospitalization	0.71	28	61	NR
Total complications	9.05	56	61	NR

NR, not reported.

improved techniques of abortion and greater sophistication in managing complications [7].

Reports published since 1980 from around the world (Table 6.1) consistently indicate complication rates for first-trimester abortion of less than 10 per 100 operations [8–14]. A recent large report described the experience of a few highly experienced physicians operating on low-risk patients with established protocols. The overall complication rate among 170 000 first-trimester abortions was nine per 1000 abortions; fewer than one per 1000 required hospitalization [12].

Mortality

Where legal abortion is accessible, mortality trends have paralleled those of morbidity. In countries such as Sweden and the USA, deaths from abortion have become rare [7,15]. In these two countries, the risk of death from abortion is about one-tenth that of giving birth. For example, in Sweden the mortality rate for legal abortions between 1971 and 1980 was 0.7 per 100 000 procedures, while the corresponding figure for the USA between 1979 and 1985 was 0.6 [7,15]. Recent national data from countries in Europe and North America have revealed abortion mortality rates of two deaths per 100 000 procedures or less (Fig. 6.3) [1]. In this figure, the wide confidence intervals around the rates reflect the statistical instability resulting from small numbers of deaths.

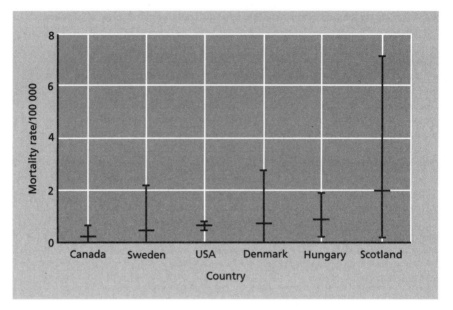

Fig. 6.3 Abortion rates (with 95% confidence intervals) in selected countries (Canada 1980–89, Sweden 1980–87, USA 1981–85, Denmark 1976–87, Hungary 1980–87, Scotland 1976–87). From Henshaw [1].

Specific complications

Complications are divided into three groups depending on their temporal relationship to the abortion: (i) immediate complications which occur during or within 3 h of the procedure; (ii) delayed complications which develop after 3 h but within 28 days of the procedure; and (iii) late complications which occur thereafter.

Immediate

Uterine perforation

Uterine perforation is an infrequent but potentially serious complication associated with haemorrhage, infection and injury to abdominal contents [16]. Recent case-series reports (see Table 6.1) reveal low rates of this complication. Nevertheless, reported rates appear to be a gross underestimate. A recent report of laparoscopic tubal sterilization after abortion [17] found the number of unsuspected perforations to be six times the number detected during the abortion; this increased the rate from three to 20 perforations per 1000 operations. Perforations of the uterus during second-trimester dilatation and evacuation (D & E) abortions are much more serious. In a series of 15 from one hospital [18], all patients ultimately required laparotomy. Two-thirds had suffered bowel injury, and two patients required hysterectomy.

Physician experience and use of osmotic dilators protect against uterine perforation during first-trimester abortion [19]. For second-trimester D & E abortions, careful estimation of gestational age, adequate preoperative cervical dilatation and ultrasound guidance of the evacuation may reduce the risks [18].

Haemorrhage

The true incidence of haemorrhage associated with abortion is unknown because of inconsistent definitions and lack of measurement. Reported rates vary widely (see Table 6.1). In older studies, use of blood transfusion was a useful proxy for clinically troubling bleeding. Transfusion rates today are so low that this index is no longer helpful. Recent advances in the management of haemorrhage after curettage procedures include paracervical injection of vasopressin solution, assessment of the endometrial cavity with hysteroscopy and internal compression of the cavity with a large Foley catheter balloon or a pack soaked in vasopressin solution [20].

Coagulopathy rarely complicates abortion. In a series of patients from a single institution with a stable staff of physicians, coagulopathy was defined as clinical evidence of non-clotting blood and a plasma fibrinogen < 200 mg/dl. The rates of coagulopathy were eight per 100 000 suction curettage procedures, 191 for D & E procedures and 658 for saline instillation [21].

Unrecognized ectopic pregnancy

Failure to identify a pre-existing ectopic pregnancy [22] is potentially lethal [23]. For example, over 20 women in the USA have died from ruptured ectopic pregnancies after ostensibly having had suction curettage abortions. For this reason, and to confirm the completeness of a curettage abortion, aspirated tissue must be examined for the presence of fetal tissue before each woman leaves the abortion facility. Routine examination of aspirated tissue by a pathologist is not medically necessary and may delay the recognition of failure to obtain fetal tissue [23]. Inspection of suspended tissue with back lighting is rapid, inexpensive and sensitive [24]. This precaution will eliminate this dangerous complication, except for the rare twin intrauterine and extrauterine pregnancies [12].

Cervical injury

Laceration of the cervix can occur if the tenaculum pulls off during dilatation. This complication can be almost eliminated by placing the tenaculum on the cervix vertically, with one tooth in the os and the other high on the anterior lip. In addition, use of osmotic dilators can significantly reduce the risk of cervical injury during abortion [25]. In a small randomized trial [26], hypan osmotic dilators appeared preferable to either laminaria or meteneprost vaginal suppositories. Mechanical dilatation of the cervix to 11 mm in diameter is associated with a fall in cervical resistance in most women, which may be due to minor injury; the clinical import of this is unknown [27].

Osmotic dilators carry risks of their own. Both hypan dilators and laminaria can fragment, leading to prolonged retention of the fragments. Rarely, a patient with overnight osmotic dilator placement changes her mind about having an abortion and requests their removal; some patients have uneventful pregnancies [28], while others abort soon after, occasionally with chorioamnionitis.

Anaesthesia complications

Pain during abortion is related not only to the method of anaesthesia chosen but also to the personality of the woman. In a study using the McGill pain questionnaire and verbal and visual analogue scales, pain scores were significantly higher for women who reported moderate to severe depression before the abortion. Similarly, young age (13–17 years) was significantly associated with greater reported pain [29].

Local anaesthesia appears safer than general anaesthesia for curettage abortions in the first and second trimesters. In an Italian centre, use of general anaesthesia was associated with a significant increase in the risk for all complications (relative risk 1.8; 95% confidence interval 1.4–2.5) [30]. The largest increase in risk was for haemorrhage (relative risk 4.6; 95% confidence interval 2.2–9.5), which confirms the findings of studies done in the 1970s.

Local anaesthesia is safer for second-trimester D & E abortions as well. In a large USA cohort study [31], the relative risk of serious complications associated with general anaesthesia was 2.6 times (95% confidence interval 1.4–4.9) that associated with the use of local anaesthesia. Indeed, in the USA, complications associated with general anaesthesia (usually hypoventilation or failure to maintain an airway) have emerged as the leading causes of abortion-related mortality [32]. Hence, the use of local anaesthesia is preferable to general anaesthesia in terms of both safety and cost.

Amniotic fluid embolism

Amniotic fluid embolism is an important cause of morbidity and mortality in the second trimester. The risk of this occurrence increases with advancing gestational age, presumably reflecting larger volumes of fluid capable of embolization [33]. In addition, labour-induction abortions and hysterotomy appear to increase the risk of this complication. A recent report [34] has confirmed the presence of fetal tissue and placental fragments in the uterine and parametrial veins of a woman who sustained an embolism during a D & E abortion at 19 weeks gestation. Draining amniotic fluid at the beginning of such procedures may reduce this risk.

Delayed

Infection

Infection is one of the more common complications of abortion, particularly when the abortion is incomplete or the woman harbours pathogens in her cervix. In the large series of suction curettage procedures from Planned Parenthood in New York [12], mild infection occurred in five per 1000 cases, and sepsis requiring hospitalization in two. In contrast, reported infection rates are lower in vital statistics systems [8] and higher in single-institution reports [10,11].

The presence of *Neisseria gonorrhoeae* or *Chlamydia trachomatis* in the cervix before abortion dramatically increases the risk of infection afterwards [35–38]. Hence, when identified, these infections should be treated before abortion is performed.

In some settings, such as the USA, women often make a single visit for abortion services; preoperative screening for sexually transmitted diseases is not practical. Hence, a number of studies have addressed the potential benefit of prophylactic antibiotics at the time of abortion for women without preoperative screening. In the early 1980s, a review of the literature provided strong evidence for this being cost-effective [39]. Since then, several large, well-done randomized controlled trials have confirmed this assessment. For example, in a trial of 800 women [40] the relative risk of postoperative infection in the group receiving doxycycline was 0.32 (95% confidence interval 0.14–0.73), while in another [41] the relative risk with doxycycline was 0.13 (95% confidence interval 0.03–0.57). Other smaller trials have found protection with erythromycin [42], lymecycline [43] and metronidazole in women with bacterial vaginosis [44]. Given the potential seriousness of upper genital tract infection and the safety and low cost of perioperative antibiotic administration, use of prophylaxis should be strongly considered.

Late complications

Reproductive sequelae

Because so many women who have abortions intend to have children in the future, the issue of potential adverse effects on later reproduction is important. Extensive research has documented that induced abortion has few late sequelae.

Secondary infertility is not increased after suction curettage abortion [45–48]. Indeed, several reports have found shorter intervals between pregnancies, possibly reflecting a higher fertility of women with unintended pregnancies [49]. While secondary infertility may rarely result from an abortion complication, this occurs so infrequently that no overall effect is seen. Similarly, infertility is not increased after second-trimester abortion by prostaglandin induction [50]. Most prospective cohort and case–control studies concur in this assessment, although a recent case–control study from Greece has suggested an increase in secondary infertility that was marginally statistically significant [51].

Induced abortion has no overall effect on the risk of later ectopic pregnancy. Several large case–control studies have shown no increase in risk, even after multiple induced abortions [52,53]. However, abortions complicated by infection or retained products of conception may add to the risk [45,54].

Spontaneous abortions are not increased by prior suction curettage abortion. Several studies have examined the potential risk of spontaneous abortion in the mid-trimester of pregnancy. Here, the method of abortion appears to be important. Having a first pregnancy aborted by suction curettage does not increase risk, while abortion by sharp curettage probably does. The latter finding has been consistent in four studies [45]. While the mechanism for the effect is unclear, cervical injury has been suggested as a possible explanation. The potential effect of multiple induced abortions on the risk of subsequent spontaneous abortion has been less well studied. Nevertheless, existing data [55] suggest that repeated induced abortions do not increase the risk.

The risk of adverse outcomes does not appear to be increased for later pregnancies carried to delivery [56]. Outcomes studied have included prematurity, low birthweight, congenital anomalies and maternal morbidity. In general, no consistent effect has been found. This appears to hold true even after multiple induced abortions [57–60]. Concerning the potential effect of labour-induction abortion, one report found a higher rate of low-birthweight infants born after a first pregnancy aborted by prostaglandin induction as opposed to saline abortion; however, this difference was not statistically significant [61].

One unsettled issue, however, is placenta previa. Early studies with before–after design and inadequate control for potential confounding suggested an increased risk of placenta previa after induced abortion [62]. More sophisticated studies have either shown no [63] or a marginally significant increase in risk (relative risk 1.3; 95% confidence interval 1.0–1.6), which was comparable to that associated with spontaneous abortion (relative risk 1.3; 95% confidence interval 1.0–1.7) [64].

Psychological sequelae

Induced abortion does not pose a threat to the psychological health of women. Rather, a number of studies suggest a therapeutic benefit of abortion in measures of emotional well-being. In other words, abortion resolves a personal crisis for many women [65–67].

The predominant emotional reaction to abortion is a sense of relief and happiness [66]. In one survey conducted 2 weeks after suction curettage, reports of relief were over four times as frequent as those of guilt (76 versus 17%) [68]. Formal testing of emotional status has revealed a steady decline in measures of distress from before abortion to immediately after abortion to several weeks later [66].

Reactions to abortion cannot be viewed in a vacuum. One must consider the emotional sequelae of the alternative to abortion: childbirth. One study found scores on the Minnesota multiphasic personality inventory to be similar, while another study of adolescents suggested a more favourable psychological response to abortion than to childbirth [69].

Several important determinants of poor psychological outcomes after abortion are known. Women who find the decision to abort difficult tend to fare less well than other women. The likelihood of adverse outcomes increases with advancing gestational age: second-trimester abortions are more emotionally stressful than first-trimester procedures. Women who abort desired pregnancies because of fetal indications, such as congenital anomalies, experience more emotional distress than other women. Previous psychiatric contact is also a strong predictor for adverse outcomes after abortion.

The impact of social support surrounding abortion is more complex. In general, women with strong social support tend to do better after abortion, but a paradoxical effect has been seen in two studies. In one study, if the partner of the woman accompanied her to the clinic, she was more likely to report postoperative depression and somatic complaints [70]. A strong ongoing relationship with the partner has also been found to be associated with poorer outcomes at 6 and 13 months in another study [71].

Thus, symptoms of emotional distress are observed in many women after abortion. 'However, these symptoms seem to be continuations of symptoms present before the abortion and more a result of the circumstances leading to the abortion than a result of the procedure itself' [67]. Case studies of women with dysphoric reactions to abortion confirm that such women were often disturbed before the procedure. For example, women with multiple abortions in one study tended to be depressed before the abortions [72].

Cancer

Since several cancers are influenced by reproductive events, such as timing and number of pregnancies, the potential effect of abortion has been of concern. Most attention has centred around breast cancer. A large number of studies have led to conflicting results [73]. Recent studies from Europe have found no effect [74,75], including one large cohort study from Sweden, a country with comprehensive computer records and a unique identification number for all citizens [76]. Indeed, in this study, in which recall bias should have been minimized, first-trimester abortion had a statistically significant protective effect against breast cancer (relative risk 0.8; 95% confidence interval 0.58–0.99). At present, the issue remains unresolved, with most concern relating to abortion of a first pregnancy and nulliparous women [73].

Little is known of the potential link between abortion and other genital cancers. While several studies have suggested a link between abortion and cervical cancer [73], this association is probably confounded by sexual behaviour. Given that cervical cancer is probably caused by viral infection of the epithelium, this potential association lacks biological plausibility. No consistent evidence indicates an effect on endometrial or ovarian cancers. A recent case–control study from Japan found a protective effect against ovarian cancer (relative risk 0.6; 95% confidence interval 0.3–0.9) [77]; this may be mediated through pregnancy-induced anovulation, rather than the abortion *per se*. No effect has been seen for endometrial cancer.

Choice of abortion method

The choice of abortion method greatly influences safety. In the first trimester, suction curettage remains the gold standard against which other methods should be compared. While prostaglandins can successfully induce medical abortions, the incidence of incomplete abortion, severe pain, nausea and vomiting are usually prohibitive [78]. In one study first-trimester abortion induced by ethacridine lactate was associated with a febrile morbidity rate of 4.8% and 'profuse bleeding' in 4.9% [79].

In contrast, medical abortion with mifepristone plus prostaglandin has been shown to have very low complication rates. Large series [80–82] have demonstrated morbidity rates similar to those of suction curettage; in the largest [80], the rate of transfusion because of haemorrhage was only 0.1 per 100 cases. The mean measured blood loss with mifepristone followed by gemeprost suppository at $\leqslant 63$ days of amenorrhoea was 74 ml (range 14–512 ml) [83]. To date, no large randomized controlled trials have compared mifepristone plus prostaglandin versus suction curettage abortion.

In the early second trimester, D & E abortion is significantly safer than induction of labour [84]. A randomized controlled trial [85], large cohort studies [84,86], case–series reports [87] and a nationwide mortality surveillance in the USA [84] support this conclusion. Indeed, a recent cohort study from Canada [88] has suggested a lower risk of complications from D & E at 15–20 weeks than from earlier suction curettage (relative risk 0.57; 95% confidence interval 0.33–1.00).

In the late second trimester, no recent studies have compared D & E with labour-induction abortion. Abortions induced with prostaglandins carry substantial risks of morbidity. Recent series have reported hysterectomy rates as high as 1% [89,90], a posterior cervical laceration rate as high as 4% in nulliparous women [91,92], myocardial infarction [93] and death [89]. However, mortality data from the USA suggest that both D & E and labour-induction abortion carry similar low risks of death [94].

Risk factors for abortion complications

Several personal and technical factors strongly influence the likelihood of complications from abortion. Older women, those at an advanced gestational age and parous women are at increased risk of serious complications from abortion [95].

While none of these factors can be controlled by the clinician, several factors can be. Suction curettage, the most thoroughly studied method, has been shown to have the lowest complication rate of widely available methods. D & E has a morbidity rate higher than that of suction curettage in most reports. Labour-induction methods have higher complication rates, followed by major operations (hysterotomy and hysterectomy) [7]. However, hysterotomy was safer than labour-induction abortions in Canada, although the former is rarely used [8]. In contrast, the risk of death from hysterotomy and hysterectomy in the USA has been prohibitive [94].

Safe abortion depends upon easy access to skilled providers. Delays of any cause lead to increased risks of complications. Gentle, thorough technique reduces the risk of complications. Should complications occur, prompt care in a compassionate setting can limit the adverse sequelae.

Abortion has been intensively studied because of its controversial nature. Indeed, more is known today about the safety of abortion than any other operation. In much of the world, it remains one of the safest operations in contemporary practice. With continued refinement in surgical technique and the growing use of antiprogestogens, abortion should become even safer in the future.

References

1 Henshaw SK. How safe is therapeutic abortion? In: Teoh ES, Ratnam SS, Macnaughton M, eds. *Pregnancy Termination and Labour*. Volume 5. Carnforth: Parthenon Publishing, 1993: 31–41.

2 Royston E, Armstrong S. *Preventing Maternal Deaths.* Geneva: World Health Organization, 1989: 107–136.
3 Pardo F, Uriza G. Estudio de morbilidad y mortalidad pro aborto en 36 instituciones de Bolivia, Colombia, Peru y Venezuela. *Rev Colomb Obstet Ginecol* 1991; 42: 287–297.
4 Weissman A, Elhalal U, Blickstein I, Caspi B. Self-induced abortion—the peril is still real. *Adv Contraception* 1992; 8: 81–88.
5 Okonofua FE, Onwudiegwu U, Odunsi OA. Illegal induced abortion: a study of 74 cases in Ile-Ife, Nigeria. *Trop Doct* 1992; 22: 75–78.
6 Villareal J. Responsabilidad profesional frente al aborto. *Rev Colomb Obstet Ginecol* 1992; 43: 87–94.
7 Council on Scientific Affairs, American Medical Association. Induced termination of pregnancy before and after *Roe v Wade*. *JAMA* 1992; 268: 3231–3239.
8 Wadhera S. Early complication risks of legal abortions, Canada, 1975–1980. *Can Med Assoc J* 1982; 73: 396–400.
9 Sotnikova EI. Short- and long-term results of pregnancy termination by different methods. *Acta Med Hung* 1986; 43: 139–143.
10 Heisterberg L, Kringlebach M. Early complications after induced first-trimester abortion. *Acta Obstet Gynecol Scand* 1987; 66: 201–204.
11 Fried G, Ostlund E, Ullberg C, Bygdeman M. Somatic complications and contraceptive techniques following legal abortion. *Acta Obstet Gynecol Scand* 1989; 68: 515–521.
12 Hakim-Elahi E, Tovell HMM, Burnhill MS. Complications of first-trimester abortion: a report of 170 000 cases. *Obstet Gynecol* 1990; 76: 129–135.
13 Joint Study of the Royal College of General Practitioners and the Royal College of Obstetricians and Gynaecologists. Induced abortion operations and their early sequelae. *J Roy Coll Gen Pract* 1985; 35: 175–180.
14 Nesheim BI. Induced abortion by the suction method. *Acta Obstet Gynecol Scand* 1984; 63: 591–595.
15 Hogberg U, Joelsson I. Maternal deaths related to abortions in Sweden, 1931–1980. *Gynecol Obstet Invest* 1985; 20: 169–178.
16 Mittal S, Misra SL. Uterine perforation following medical termination of pregnancy by vacuum aspiration. *Int J Gynaecol Obstet* 1985; 23: 45–50.
17 Kaali SG, Szigetvari IA, Bartfai GS. The frequency and management of uterine perforations during first-trimester abortions. *Am J Obstet Gynecol* 1989; 161: 406–408.
18 Darney PD, Atkinson E, Hirabayashi K. Uterine perforation during second-trimester abortion by cervical dilation and instrumental extraction: a review of 15 cases. *Obstet Gynecol* 1990; 75: 441–444.
19 Grimes DA, Schulz KF, Cates W Jr. Prevention of uterine perforation during curettage abortion. *JAMA* 1984; 251: 2108–2111.
20 Townsend DE, Barbis SD, Mathews RD. Vasopressin and operative hysteroscopy in the management of delayed post-abortion and postpartum bleeding. *Am J Obstet Gynecol* 1991; 165: 616–618.
21 Kafrissen ME, Barke MW, Schulz KF, Grimes DA. Coagulopathy and induced abortion methods: rates and relative risks. *Am J Obstet Gynecol* 1983; 147: 344–345.
22 Holmgren K. Women's evaluation of three early abortion methods. *Acta Obstet Gynecol Scand* 1992; 71: 616–623.

23 Rubin GL, Cates W Jr, Gold J, Rochat RW, Tyler CW Jr. Fatal ectopic pregnancy after attempted legally induced abortion. *JAMA* 1980; 244: 1705–1708.

24 Munsick RA. Clinical test for placenta in 300 consecutive menstrual aspirations. *Obstet Gynecol* 1982; 60: 738–741.

25 Schulz KF, Grimes DA, Cates W Jr. Measures to prevent cervical injury during suction curettage abortion. *Lancet* 1983; i: 1182–1184.

26 Darney PD, Dorward K. Cervical dilation before first-trimester elective abortion: a controlled comparison of meteneprost, laminaria, and hypan. *Obstet Gynecol* 1987; 70: 397–400.

27 Molin A. Risk of damage to the cervix by dilatation for first-trimester induced abortion by suction aspiration. *Gynecol Obstet Invest* 1993; 35: 152–154.

28 Van Le L, Darney PD. Successful pregnancy outcome after cervical dilation with multiple laminaria tents in preparation for second-trimester elective abortion: a report of two cases. *Am J Obstet Gynecol* 1987; 156: 612–613.

29 Belanger E, Melzack R, Lauzon P. Pain of first-trimester abortion: a study of psychosocial and medical predictors. *Pain* 1989; 36: 339–350.

30 Osborn JF, Arisi E, Spinelli A, Stazi MA. General anaesthesia, a risk factor for complication following induced abortion? *Eur J Epidemiol* 1990; 6: 416–422.

31 MacKay HT, Schulz KF, Grimes DA. Safety of local versus general anaesthesia for second-trimester dilatation and evacuation abortion. *Obstet Gynecol* 1985; 66: 661–665.

32 Atrash HK, Cheek TG, Hogue CJR. Legal abortion mortality and general anaesthesia. *Am J Obstet Gynecol* 1988; 158: 420–424.

33 Guidotti RJ, Grimes DA, Cates W Jr. Fatal amniotic fluid embolism during legally induced abortion, United States, 1972–1978. *Am J Obstet Gynecol* 1981; 141: 257–261.

34 Saltzman R, Miranda P, Jerez E. Fetal parts embolization during termination of pregnancy: report of a case. *Hum Pathol* 1990; 21: 117–118.

35 Osser S, Persson K. Postabortal pelvic infection associated with *Chlamydia trachomatis* and the influence of humoral immunity. *Am J Obstet Gynecol* 1984; 150: 699–703.

36 Barbacci MB, Spence MR, Kappus EW, Burkman RC, Rao L, Quinn TC. Postabortal endometritis and isolation of *Chlamydia trachomatis*. *Obstet Gynecol* 1986; 68: 686–690.

37 Heisterberg L, Branebjerg PE, Bremmelgaard A, Scheibel J, Hoj L. The role of vaginal secretory immunoglobulin A, *Gardnerella vaginalis*, anaerobes, and *Chlamydia trachomatis* in postabortal pelvic inflammatory disease. *Acta Obstet Gynecol Scand* 1987; 66: 99–102.

38 Skjeldestad FE, Tuveng J, Solberg AG, Molne K, Dalen A, Buhaug H. Induced abortion: *Chlamydia trachomatis* and postabortal complications. *Acta Obstet Gynecol Scand* 1988; 67: 525–529.

39 Grimes DA, Schulz KF, Cates W Jr. Prophylactic antibiotics for curettage abortion. *Am J Obstet Gynecol* 1984; 150: 689–694.

40 Darj E, Stralin EB, Nilsson S. The prophylactic effect of doxycycline on postoperative infection rate after first-trimester abortion. *Obstet Gynecol* 1987; 70: 755–758.

41 Levallois P, Rioux JE. Prophylactic antibiotics for suction curettage abortion: results of a clinical controlled trial. *Am J Obstet Gynecol* 1988; 158: 100–105.

42 Sorenson JL, Thranov I, Hoff G, Dirach J, Damsgaard MT. A double-blind

randomized study of the effect of erythromycin in preventing pelvic inflammatory disease after first trimester abortion. *Br J Obstet Gynaecol* 1992; 99: 434–438.

43 Heisterberg L, Gnarpe H. Preventive lymecycline therapy in women with a history of pelvic inflammatory disease undergoing first-trimester abortion: a clinical, controlled trial. *Eur J Obstet Gynecol Reprod Biol* 1988; 28: 241–247.

44 Larsson PG, Platz-Christensen JJ, Thejls H, Forsum U, Pahlson C. Incidence of pelvic inflammatory disease after first-trimester legal abortion in women with bacterial vaginosis after treatment with metronidazole: a double-blind, randomized study. *Am J Obstet Gynecol* 1992; 166: 100–103.

45 Hogue CJR. Impact of abortion on subsequent fecundity. *Clin Obstet Gynaecol* 1986; 13: 95–103.

46 Frank P, McNamee R, Hannaford PC, Kay CR, Hirsch S. The effect of induced abortion on subsequent fertility. *Br J Obstet Gynaecol* 1993; 100: 575–580.

47 Daling JR, Weiss NS, Voigt L *et al*. Tubal infertility in relation to prior induced abortion. *Fertil Steril* 1985; 43: 389–394.

48 World Health Organization Task Force on Sequelae of Abortion. Secondary infertility following induced abortion. *Stud Fam Plann* 1984; 15: 291–295.

49 Stubblefield PG, Monson RR, Schoenbaum SC, Wolfson CE, Cookson DJ, Ryan KJ. Fertility after induced abortion: a prospective follow-up study. *Obstet Gynecol* 1984; 63: 186–193.

50 MacKenzie IZ, Fry A. A prospective self-controlled study of fertility after second-trimester prostaglandin-induced abortion. *Am J Obstet Gynecol* 1988; 158: 1137–1140.

51 Tzonou A, Hsieh CC, Trichopolous D *et al*. Induced abortions, miscarriages, and tobacco smoking as risk factors for secondary infertility. *J Epidemiol Comm Health* 1993; 47: 36–39.

52 Burkman RT, Mason KJ, Gold EB. Ectopic pregnancy and prior induced abortion. *Contraception* 1988; 37: 21–27.

53 Daling JR, Chow WH, Weiss NS, Metch BJ, Soderstrom R. Ectopic pregnancy in relation to previous abortion. *JAMA* 1985; 253: 1005–1008.

54 Hogue CJR, Cates W Jr, Tietze C. The effects of induced abortion on subsequent reproduction. *Epidemiol Rev* 1982; 4: 66–94.

55 Bracken MB, Bryce-Buchanan C, Srisuphan W, Holford TR, Silten R. Risk of late first and second trimester miscarriage after induced abortion. *Am J Perinatol* 1986; 3: 84–91.

56 Frank PI, Kay CR, Scott LM, Hannaford PC, Haran D. Pregnancy following induced abortion: maternal morbidity, congenital abnormalities and neonatal death. *Br J Obstet Gynaecol* 1987; 94: 836–842.

57 Meirik O, Bergstrom R. Outcome of delivery subsequent to vacuum-aspiration abortion in nulliparous women. *Acta Obstet Gynecol Scand* 1983; 62: 499–509.

58 Mandelson MT, Maden CB, Daling JR. Low birth weight in relation to multiple induced abortions. *Am J Publ Health* 1992; 82: 391–394.

59 Bracken MB, Hellenbrand KG, Holford TR, Bryce-Buchanan C. Low birth weight in pregnancies following induced abortion: no evidence for an association. *Am J Epidemiol* 1986; 123: 604–613.

60 Lopes A, King PA, Dip Ven SJD, To WK, Ma HK. The impact of multiple induced abortions on the outcome of subsequent pregnancy. *Aust NZ J Obstet Gynaecol* 1991; 31: 41–43.

61 Meirik O, Nygren K-G. Outcome of first delivery after second trimester two-step

induced abortion: controlled historical cohort study. *Acta Obstet Gynecol Scand* 1984; 63: 45–50.

62 Barrett JM, Boehm FH, Killam SP. Induced abortion—a risk factor for placenta previa. *Am J Obstet Gynecol* 1981; 141: 769–772.

63 Grimes DA, Techman T. Legal abortion and placenta previa. *Am J Obstet Gynecol* 1984; 149: 501–504.

64 Taylor VM, Kramer MD, Vaughan TL, Peacock S. Placenta previa in relation to induced and spontaneous abortion: a population-based study. *Obstet Gynecol* 1993; 82: 88–91.

65 Stotland NL. The myth of the abortion trauma syndrome. *JAMA* 1992; 268: 2078–2079.

66 Adler NE, David HP, Major BN, Roth SH, Russo NF, Wyatt GE. Psychological responses after abortion. *Science* 1990; 248: 41–44.

67 Dagg PKB. The psychological sequelae of therapeutic abortion—denied and completed. *Am J Psych* 1991; 148: 578–585.

68 Lazarus A. Psychiatric sequelae of legalized elective first trimester abortion. *J Psychosom Obstet Gynecol* 1985; 4: 141–150.

69 Zabin LS. Hirsch MB, Emerson MR. When urban adolescents choose abortion: effects on education, psychological status and subsequent pregnancy. *Fam Plann Perspect* 1989; 21: 248–255.

70 Major BN, Mueller P, Hildebrandt K. Attributions, expectations and coping with abortion. *J Perspect Soc Psychol* 1985; 48: 585–599.

71 Robbins JM. Out-of-wedlock abortion and delivery: the importance of the male partner. *Soc Prob* 1984; 31: 334–350.

72 Franco KN, Tamburrino MB, Campbell NB, Pentz JE, Jurs SG. Psychological profile of dysphoric women postabortion. *J Am Med Wom Assoc* 1989; 44: 113–115.

73 Remennick LI. Induced abortion as cancer risk factor: a review of epidemiological evidence. *J Epidemiol Commun Health* 1990; 44: 259–264.

74 La Vecchia C, Decarli A, Parazzini F *et al.* General epidemiology of breast cancer in northern Italy. *Int J Epidemiol* 1987; 16: 347–355.

75 Kvale G, Heuch I, Eide GE. A prospective study of reproductive factors and breast cancer. I. Parity. *Am J Epidemiol* 1987; 126: 831–841.

76 Lindefors Harris B-M, Eklund G, Meirik O, Rutqvist LE, Wiklund K. Risk of cancer of the breast after legal abortion during first trimester: a Swedish register study. *Br Med J* 1989; 299: 1430–1432.

77 Mori M, Harabuchi I, Miyake H, Casagrande JT, Henderson BE, Ross RK. Reproductive, genetic, and dietary risk factors for ovarian cancer. *Am J Epidemiol* 1988; 128: 771–777.

78 Gail J. The use of PGs in human reproduction. *Popul Rep* 1980; series G, no. 8: G-77–G-118.

79 Szeverényi M, Veres L, Surányi S, Lampé L. Early complications of first trimester interruption of pregnancies with Rivanol predilatation. *Acta Med Hung* 1986; 43: 175–185.

80 Ulmann A, Silvestre L, Chemama L *et al.* Medical termination of early pregnancy with mifepristone (RU 486) followed by a prostaglandin analogue. *Acta Obstet Gynecol Scand* 1992; 71: 278–283.

81 UK Multicentre Trial. The efficacy and tolerance of mifepristone and prostaglandin in first trimester termination of pregnancy. *Br J Obstet Gynaecol* 1990; 97: 480–486.

82 Peyron R, Aubeny E, Targosz V *et al.* Early termination of pregnancy with mifepristone (RU 486) and the orally active prostaglandin misoprostol. *N Engl J Med* 1993; 328: 1509–1513.

83 Rodger MW, Baird DT. Blood loss following induction of early abortion using mifepristone (RU 486) and a prostaglandin analogue (gemeprost). *Contraception* 1989; 40: 439–446.

84 Grimes DA, Schulz KF. Morbidity and mortality from second-trimester abortions. *J Reprod Med* 1985; 30: 505–514.

85 Grimes DA, Hulka JF, McCutchen ME. Mid-trimester abortion by dilatation and evacuation versus intra-amniotic instillation of prostaglandin $F_{2\alpha}$: a randomized clinical trial. *Am J Obstet Gynecol* 1980; 137: 785–790.

86 Cates W Jr, Schulz KF, Grimes DA *et al.* D & E procedures and second trimester abortions: the role of physician skill and hospital setting. *JAMA* 1982; 248: 559–563.

87 Peterson WF, Berry FN, Grace MR, Gulbranson CL. Second-trimester abortion by dilatation and evacuation: an analysis of 11 747 cases. *Obstet Gynecol* 1983; 62: 185–190.

88 Jacot FRM, Poulin C, Bilodeau AP *et al.* A five-year experience with second-trimester induced abortions: no increase in complication rate as compared to the first trimester. *Am J Obstet Gynecol* 1993; 168: 633–637.

89 Guidozzi F, van der Griendt M, Israelstam D. Major complications associated with extra-amniotic prostaglandin $F_{2\alpha}$ termination of the mid-trimester pregnancy. *S Afr Med J* 1992; 82: 102–104.

90 Lurie S, Katz Z, Insler V. Mid-trimester induction of abortion: comparison of extraovular prostaglandin E_2 and intra-amniotic prostaglandin $F_{2\alpha}$. *Contraception* 1993; 47: 475–481.

91 Kajanoja P. Induction of abortion by prostaglandins in the second trimester of pregnancy. A review. *Acta Obstet Gynecol Scand* 1983; 113 (Suppl.): 145–151.

92 Lange AP. Prostaglandins as abortifacients in Denmark. *Acta Obstet Gynecol Scand* 1983; 113 (Suppl.): 117–124.

93 Meyer WJ, Benton SL, Hoon TJ, Gauthier DW, Whiteman VE. Acute myocardial infarction associated with prostaglandin E_2. *Am J Obstet Gynecol* 1991; 165: 359–360.

94 Atrash HK, MacKay HT, Binkin NJ, Hogue CJR. Legal abortion mortality in the United States: 1972–1982. *Am J Obstet Gynecol* 1987; 156: 605–612.

95 Buehler JW, Schulz KF, Grimes DA, Hogue CJR. The risk of serious complications from induced abortion: do personal characteristics make a difference? *Am J Obstet Gynecol* 1985; 153: 14–20.

7 Counselling for Abortion

Anna Glasier

The counselling process

In many countries abortion is common. In the UK a woman's lifetime chance of having an abortion is around one in 40, while presently in the USA one in four recognized pregnancies ends in induced abortion. Nevertheless, the decision to have a pregnancy terminated is never an easy one. A multitude of personal feelings and emotions have to be taken into account and even when abortion may seem to be the only option the decision is never a simple process of logical evaluation. In recognition of the difficulties most women face in making the decision, specific counselling for women seeking abortion is available in many countries. In the USA shortly after abortion was legalized in all states in 1973 a new profession—abortion counsellor—was created [1]. Some states have no laws regulating abortion counselling; others have strict informed consent laws detailing precisely what information must be given to women considering abortion [2]. In the UK, the Committee on the Working of the Abortion Act (the Lane Committee) reporting in 1974—some 7 years after legalization of abortion—recommended that every woman should have the opportunity of adequate counselling before making the decision to have her pregnancy terminated [3]. In some countries abortion counselling is mandatory.

Counselling has become a rather fashionable term and much value is placed on the concept by laypeople. Despite its popularity there is no standard definition of counselling and the term means different things to different people. The then Department of Health and Social Security in England in a circular published in 1977 described abortion counselling as, 'providing opportunities for discussion, information, explanation and advice' in a manner which is both 'non-judgemental and non-directional' [4]. In Britain, most women are 'counselled' by one or more of the professionals involved in the process of arranging and carrying out the abortion; the majority, however, do not see a professional counsellor. But, whoever does the counselling and however it is done, every woman

112

should ideally feel that she has had an opportunity to explore her feelings and anxieties and to make an informed choice. She may be sad about the decision she has had to make but should have no long-term regrets.

Professionals who counsel women about abortion usually cover three areas: (i) decision-making; (ii) information provision; and (iii) emotional support.

Decision-making

Most women faced with an unplanned pregnancy, even if they had taken no precautions to prevent it, are surprised or shocked to find themselves pregnant. Allen, in her book *Counselling Services for Sterilisation, Vasectomy and Termination of Pregnancy* [5], describes a series of in-depth interviews of 231 women who had just undergone induced abortion between 1982 and 1983 in the UK. Of the women interviewed, 56% knew immediately they suspected a pregnancy that they wanted an abortion, only 16% initially wanted to continue with the pregnancy, 10% were undecided and 11% did not know what to do.

Most women discuss their situation with their partner, a relative or friend before consulting a doctor and when they do consult their minds are made up. Even if they are quite certain of their decision these informal discussions often serve to confirm it. In Allen's study [5], conversations with partners were the most important influence in helping women to make the decision. Young women—particularly teenagers— sometimes talk to their mothers but often to girlfriends who are perceived to be particularly helpful because they are female, of a similar age and know the woman personally. Allen also interviewed a substantial number of professionals involved in counselling for abortion. Most professionals involved with counselling see the decision-making process as being of fundamental importance. They want to encourage the woman to think of both the practical and emotional consequences of all the possible options: abortion, continuing with the pregnancy and adoption. They are particularly concerned that unless a woman is quite certain of her decision she will be more likely to regret it later. A small number of women will need more time and perhaps more counselling to help them to make up their minds. The decision may, ironically, be more difficult for teenagers who can sometimes feel caught in the middle if their family and perhaps the partner's family become involved in the deliberations.

Some women do change their minds. In a small survey in Edinburgh [6], 10% of women who had been seen by at least one doctor and referred to the gynaecologist failed to keep their appointment at some stage during the process. Some left it to the last minute and simply did not turn up for the operation. Many women are afraid that they may be refused an abortion and perhaps for some it is not possible to make the final decision until they are quite certain that they really do have a choice. For others, the reality of abortion may not become apparent until they are faced with the practicalities of attending for surgery and find that at the last minute they cannot go through with it. In some countries such as France, statute demands a waiting period between the time the abortion has been agreed and the time it is carried out to allow women the opportunity to reflect on their decision free from the worry that the request may be refused. Last minute changes of mind may cause particular problems with first-trimester medical abortion where the 48-h delay between the antiprogesterone and the prostaglandin treatment allows time for a change of heart.

In the UK every woman seeking an abortion must see two doctors, both of whom must sign a form stating that there are legitimate grounds for terminating the pregnancy. Most women see their general practitioner (GP) first and then a gynaecologist who provides the second signature and performs the abortion. Professionals involved with abortion often feel that the GP is the best person to counsel the woman as he or she is most likely to know her and her personal circumstances. Some women, however, prefer to see a doctor who does not know them—this applies particularly to teenagers and married women whose pregnancy may be the result of an extramarital relationship. These women may attend a community family planning clinic (although not all clinics are able to make direct referral to gynaecologists), or they may, for reasons of perceived privacy, choose to go privately, thus having to pay for the abortion. The majority of women do not attend the doctor for help with making the decision (only 12% did so in the Allen study [5]) or for emotional support (only 3%). Seeing a doctor is a necessary part of getting an abortion and women attend expecting a pregnancy test, information and referral. In order to satisfy themselves that there are grounds for termination most doctors and counsellors discuss the reasons why the pregnancy is unwanted and the practical and emotional consequences of all the options: abortion, continuing with the pregnancy and keeping the baby and adoption. Most usually explore whether the woman is absolutely certain about her decision since uncertainty may be more likely to lead to regret. By the time they see the second doctor most women are certain that they want an abortion and few expect help with decision-making from the gynae-cologist. Since the gynaecologist also has to satisfy himself or herself that there are legitimate grounds for the abortion, he or she usually explores the same areas of discussion. Some women find these inevitable questions personal and intrusive; they do not expect to discuss the reasons, merely the details. Others feel that they have to 'make the case' to the gynaecologist for having their pregnancy terminated.

Allen concluded from her study that in the 1980s abortion counselling in the UK was 'patchy' [5]. In the USA, women receive more counselling in non-profit-making clinics than in those which are profit making [2]. Not all doctors are sympathetic and often the counselling depends more on the personality of the doctor than on the circumstances of the woman. Young unmarried women are less likely to be treated sympathetically and women who have had one or more abortions in the past may even be treated punitively. Women who are seen to have conceived because of a true method failure, such as an intrauterine contraceptive device (IUCD) failure, are more likely to receive a sympathetic hearing. Many women suspect intuitively that this may be the case and some will claim method failure even when they have not been using contraception.

Some women also see either a social worker or someone specifically trained in abortion counselling. In the UK, this is more likely to be the case in private agencies such as the British Pregnancy Advisory Service or Brook Advisory Centres. Although these professionals may often be seen to be particularly helpful—perhaps because they have more time—most women feel that they do not need to see a social worker or psychiatrist. In the Allen study [5], 28% of women were seen by a medical social worker, most thought that it was a waste of time and only one-quarter of them found the discussion helpful. In the UK, it is rare for a woman to be referred to a social worker—indeed, the need for such referral may be greater among those women who decide to continue with their pregnancy.

As discussed above, most women have made their decision long before they see a doctor and they see no need for prolonged discussions. The skill of the counsellor lies in the ability to detect those women who do need lengthy discussions and more support and those who may be at risk of severe regret. In Allen's study, only 7% of women felt that they had not had enough counselling. When asked what they wanted most women felt that abortion should be quicker and easier to obtain—they wanted information, understanding and emotional support, but most of all they wanted the abortion.

Information provision

Women perceive doctors involved in the counselling process more as a source of information than as a source of help with decision-making or emotional support. The information that doctors want to give and that the women want to receive may not always be the same. Most women want to know, in varying degrees of detail, what happens when a pregnancy is terminated. In the UK, France and Sweden women who present early enough may have a choice of medical or surgical abortion. Clinicians should discuss the different techniques together with their advantages and disadvantages, to enable a choice to be made. Doctors want to discuss the risks and side effects of abortion and both parties may be concerned with the question of the effect of abortion on future fertility. The information should be realistic, non-biased and apolitical. In some states in North America, the information that is given is sometimes designed to be off-putting with graphic—and sometimes pictorial—descriptions of fetal development.

The women who were interviewed in Allen's study felt they would have liked more information about abortion before they 'got into the system' [5]. An explanatory leaflet available from GPs and family planning doctors, which the woman can keep, is very helpful. Women also need information about what happens after the abortion, the expected duration of bleeding, how soon intercourse is permitted, even such details as when to have a bath. This is probably best given after the procedure, perhaps by nursing staff, and a separate information leaflet may be more sensitive.

Counsellors and particularly doctors regard discussion about contraception as being a vital part of the counselling process. In a Scottish study [7], 119 consultant gynaecologists strongly agreed that contraceptive advice should be given after the abortion. Interestingly, they did not think that all abortion patients should be offered a follow-up appointment with either themselves or the referring doctor. In the Allen study, most consultants discussed future contraception with the woman but few gave much information. Future contraceptive plans are usually discussed before the abortion is carried out. This may not be the best time. A woman who is anxious about being pregnant and worried that her request for an abortion may be denied, may not be receptive to a detailed discussion about contraception. Frequently, the decision to have a termination arises because a relationship has ended and the woman may not see an immediate need for future contraception. Some younger women are so devastated by the unwanted pregnancy that their reaction to any discussion of the future is to swear that they plan never to have intercourse again. While a discussion about future contraception prior to or even immediately after the abortion may not be ideal, in some cases it may be the only chance the professional has. Even if a follow-up appointment is given after the abortion many patients default.

Emotional support

Counselling for abortion should provide emotional support. For most women, abortion is emotionally painful. The decision and the procedure may cause sadness but it should not cause regret. Although many women having an abortion will receive emotional support from their families or friends, good professional counselling at the time of the decision can be extremely helpful and can reduce the psychological trauma of abortion. Women who are well counselled usually feel less guilty, less depressed, less isolated and at the time of the procedure they also feel less pain. In a study of patients undergoing first-trimester medical abortion in Edinburgh [8], women were admitted to a hospital bed in a single room or to a shared sitting room or hospital ward with a number of others undergoing the same experience. Treatment in small groups enabled women to share their experiences and they felt the benefit of this kind of supportive companionship. In France, some centres now recommend treatment in small groups for this reason [9].

Post-abortion counselling

While most women experience a huge sense of relief after an unwanted pregnancy has been terminated and many studies have demonstrated a significant improvement in psychological well-being after compared with before abortion [10], a small number do have difficulty in coming to terms with having an abortion. In the USA [2], it is estimated that 20% of women suffer from severe feelings of loss, grief and regret. These feelings may progress to anger (at herself and at her partner), or to depression and even obsession. These feelings are more likely to arise in women who: lack social support; whose decision to terminate the pregnancy is in conflict with their family or their religious beliefs; who feel they were pressurized into having an abortion; who have abortion because of fetal anomaly; and who are very young or have a very late abortion. Some women may need prolonged counselling by trained experts, although many find that a few sessions of post-abortion counselling allows them to come to terms with their emotions.

Template for services

The worldwide trend towards the liberalization of abortion laws which started in Europe in the 1930s has continued over the last decade. Some 63% of the world's population live in countries where abortion is either available on request or where social factors can be an indication [11]. However, 25% of women still have access to abortion only if pregnancy is life-threatening. Liberalization of the abortion laws leads to but does not guarantee a safe abortion service. In most countries in which abortion is legal only licensed medical personnel provide it, although the policies and practices regarding the setting vary widely.

In many developed countries, there is a move away from the provision of abortion within a hospital setting. For example, in the Netherlands, Norway and the USA, specialized abortion clinics have been established. In the USA, larger clinics have a caseload of more than 10 000 abortions each year [12]. In France, New Zealand and the UK abortion is provided almost only in hospital. Abortion within dedicated clinics may be more economical and the service is provided by experts who may be more sensitive and sympathetic to women undergoing pregnancy termination. However, this approach separates abortion from other aspects of reproductive health care. In Scotland, where over 95% of abortions are performed in National Health Service hospitals, counselling for and performing abortions is part of the training of all gynaecologists unless they have moral or religious objections. Medical students and doctors planning to enter general practice are also exposed to all aspects of unwanted pregnancy [13]. In countries where abortion is largely confined to specialized clinics such as the USA, abortion is not always part of gynaecological training. Without exposure during their training to the relevant issues and to women who are seeking abortion, doctors may become increasingly reluctant to be involved with the provision of services.

While the manner in which abortion services are provided varies widely between countries it is possible to devise a set of guidelines for a high-quality service that is universally applicable to all providers. Such a template for abortion services should aim for a safe, efficient and comprehensive service that allows women to exercise choice over their treatment and which respects their dignity. This template can be divide into four elements:

1 pregnancy diagnosis and determination of gestational age;
2 information, medical assessment and counselling;
3 provision of the abortion;
4 post-abortion services.

Pregnancy diagnosis and determination of gestational age

An abortion service should be able to offer immediate biochemical pregnancy testing, as waiting for results may cause delay and certainly increases anxiety. Ultrasound scanning facilities should be available to determine the gestational age and viability of the fetus when there is clinical doubt. A few women will not be pregnant or will have an ectopic or non-viable pregnancy. In such cases, referral for the management of abnormal pregnancy or investigation of amenorrhoea should be available and women should receive advice about contraception (and supplies) if appropriate. The ability to scan the patient is also useful in the assessment of incomplete or failed abortion at follow-up.

Information, medical assessment and counselling

Counselling and written information about abortion, as described above, should be available to all women seeking abortion. It must be possible for women who are uncertain about their decision to see a counsellor on more than one occasion. In the UK, it is estimated that 90% of women who approach a doctor to discuss it will choose abortion, 8% will choose to continue with the pregnancy, 1% will present too late for legal abortion and 1% will not be pregnant. For those women who are too late and for some of those who choose to have the baby, information about social security benefits and adoption, and referral to social services where they exist, should be available.

Abortion services should have the ability to assess the general health of the woman and her suitability for the various methods of abortion. A check-list of indications and contraindications to the available techniques is useful in a clinic setting. Blood should be taken for ABO and rhesus (D) testing and for any other appropriate investigations such as sickle cell screening. Whether the service chooses to screen for genital tract infection, particularly *Chlamydia*, or simply to treat everyone with prophylactic antibiotics will depend on the background incidence of infection in the local population. Women considered to be at high risk of hepatitis B or human immunodeficiency virus (HIV) should be offered screening with appropriate counselling. Such tests should never be made a condition of having the abortion and women who refuse screening should be treated as high risk during the abortion procedure. Cervical screening should be offered in accordance with national screening policies.

Provision of the abortion

In general, the earlier the abortion is done, the safer it is. Surgical abortion is associated with a higher failure rate, however, if performed before 7 weeks of gestation. The abortion should be provided at the earliest possible gestation and preferably completed within 7 days of the initial request. It is well recognized that the mortality and morbidity associated with the procedure increase with the gestation of the pregnancy at the time of termination. The risk of major complications doubles when termination is carried out at 15 as compared with 8 weeks gestation [14]. International comparisons of gestational age at the time of abortion are difficult to obtain but there are wide variations in the proportion of abortions performed at different gestations in different countries. In former Czechoslovakia, late abortions involve a prolonged stay in hospital and a charge to the woman, early abortion is encouraged and some 85% are performed before 9 weeks. In some countries such as India, lack of medical resources mean that women have to wait for abortion until they are in the second trimester. The same is true in parts of England where National Health Service provision of abortion is insufficient for the demand among women who cannot afford private treatment.

Gestational age also determines the method of choice. Medical abortion is only available to women in the UK and Sweden up to 63 days of amenorrhoea and up to 49 days in France. Clearly, early treatment increases the opportunities for a choice of method in the first trimester. Long delays also increase the woman's anxiety over her unwanted pregnancy.

Abortion should be available to women of any gestation up to the legal limit for that country, and this means having a variety of methods available. Women who present early enough should have a choice between medical or surgical induction of abortion. Vacuum aspiration has been the method of choice for early surgical termination of pregnancy in industrialized countries for more than two decades. In his world review made in 1990, Henshaw [12] reports that over 95% of surgical abortions were performed by suction in most of northern Europe and the USA. Yet, dilatation and curettage (D & C) is still the standard method for uterine evacuation in many Eastern European countries—52% in Hungary [12]—and in developing countries [15] where most physicians are not trained in suction aspiration. D & C requires more cervical dilatation, carries more risk of uterine injury and a higher incidence of retained products of conception and, is thus associated with a significantly higher complication rate and adverse future reproductive outcome [16]. Vacuum aspiration is less painful than D & C and is thus associated with less need for analgesia.

Vacuum aspiration can be achieved by the use of either electric or manual pump, the latter (manual vacuum aspiration, MVA) involves the use of a hand-held syringe allowing its use in clinics without electricity. MVA is a simple procedure [15] appropriate for use by trained non-medical health workers. Its use in the management of abortion complications in countries such as Nigeria and Nicaragua where previously D & C under general anaesthesia was used, has had a significant effect on maternal mortality and morbidity from illegal abortion [17].

Vacuum aspiration can be performed under either local or general anaesthesia. In many countries, developed and developing, local anaesthesia is the method of choice, although in the UK the great majority of abortions are performed under general anaesthesia. General anaesthesia necessitates the use of an operating theatre, a trained anaesthetist and a longer recovery period and these requirements may add to the delay in treatment particularly in the developing world where the demands on operating theatre time can be immense. Some evidence suggests that the use of general anaesthesia increases the risk of the procedure. In the USA, the mortality rate is two to four times greater when general rather than local anaesthesia is used for first-trimester abortion [18]. In countries where both techniques are available with safety, the woman should have some involvement in the choice of anaesthetic.

Preoperative treatment with a cervical priming agent has been shown to reduce the risk of haemorrhage and genital tract trauma associated with vacuum aspiration. Prostaglandins, laminaria tents and the anti-progesterone RU 486 are all effective. Pretreatment of the cervix adds to the cost of the procedure and may be difficult to organize because of time constraints. Cervical trauma is more common in women under the age of 17 years and uterine perforation is associated with increasing parity and increasing gestation [19]. It would seem reasonable to select women for cervical priming on the basis of age, parity and gestation.

Medical termination of early first-trimester pregnancy using a combination of RU 486 and prostaglandin has been available in France since 1988, the UK since 1991 and Sweden since 1993. The incidence of serious complications is probably similar to that associated with surgical abortion, but because 95% of women need neither anaesthesia nor instrumentation of the uterus, large randomized trials may eventually show medical abortion to be safer. In France and the UK, around 20–25% prefer medical abortion [20] and, in countries where RU 486 is licensed, women who have no contraindications to either method should have a choice.

Second-trimester abortion is less common—it accounts for 10–15% of all legal abortions in the UK—but, is associated with a disproportionately high level of morbidity, with many of the complications relating to the specific method used to terminate the pregnancy. There are very few large randomized studies and it is difficult to determine whether there is a 'best method' for mid-trimester abortion. D & E is the most widely used method in many countries including the USA, Canada, Denmark, England and Wales, New Zealand, Norway and the former West Germany, and the method has proved to be consistently safer than instillation procedures (at least in the USA at gestations up to 16 weeks). The latter involve the instillation, either intra- or extra-amniotically, of prostaglandins, hypertonic saline, urea or ethacridine lactate. Skilled personnel are required to carry out these procedures and the abortion (the woman is conscious) tends to be painful and prolonged. With the exception of ethacridine lactate all the substances are potentially toxic (for review see [21]). The development of stable prostaglandin analogues has allowed the vaginal administration of prostaglandins, a route that is much safer than instillation. In 1990, Scotland and Finland were the only countries with a significant incidence of medically induced—rather than surgical—second-trimester abortions. In Scotland, the administration of prostaglandin vaginally is the method of choice, instillation being rarely used. The induction–abortion interval is significantly reduced by pre-treatment with RU 486 [22], and where the compound is available the combination of vaginal prostaglandins with antiprogesterone pretreatment may be recommended.

Abortion beyond 18 weeks gestation is rare and in many countries it is either illegal or only available for pregnancies complicated by severe fetal malformation. Particularly distressing for both the mother and the staff, these late abortions are often effectively managed with vaginal prostaglandins in combination with RU 486 with intra-amniotic urea or fetal intracardiac injection of potassium to minimize the chances of a live birth.

Whatever the method used, abortion should be available as a day-case or office procedure since this minimizes inconvenience to the woman concerned and reduces the cost. There is a worldwide trend towards shorter hospital stays in those countries where abortion is performed within a hospital setting. Overnight stay should be possible for women who have to travel long distances or who are unfit to go home after the procedure is completed.

Post-abortion services

All women should receive contraceptive advice and, if appropriate, supplies before going home. They should also, as discussed above, receive written information about side effects, bleeding patterns and the resumption of fertility. All should be given a follow-up appointment within 3 weeks, either with the clinic that carried out the abortion or a suitable alternative doctor. At follow-up a pelvic examination should confirm complete abortion and the absence of infection. Discussion should include contraceptive advice and post-abortion counselling if required.

Abortion providers should participate in relevant health promotion programmes and should undertake regular audit of their service. They should be aware of and able to incorporate developments in technical and clinical practice. The service should be sensitive to the special needs of certain groups of patients including the very young, women from ethnic minorities and those with disabilities. In 1992–93 in the UK, the Birth Control Trust (BCT) circulated a model service specification for women requesting abortion [23]. Although written specifically for service provision in the UK, where abortion is provided free of charge on the National Health Service, the BCT's template for a service is a detailed and useful document for providers wishing to improve or audit their service.

Conclusion

As we approach the next century, unsafe abortion is one of the major concerns facing people involved in reproductive health care. Worldwide it results in about 70 000 maternal deaths each year [11] and, yet, if provided under modern medical conditions in developed countries it is safer than pregnancy and childbirth. In their paper on the role of health care systems in abortion provision, McLaurin *et al.* [17] argue that providers 'need to examine existing services in light of women's needs, discover the barriers that hinder women's access to abortion care, and implement mechanisms to ensure that appropriate care is both available and accessible'.

References

1 Landy U. Abortion counselling—a new component of medical care. *Clin Obstet Gynaecol* 1986; 13: 33–41.
2 Steinberg TN. Abortion counselling: to benefit maternal health. *Am J Law Med* 1989; 15: 483–517.

3 Committee on the Working of the Abortion Act (Chair: Mrs Justice Lane) *Report*. Volume 1, Cmnd 5579. London: HMSO, 1974.

4 Department of Health and Social Security. Health Services Development. *Arrangements for Counselling of Patients Seeking Abortion*. Health Circular HC(77)26. London: HMSO, 1977.

5 Allen I. *Counselling Services for Sterilisation, Vasectomy and Termination of Pregnancy*. No. 641. London: Policy Studies Institute, 1985.

6 Glasier A, Thong JK. *The Establishment of a Centralised Referral Service Leads to Earlier Abortion*. Health Bulletin no. 49. Edinburgh: HMSO, 1991: 254–259.

7 Penney GC, Glasier A, Templeton AA. Agreeing criteria for audit of the management of induced abortion: an approach by national consensus survey. *Quality in Health Care* 1993; 2: 167–169.

8 Thong KJ, Dewar MH, Baird DT. What do women want during medical abortion? *Contraception* 1992; 46: 435–442.

9 Baulieu EE, Rosenblum M. *The Abortion Pill, RU 486; a Woman's Choice*. New York: Simon and Schuster, 1991: 97.

10 Adler NE, David HP, Major BN, Roth SH, Russo NF, Wyatt GE. Psychological responses after abortion. *Science* 1990; 268: 41–44.

11 Maternal Health and Safe Motherhood Programme. *Abortion. A Tabulation of Available Data on the Frequency and Mortality of Unsafe Abortion*, 2nd edn. Geneva: World Health Organization Division of Family Health, 1993.

12 Henshaw SK. Induced abortion: a world review. *Fam Plann Perspect* 1990; 22: 76–89.

13 Glasier A. The organisation of abortion services. *Curr Obstet Gynaecol* 1993; 3: 23–27.

14 Filshie GM. Abortion. In: Filshie GM, Guillebaud J, eds. *Contraception. Science and Practice*. London: Butterworths, 1989: 265–267.

15 Greenslade FG, Benson J, Winkler J, Henderson V, Wolf M, Leonard A. Summary of clinical and programmatic experience with manual vacuum aspiration. *Adv Abortion Care* 1993; 3(2): 1–6.

16 Henshaw RC, Templeton AA. Methods used in first trimester abortion. *Curr Obstet Gynaecol* 1993; 3: 11–16.

17 McLaurin KE, Hord CE, Wolf M. *Health Systems' Role in Abortion Care: the Need for a Pro-active Approach. Volume 1. Issues in Abortion Care*. Carrboro: International Projects Assistance Services, 1991.

18 Peterson HB, Grimes DA, Cates W Jr, Rubin GL. Comparative risk of death from induced abortion at 12 weeks or less gestation performed with local versus general anesthesia. *Am J Obstet Gynecol* 1981; 141: 763–768.

19 Schulz KF, Grimes DA, Cates W Jr. Measures to prevent cervical injury during suction currettage abortion. *Lancet* 1983; i: 1182–1184.

20 Henshaw RC, Naji SA, Russel IT, Templeton AA. Comparison of medical abortion with surgical vacuum aspiration: women's preferences and acceptability of treatment. *Br Med J* 1993; 307: 714–717.

21 Urquhart DR. Methods used in second trimester abortion *Curr Obstet Gynaecol* 1993; 3: 17–22.

22 Rodger MW, Baird DT. Pretreatment with mifepristone (RU 486) reduces interval between prostaglandin administration and expulsion in second trimester abortion. *Br J Obstet Gynaecol* 1990; 97: 41–45.

23 Birth Control Trust. *Model Service Specification: Services for Women Requesting Abortion*. London: Birth Control Trust, 1993.

8   Introducing Medical Abortion Technologies into Service-Delivery Systems

Forrest C. Greenslade, Traci L. Baird,
Brooke R. Johnson, Judith Winkler & Ann H. Leonard

Introduction

Debate and controversy continue over the introduction of medical abortion technologies, such as the regimen of RU 486 and prostaglandin (RU/PG), into service delivery. On the one hand, some advocates assert that RU/PG will remove most obstacles to safe abortion. On the other hand, some opponents are concerned that the safety of such drugs has not been adequately documented and their introduction will interfere with the provision of existing abortion services [1–5]. While these statements may reflect the extreme points of view, each has some merit. The potential of medical methods for early abortion presents both opportunities and challenges. The opportunities lie in expanding the options available to women for safely regulating their own fertility and improving the quality of care they receive. The challenges are determining whether, where, when and how to incorporate such new technologies into existing services in ways that improve the quality of abortion care.

The issues include the cultural, social, political and economic contexts where introduction might occur. The regulatory requirements of most developed countries mandate documentation of safety and effectiveness and involve a time-consuming, resource-intensive process. Health care infrastructures are generally well developed, but mechanisms for training providers in new technologies are often not well organized. Also, the costs of broad access, especially among low-income groups, are an increasingly problematic issue.

In developing countries, preparing overburdened health care systems to deliver new technologies safely and effectively is even more daunting. The legal, cultural, political and economic issues usually differ from those of developed countries and may vary from one low-resource setting to the next. Underpinning the introduction of RU/PG are values and standards regarding quality of care, women's perspectives and even biomedical issues. Successful introduction of RU/PG into developing countries or 'low-resource' contexts will require answers to many of

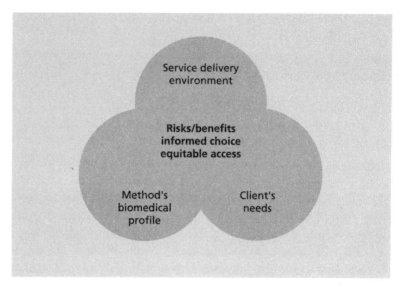

Fig. 8.1 Factors essential to the introduction of new technology. From Macklin [8].

the questions raised in this chapter through comprehensive research.

The bioethical issues of introducing a medical abortion technology into service delivery are those for any health care intervention [6,7]: assessment of risks versus benefits for the client, analysis of rights and obligations and consideration of just distribution. As shown in Fig. 8.1, three factors are central to the introduction of a new technology [9]: (i) the biomedical profile of the technology; (ii) the needs of clients; and (iii) the service-delivery environment.

This chapter highlights the biomedical profile of the early first-trimester medical abortifacient RU/PG. The available information on women's experiences with RU/PG is reviewed and the requirements for introducing the technology into service delivery are outlined. Finally, management guidance is provided about whether and how to introduce RU/PG into service-delivery programmes focusing on health systems research for service delivery.

Technology introduction and quality of abortion care

The mix of approaches available will influence the opportunities that medical abortion technologies may hold for improving the quality of abortion care. The more safe and effective technologies that are available, the better. No one technology is without risks or drawbacks or is acceptable to all women or providers. The limited availability of methods leaves many problems unresolved and can restrict women's access to safe and acceptable services. Each health care technology has specific biomedical characteristics that, to a large extent, determine the risks and benefits for clients and the requirements for service delivery. This section outlines the biomedical profile of RU/PG, the experiences that women have had with the drug regimen to date and service-delivery requirements for the introduction of the technology.

Biomedical profile of RU/PG

The World Health Organization (WHO) Special Programme of Research, Development and Research Training has conducted clinical evaluations of RU/PG in a number of countries, including Cuba, Georgia, Hong Kong, Hungary, Scotland, Sweden and Zambia. Based on this experience, medical guidelines were recently prepared which provide the following profile [10].

1   **Indications.** RU/PG may be used to terminate early pregnancy up to 63 days (9 weeks) since the beginning of the last menstrual period (LMP).

2   **Dose regimen.** The current recommended regimen is a 600 mg oral dose of RU 486 (mifepristone) followed 36–48 h later by a prostaglandin (a 1 mg gemeprost vaginal pessary, or a 400 μg oral dose of misoprostol).

3   **Effectiveness.** The combination with gemeprost results in complete abortion in approximately 95% of women. The patient usually expels the products of conception a few hours after administration of the prostaglandin.

4   **Side effects and complications.** Drug actions produce uterine bleeding and contractions (described in Chapters 2 and 3). Abdominal pain and blood loss usually accompany abortion. Bleeding continues for 5–30 days. Although total blood loss is modest in most women (median 80 ml; range 15–500 ml), about 1% of women bleed heavily and require curettage to stop bleeding. Another 3% of women require evacuation for incomplete abortion, and an additional 1% for continuing pregnancy. In general, complications are similar to those encountered following vacuum aspiration or sharp curettage, except that uterine perforation and operative trauma are not associated with medical abortion. Gastrointestinal problems are commonly reported. Rarely, myocardial infarction and cardiac arrhythmia (presumably related to the use of sulprostone) occur.

5   **Client selection criteria.** Women with legal indication for pregnancy termination and with intrauterine pregnancy up to 63 days LMP can use RU/PG. Use in ectopic pregnancy is contraindicated. Anaemia (haemoglo-

bin concentration less than 100 g/l), heart disease including myocardial infarction, coagulation disorder and asthma are contraindications. Caution is appropriate with women over 35 years of age and those who are heavy smokers. Caution is also appropriate for women with a family history of risk factors (e.g. elevated cholesterol, diabetes) for cardiovascular disease, epileptic women and women on glucocorticoid therapy.

Women's experiences with RU/PG

Acceptability studies

Investigators have evaluated acceptability of RU/PG in China, Cuba, England, France, Hong Kong, India, Scotland, Sweden and the USA [11–21] (B. Winikoff, personal communication, 1993). Study methodologies include interviews, questionnaires or surveys of women considering abortion or subsequent to abortion procedures. The responses to questions designed to assess women's perceptions of the experience indicate a high level of acceptability. However, in studies comparing medical abortion with vacuum aspiration, women indicated a high level of acceptability with both technologies. To date, few studies have objectively compared the acceptability of medical and vacuum aspiration technologies.

The characteristics of RU/PG that women reported liking the most are that it is non-surgical [5,15] and that it was perceived as causing less injury or trauma [12,22]. It was also perceived to be more natural and convenient [12,22,23]. Women reported that they had greater awareness of what was happening during the termination [15] and that they had a feeling of being more in control [23]. They also noted that the process was more discreet [15]. Women did not like some characteristics. Some expressed concern about the effectiveness of the medical abortion and the potential side effects of drugs [12]. Some women did not like the long period that it took between taking the drug and the expulsion [12]. Most women were aware of uterine bleeding with RU/PG (B. Winikoff, personal communication, 1993).

The perceptions of women's health advocates

The opinions of women's health advocates have varied widely concerning the appropriateness of medical abortion technologies such as RU/PG in different settings. These issues are complex in any country, but particularly so in most of the developing countries. In countries where women's access to reproductive health care services (including supplies and practitioners) is limited, their concerns warrant special evaluation [24–28]. Some women's health leaders question whether the current formulations of RU 486 and prostaglandins are appropriate for settings such as Bangladesh [4].

Berer [29] has posed the following questions relating women's perspectives to the issue of service delivery of RU/PG.

1   What is the overall experience of abortion? Will a medical approach be more like 'inducing a miscarriage' for women? Spontaneous miscarriage is almost always an unwanted experience of loss. The experience of a medical abortion is similar, except that it is sought and therefore experienced differently at an emotional level. The medical approach could, therefore, provide a totally different alternative to surgical approaches to abortion.

2   What are the time limits on the efficacy of the method? Can women and health care systems accommodate the narrow window in which technologies such as RU/PG are effective?

3   Who is in control of the procedure and process of abortion? How will different women perceive their involvement in the process, and how will it change relationships between clients and providers?

4   How long does it take to complete the abortion? How will different women experience a medical abortion, which may take several days, as compared to a vacuum aspiration abortion which takes just minutes to complete?

5   What is the abortion setting? How will medical abortion change the quality of services and women's access to them?

6   How many visits are required? How will women and health care systems accommodate multiple visits?

7   Who can use the method? How will policies, management practices, logistics and provider attitudes affect different women's access to medical abortion services?

8   How likely are adverse effects, especially prolonged bleeding? How will the relative medical risks and benefits of medical versus vacuum aspiration abortion be communicated by providers and perceived by women? Such issues clearly need to be addressed in determining the service-delivery requirements for RU/PG.

Service-delivery requirements for RU/PG

Experience specific to RU/PG and other reproductive health technologies provides valuable guidance for the development of management strategies for service delivery. This section defines the service-delivery requirements for such medical abortion technologies.

Initial experience with RU/PG

Experience with medical abortion comes primarily from developed countries. Even in these settings, the introduction of RU/PG into service delivery has had difficulties. The 1991 regulatory approval for use of RU/PG in the UK has presented the opportunity to evaluate issues related to setting up services. A symposium was held by the Birth Control Trust in 1993 to share this early information [30–37]. In general, the medical abortion technology was well accepted by clients and providers, although incorporation into the National Health Service is proceeding far more slowly than was predicted. A number of problems have been encountered in adapting the management and clinical practices for surgical abortion to accommodate medical termination; some provider stress in organizing the new service did occur. Training and preparing professional staff for providing the service was time consuming. A common set of problems centred around assessing women for appropriateness of medical abortion and referring them within the acceptable time period for treatment. Arranging with pharmacies for medications, including analgesics, was an important issue; pharmacy costs increased when compared to surgical abortion. Managing appointments was a problem. Women remain in bed longer after prostaglandin administration than after surgical abortion, therefore, negotiating beds for clients was challenging. An unexpected problem was providing enough toilet and bedpan facilities.

Extrapolating from this limited experience to developing countries is difficult. The Program for Appropriate Technology in Health (PATH) conducted in-depth interviews with health, family planning and women's health leaders about medical abortion technologies in Turkey, India, Thailand and Zambia [24–26]. Physicians and family planning practitioners expressed interest in technologies such as RU/PG, but expressed concerns about incorporating them into health services. A major concern was the ability of women to meet the demands of the multiple visits, given that in many developing countries they face great difficulties in accessing health services. A second issue was the logistics of drug supply, especially the ability to keep RU 486 from leaking into unauthorized distribution. A third area of concern was the cost of commodities and services of a medical abortion as compared to the existing practice.

Quality of care framework

Given the paucity of information on developing countries, lessons learned from services for other abortion care methods must be drawn upon. The IPAS (International Projects Assistance Services) has worked for 20 years to improve the quality of abortion care through introducing manual vacuum aspiration (MVA) into various health care systems, especially in developing countries. This method is indicated for abortion within 12 weeks LMP, menstrual regulation, treatment of incomplete abortion and endometrial biopsy [38,39]. The work of IPAS has led to a conceptual framework for quality abortion care [40]. The framework, depicted in Fig. 8.2, is a management tool to identify service-delivery requirements for introducing new abortion technologies [9,41–43]. The following analysis uses this framework to extrapolate information from the technology profile of RU/PG, including insights gained from investigators at WHO collaborating research centres (M. Bygdeman, A. Calder and M. Gomez Alzugaray, and O. Mateo de Acosta *et al.*, personal communications, 1993) and women's perspectives to define service-delivery requirements for programmatic use. Table 8.1 shows how to use this approach to organize issues related to the different abortion technologies.

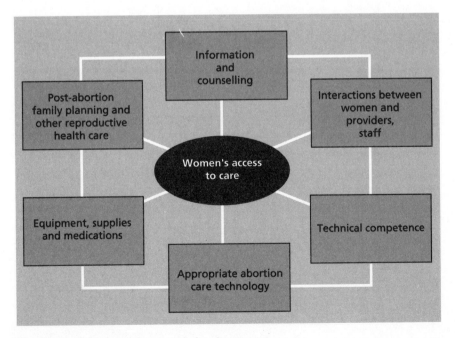

Fig. 8.2 Quality of care framework for abortion care.

Table 8.1 Early abortion technologies: opportunities and/or requirements for high-quality care. From Greenslade et al. [44]

	Profile of technology	Technical competence	Equipment, supplies, medications	Information, counselling	Interactions women/ providers	Post-abortion FP	Women's access to care
RU/PG	Drug action to produce uterine bleeding and contraction. Two-drug regimen currently administered in separate clinic visits. Very effective when given up to 9 weeks after the first day of LMP. Heavy bleeding, uterine pain, and gastrointestinal problems most commonly reported side effects. Prolonged bleeding and spotting also reported. Rarely, myocardial infarction and cardiac arrhythmia, presumably related to PG. Currently contraindicated for women with diabetes, liver or renal insufficiency, adrenal abnormalities, blood clotting disorders, bronchial asthma, history of heart disease or hypertension, and anaemia	Training in risks and benefits of RU/PG regimen, protocol and follow-up. Early pregnancy diagnosis. Linkage to surgical back-up for failure	Secure logistics for two drugs. Supplies of both RU and PG. Cold storage required for some PGs currently in use. Sensitive tests for early pregnancy detection. Medications for side effects and treatment of complications	Early pregnancy detection. Drug effects, complications, clinic protocol. Referral for back-up services	Continuity of care more difficult given clinic protocol	Appropriate timing of counselling and referral given multiple visit protocol. Research needed on FP methods most appropriate for use after RU/PG	Potential for further decentralized care. Increases access to early safe services. Early access critical because of time limit on effective use. Clinic protocol and need for back-up for incompletes or complications may restrict access. Cost may be prohibitive

Method	Description	Training and monitoring	Logistics and supplies	Information and verbal support	Client support during procedure	Linkages to FP	Service delivery level
VA MVA EVA	Uterine contents evacuated by vacuum through cannula introduced through cervical os. Requires minimal cervical dilatation, minimal pain control and medication. Very effective throughout first trimester, less effective prior to 7 weeks LMP. Heavy bleeding most commonly reported complication. Rarely, uterine and cervical injuries and pelvic infection reported. Contraindicated for women with acute purulent cervicitis or pelvic infection until infection is controlled, unless emergency attention is required	Training in VA procedure, aseptic techniques and follow-up. Monitoring of above and infection control protocols for use by personnel and for medical instruments	Secure logistics for VA instruments. Supplies and facilities for asepsis and infection control. Pain control medications	Information and verbal support		Decentralized services can facilitate linkages to FP services	Can be decentralized to primary care level. Single out-patient or clinic visit for procedure. Serves as its own back-up for complications. Service costs reduced from sharp curettage
Sharp curettage	Uterine contents removed by scraping of uterine lining with metal curette. Requires more cervical dilatation and pain control than VA. Not recommended for early first-trimester abortion. Heavy bleeding most commonly reported complication. Uterine and cervical injuries, pelvic infection and anaesthesia-related complications reported. Serious complications twice as frequent as with VA	Training in sharp curettage procedure, aseptic techniques, follow-up, infection control for use by personnel and for medical instruments and anaesthesia. Monitoring for above	Secure logistics for sharp curettage instruments. Supplies and facilities for asepsis and infection control. Pain control medications. In many cases, supplies and facilities for general anaesthesia	Higher level of anaesthesia or sedation makes woman less able to be fully involved in her own health care and makes communication at time of procedure more difficult	· Interaction with client during procedure limited by higher level anaesthesia or sedation	Linkages to FP more difficult with more centralized care	More centralized care, anaesthesia and hospital stays common. Single visit for procedure. Can serve as its own back-up for complications

EVA, electric (pump) vacuum aspiration; FP, family planning; VA, vacuum aspiration.

Technical competence

Assuring technical competence with a new technology at all levels of the system is the first priority. Training, supervision, adherence to protocols and systematic review of complications are essential. The categories of health personnel that need to be trained may differ according to local laws and regulations pertaining to provision of abortion services. Registered medical practitioners, including gynaecologists, residents, nurses and paramedical staff have successfully provided RU/PG. Physicians, nurses, midwives or other paramedics can learn to provide medical abortion within a few days. Additionally, counselling staff for abortion and family planning must be trained. To date, RU/PG abortions have primarily occurred in hospital settings, but clinics within approximately 30 min of a hospital may also be appropriate. Local laws may govern the clinical setting for provision of medical abortions. In-service training, in which new personnel work with experienced staff over a 1–2-week period, has been successful. Regular staff meetings to update information, especially complications, have been useful.

Quality assurance mechanisms are important. These include client records on diagnosis, complications and other critical outcomes. Review of cases on a regular basis is needed to improve services.

Many aspects of the multiple-visit protocol in effect in France, the UK and Sweden will present training and related logistical challenges [45]. The limitation of use to very early gestation requires careful determination of LMP, pregnancy testing with a sensitive method and/or ultrasound scan. Physical examination and discussion with the client may well be adequate, but further research on this is needed. Clinicians administer the prostaglandin under controlled clinical conditions followed by an observation period of up to 4 h. The availability of providers trained in vacuum aspiration or sharp curettage, either on-site or through referral to a nearby facility, is critical. Some women will probably choose vacuum aspiration. Some will not be eligible for RU/PG because of medical contraindications or duration of pregnancy, and aspiration will be required in cases in which the medical treatment fails to produce complete abortion (currently estimated at 5% of cases) [46,47]. It is imperative that the infrastructure for referral to back-up services be in place *before* the introduction of the method.

Equipment, supplies and medication

The continuous availability of appropriate equipment, supplies and medication is central to the provision of safe and effective care. Logistical and supply issues are often among the most intransigent introduction problems, often becoming more acute with decentralization of services. Introduction of a new technology usually requires adaptation of existing networks, which often do not work effectively even for currently available methods. It is essential to ensure the security of abortion commodities, both surgical supplies and medical agents, because of the potential danger of unauthorized use. With RU/PG, distribution plans must provide for the security of both RU 486 and prostaglandins. A prostaglandin currently in use with RU 486 (gemeprost) requires special cold storage conditions. Another, misoprostol, is stable under dry, temperate conditions. In addition, the limited time during pregnancy that RU/PG is effective may make availability of sensitive pregnancy tests crucial.

In addition to the abortion medicines, uterotonic agents, anaesthetics, blood transfusion supplies, analgesics, antiemetics, antibiotics and drugs for the rare cardiovascular complications should be available. Access to a range of contraceptive drugs and devices is important. Facilities and instruments for back-up vacuum aspiration must be available.

Information and counselling

Although critical to the effectiveness and acceptability of any technology, adequate counselling and education are very difficult to implement. The health system must be able to provide women with complete information about abortion and ensure their ability to make informed choices among treatment methods. Clear information about the symptoms of complications and what to do if they occur is also required. Completely new protocols may be required for discussing risks and benefits of the new method in comparing it to other available approaches. Developing and instituting these protocols requires staff, time and commitment.

A major task in introducing RU/PG is educating women about the method. Specifically, the limited period in early pregnancy for effective use of this method necessitates that women recognize the early signs of pregnancy and/or obtain early pregnancy testing. Informing women fully about the effects of the method will also be vitally important. Especially in cultures where women are considered 'unclean' or are even sequestered during their menses, the prolonged bleeding that can occur with RU/PG may not be acceptable. A variety of materials, including locally produced written materials and videotapes, are currently used in different settings. At the WHO collaborating research centres, physicians, nurses, social workers and specially trained counsellors provide information and counselling. Counselling occurs at the pre-admission visit, at the time of the abortion and at a follow-up appointment.

It is imperative that women understand that the visit to receive the prostaglandin dose is an important part of the therapy. It is also critical that women feel confident that they can gain access to back-up services in the event of an incomplete abortion or complication.

Interactions between women and providers/staff

In interactions with clients, health care providers and staff need to be supportive and respectful of women and their situations. By respecting women's confidentiality and autonomy, providers should create an atmosphere of trust in which women can freely express their concerns. This environment is most conducive to the provision of high-quality care. Introduction of a new technology requires examination of how it will affect relationships among women, providers and staff. Managers should consider the need for special training and practices to promote supportive interactions. Women's needs for support throughout their care may differ for medical abortifacients and surgical procedures.

Post-abortion family planning

This and other reproductive health services are important. Managers should identify and modify administrative practices and policies to enhance access to such services. More research is needed to learn whether contraceptive method selection may be different after RU/PG than after other abortion technologies.

Access to care

The goal of abortion care is not simply that services be available but that the largest number of women be able to benefit from high-quality care. Meeting this objective requires that services be effectively and appropriately managed and that women understand how to obtain them.

Introducing medical abortion technologies into service delivery

Introduction programmes must focus on management and technical issues that affect the technology's appropriate delivery into specific countries. System management issues such as training, counselling and product logistics need planning. Major emphasis must be placed on assessing women's experiences with the technology and its delivery. The availability of a new technology provides a special opportunity to evaluate and possibly improve the quality of care provided by the service-delivery system [9,43,48–52].

Management strategy for decision-making

This management strategy for decision-making in establishing reproductive health services reflects the experience of the following: (i) the Population Council in introducing Norplant implants and copper T intrauterine contraceptive devices (IUCDs); (ii) WHO in introducing Cyclofem; (iii) IPAS in providing MVA services; and (iv) PATH in exploring programmatic potential for RU/PG. The strategy recently developed by the WHO Task Force on Research on the Introduction and Transfer of Technologies for Fertility Regulation [53] provides operational principles appropriate for introducing medical abortion technologies. The basic tenet of the approach is as follows: technology should be assessed with greater emphasis on the ability of the service environment to provide it appropriately to the user (client) community. Introduction can play an important role in that it provides a window of opportunity for strategic decision-making.

Technology introduction programmes should do the following:

1   offer a choice of technologies rather than be directed by a single product;

2   emphasize the ability of the system to manage the services needed for the new technology;

3   stress the importance of assessing the potential of the technology at each stage of the introduction process;

4   encourage collaborative research and decision-making to increase resources and commitment to a positive outcome;

5   recognize that successful and sustainable programmes are country-specific, yet benefit from partnerships between interested agencies and non-governmental organizations;

6 focus on quality of care, considering whether the technology will improve existing levels of care or expand the range of options offered by the programme.

WHO recommends a multistage decision-making process (Fig. 8.3). This process recognizes that in each setting there are differences among clients and among service-delivery infrastructures. Decisions concerning whether and how to introduce a medical abortion technology such as RU/PG must be made locally. Those charged with these decisions should analyse at each stage whether introducing this technology will improve the quality of care provided.

Health systems research for service delivery

Medicines such as RU/PG should be appropriate for the setting of the developing country. However, there is a great deal to learn about service-delivery infrastructure and management changes that must be made [54,55]. The issues identified in the following section form the basis of health systems research projects needed to inform decisions about whether and how to introduce this technology.

To date, few research projects have compared RU/PG to other procedures (such as MVA) to terminate pregnancy. New research should focus on how the introduction of RU/PG affects abortion service delivery. What changes in provider training and attitudes, and administrative and client management, are necessitated by the introduction of the new technology? What are the cost differences? What is the most appropriate back-up technology for RU/PG? Answers to these questions will require detailed examination of the infrastructure requirements, client/provider acceptability of RU/PG and alternative technologies. If conducted in a setting in which many women have had multiple abortions (e.g. Eastern Europe), researchers could assess the attitudes of clients and providers who have experienced both RU/PG and vacuum aspiration.

Additionally, many questions remain unanswered about the potential use of RU/PG for abortion in developing or low-resource countries. In most developing countries, policymakers must first contend with the issue of legalizing abortion on request before they can consider introducing RU/PG. Another issue policymakers must consider is whether RU/PG will be appropriate in the public health system or in the private sector. The need for restricted distribution of RU/PG to appropriately licensed providers will likely influence its introduction. Furthermore, those introducing RU/PG in developing countries should consider some unre-

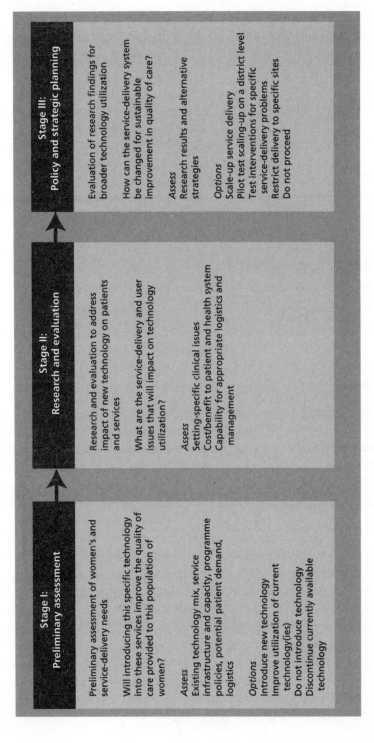

Fig. 8.3 Multistage decision-making process for the introduction of a new technology for fertility regulation. From Spicehandler and Simmons [53].

solved cultural issues, including whether or not women will complete the multiple-visit protocol and if women will accept seeing the products of conception and the additional bleeding associated with RU/PG procedures.

Many specific issues must be considered by those charged with the responsibility of making decisions related to introducing this technology into service-delivery systems. Table 8.2 presents a partial list of these issues and is designed to guide the method-introduction decision-making process. Decision-makers first need to decide what questions they want to answer. Researchers should devise strategies to study both clients and providers of abortion services. If questions extend beyond the clinical setting, researchers should expand the sample to include administrators, policymakers and local community members. Service-delivery issues for RU/PG exist in a wide range of cultural, social, political and economic contexts. Data collection methods should be relevant for each group. Structured and open-ended individual interviews should complement, and help to focus, group discussions; additionally, general observations of service-delivery and time–motion studies of client management should occur.

Conclusion

Unsafe abortion is a major cause of morbidity and mortality for women throughout the world. Improving women's access to safe, high-quality abortion care is a growing need in developed and developing countries. The medical abortion technologies clearly present many opportunities to extend women's access to care. This presents a special opportunity for health policymakers, programme managers, health care providers and women's health advocates to address critical issues concerning the general quality of abortion care. What emerges from past experience is that there is no quick fix to the problem of unsafe abortion. Twenty years after the development of MVA, the incorporation of this technology into health care systems is far from complete. A similar experience awaits any new technology—RU/PG and others that may follow. To believe either that medical abortion technologies will resolve the unsafe abortion problem or, conversely, that drugs like RU/PG face unique and formidable introduction challenges, is naive. The debate should focus on the pragmatic policy and management changes needed to provide women with access to all appropriate technologies and services required to improve the quality of abortion care.

Table 8.2 Decison-making issues

Health care system infrastructure
Availability of existing services to adapt for RU/PG implementation
Existing infrastructural resources to accommodate RU/PG (e.g. cold chain, pregnancy tests, analgesics, central instruments, treatment space)
Resources for back-up uterine evacuation
Staffing patterns at potential RU/PG sites
Staffing for back-up services
Present caseload and client profiles at current abortion providers
Procedures for logistics and inventory control
Procedures to monitor multiple visits
Procedures to monitor women with complications
Availability of pre-abortion counselling
Mechanisms to ensure family planning counselling
Financing of equipment, training, evaluation and outreach needs
Level within health care system at which women have greatest access to appropriate services

Regulatory requirements
National and local regulations and policies that govern the procurement, prescription and administration of RU/PG
Approval to conduct clinical trials and acceptability studies
Approval for distribution and general use

Logistics/supplies
Arrangements and accounts for obtaining RU 486, a prostaglandin and other supplies
Inventory and distribution systems
Facility space for activities defined in protocol

Training
Training needs for personnel providing RU/PG
Provision of training for personnel
Evaluation and monitoring of technical competence
Evaluation of training programmes

Client care
Protocols for practice (e.g. client screening, informed consent, counselling, use of analgesia, family planning services)
Protocols for managing complications
Provision and monitoring of family planning services
Responsibilities of staff for RU/PG services
Monitoring and evaluation of RU/PG services
Record-keeping procedures for clients
Facilitation of clients' return for required visits
Availability of/demand for other abortion technologies at facility
Provision of or referral for family planning services
Scheduling services to facilitate women's access
Prices of abortion and medical services

Informational needs
Educational materials necessary for women treated with RU/PG
Information needed by practitioners
Information needed in community to raise awareness of services and to encourage early recognition of pregnancy
Documentation of programmes and dissemination of programme results

---

Appropriate policies and management practices must be based on solid research information. While the basic biomedical research of RU/PG has been extensive, women's experiences with and perceptions of the technology and its delivery are poorly understood. Acceptability research should be extended to a variety of sociocultural settings.

Examination and adaptation of health system infrastructures before implementation of a new technology is essential. A critical element of such research is the acceptability of a new technology compared to those currently in use. Evaluation of the specific niches that various technologies achieve in a health system is helpful.

The next stage is a careful analysis of the impact of introducing medical abortion technologies into different health systems. Researchers and providers must now focus on this aspect of RU/PG service-delivery implementation.

References

1 Klitsch M. Antiprogestins and the abortion controversy: a progress report. *Fam Plann Perspect* 1991; 23: 275–282.
2 Raymond JG, Klein R, Dumble LJ. *RU 486: Misconceptions, Myths and Morals.* Cambridge, MA: Institute on Women and Technology, 1991.
3 Le Grand A. The abortion pill: a solution for unsafe abortions in developing countries? *Soc Sci Med* 1992; 35: 767–776.
4 Kabir SM, Germain A. Is RU 486/PG in its current form likely to be appropriate for women in Bangladesh? In: Kamal GM, ed. *Proceedings of the International Symposium on Antiprogestins.* Dhaka, Bangladesh: BAPSA, 1992.
5 Claro A, Shallat L, Vickery K. Round table on RU 486. *Women's Health J* 1993; Feb: 29–52.
6 Cook RJ, Grimes DA. Antiprogestin drugs: ethical, legal and medical issues. *Law Med Health Care* 1992; 20: 149–153.
7 Macklin R. Antiprogestin drugs: ethical issues. *Law Med Health Care* 1992; 20: 215–219.
8 Macklin R. Antiprogestins: ethical issues. Paper prepared for the *International Symposium on Antiprogestins.* Dhaka, Bangladesh, Oct 1991.
9 Greenslade FC, Winkler J, Leonard AH. Introduction of abortion technologies: a quality of care management approach. *Law Med Health Care* 1992; 20: 161–168.
10 World Health Organization. *Medical Requirements for Use of Antiprogestogen and Prostaglandin for Induction of Therapeutic Abortion.* Geneva: World Health Organization, 1993 (unpublished document).
11 Hill NC, Ferguson J, MacKenzie IZ. The efficacy of oral mifepristone (RU 38 486) with a prostaglandin E_1 analog vaginal pessary for the termination of early pregnancy: complications and patient acceptability. *Am J Obstet Gynecol* 1990; 162: 414–417.
12 Tang GWK. A pilot study of acceptability of RU 486 and ONO 802 in a Chinese population. *Contraception* 1991; 44: 523–532.

13 Grimes DA, Mishell DR, David HP. A randomized clinical trial of mifepristone (RU 486) for induction of delayed menses: efficacy and acceptability. *Contraception* 1992; 46: 1–10.
14 David HP. Acceptability of mifepristone for early pregnancy interruption. *Law Med Health Care* 1992; 20: 188–194.
15 Urquhart DR, Templeton AA. Psychiatric morbidity and acceptability following medical and surgical methods of induced abortion. *Br J Obstet Gynaecol* 1991; 98: 396–399.
16 Bachelot A, Cludy L, Spira A. Conditions for choosing between drug-induced and surgical abortions. *Contraception* 1992; 45: 547–559.
17 Glasier A. Provision of medical abortion in the UK—organisation and uptake. In: Furedi A, ed. *Medical Abortion Services: European Perspectives on Anti-Progestins. Conference Report.* Conference held in Frankfurt, Germany, Dec 1992.
18 Thong KJ, Dewar MH, Baird DT. What do women want during medical abortion? *Contraception* 1992; 46: 435–442.
19 Holmgren K. Women's evaluation of three early abortion methods. *Acta Obstet Gynecol Scand* 1992; 71: 616–623.
20 Winikoff B, Coyaji K, Cabezes E *et al.* Studying the acceptability and feasibility of medical abortion. *Law Med Health Care* 1992; 20: 195–198.
21 Baird TL, Pearl M. Potential acceptability of ovulation detection kits and RU-486 at two college campuses. *J Am College Health* 1994; 43: 51–56.
22 Coulet MF. Anti-progestins in France: questions women ask. In Furedi A, ed. *Medical Abortion Services: European Perspectives on Anti-Progestins. Conference Report.* Frankfurt, Germany, Dec 1992.
23 Birman C. The experiences of women having an abortion with RU 486. *Women's Global Network for Reproductive Rights: Newsletter* 1989; 31: 7–9.
24 Program for Appropriate Technology in Health (PATH). *Report to the Buffett Foundation on Technology Promotion of RU 486 in India and Turkey.* Seattle, WA: PATH, 1990.
25 Program for Appropriate Technology in Health (PATH). *Interim Report to the Population Crisis Committee on Technology Promotion of RU 486.* Seattle, WA: PATH, 1991.
26 Program for Appropriate Technology in Health (PATH). *Final Report to the Population Crisis Committee on the Technology Promotion of RU 486.* Seattle, WA: PATH, 1991.
27 Program for Appropriate Technnology in Health (PATH). RU 486 in developing countries: questions remain. *Outlook* 1991; 9: 1–6.
28 Holt R. RU 486/prostaglandin: considerations for appropriate use in low-resource settings. *Law Med Health Care* 1992; 20: 169–183.
29 Berer M. 'Inducing a miscarriage': women-centered perspectives on RU 486/prostaglandin as an early abortion method. *Law Med Health Care* 1992; 20: 199–208.
30 Stewart P. *Setting up Services.* Paper presented at the Birth Control Trust Workshop, 1993.
31 Bromham D. *Setting up Services.* Paper presented at the Birth Control Trust Workshop, 1993.
32 Jones I. *Mifepristone in Practice: Setting up Services.* Paper presented at the Birth Control Trust Workshop, 1993.
33 Broome M. *Mifepristone: the Experience in Reading.* Paper presented at the Birth Control Trust Workshop, 1993.
34 Logan A. *Antiprogestins in Practice: Provision and Problems.* Paper presented at the Birth Control Trust Workshop, 1993.

35 Paterson C. *Antiprogestins in Practice: Provision and Problems*. Paper presented at the Birth Control Trust Workshop, 1993.

36 Templeton A. *Future Possibilities*. Paper presented at the Birth Control Trust Workshop, 1993.

37 Henshaw R. *Acceptability*. Paper presented at the Birth Control Trust Workshop, 1993.

38 Greenslade FC, Leonard AH, Benson J *et al*. *Manual Vacuum Aspiration: a Summary of Clinical and Programmatic Experience Worldwide*. Carrboro, North Carolina: IPAS, 1993.

39 World Health Organization. *Complications of Abortion: Technical and Managerial Guidelines*. Geneva: World Health Organization, 1995.

40 Leonard AH, Winkler J. Quality of care framework for abortion care. *Adv Abortion Care* 1991; 1: 1–4.

41 Greenslade FC, Tyrer LB. *Access to Safe Abortion Care Technology: a Challenge for Reproductive Health Professionals*. IPAS Working Paper, 1994.

42 Greenslade FC, Winkler J, Benson J *et al*. Safe abortion care: the challenges of technology introduction and quality of care. *Proceedings of the IPPF Family Planning Congress*. Delhi, Oct 1992. Carnforth: Parthenon Publishing, 1993.

43 Greenslade FC, McLaurin KE, Leonard AH *et al*. Technology introduction and quality of abortion care. *J Women's Health* 1993; 2: 27–33.

44 Bygdeman M, Van Look PFA. The use of prostaglandins and antiprogestins for pregnancy termination. *Int J Gynecol Obstet* 1989; 29: 5–12.

45 Roussel Uclaf. *Data Sheets*. Paris, 1991.

46 Baulieu EE. RU 486 as an antiprogesterone steroid: from receptor to contragestion and beyond. *JAMA* 1989; 262: 1808–1814.

47 Van Look PFA, Bygdeman M. Medical approaches to termination of early pregnancy. *Bull WHO* 1989; 67: 567–575.

48 Spicehandler J. Norplant introduction: a management perspective. In: Segae SJ, Tsui AO, Rogers SM, eds. *Demographic and Programmatic Consequences of Contraceptive Innovations*. New York: Plenum Press, 1989.

49 International Development Research Centre (IDRC). *Choice and Challenge—Global Teamwork in Developing a Contraceptive Implant*. Ottawa, Canada: IDRC, 1990.

50 World Health Organization. *Norplant Contraceptive Subdermal Implants: Managerial and Technical Guidelines*. Geneva: World Health Organization, 1990.

51 Beattie KJ, Greenslade FC, Spitzer ER. Opportunities for improving the quality of care in family planning services through introduction of new contraceptive methods. Prepared for the *118th Annual Meeting of the American Public Health Association*. New York, Sept–Oct, 1990.

52 Bradley J, Sikazwe N, Healy J. Improving abortion care in Zambia. *Studies Fam Plann* 1991; 22: 391–394.

53 Spicehandler J, Simmons R. *Contraceptive Introduction Reconsidered: a Review and Conceptual Framework. Annual Meeting of Policy and Coordinating Committee*. World Health Organization Special Programme of Research, Development and Research Training in Human Reproduction, June 1993.

54 Johnson BR, Benson J, Bradley J *et al*. Costs and resource utilization for the treatment of incomplete abortion in Kenya and Mexico. *Soc Sci Med* 1993; 36: 1443–1453.

55 Johnson BR, Benson J, Bradley J *et al*. *Costs of Alternative Treatments for Incomplete Abortion*. World Bank Working Paper, Jan 1993.

9 Acceptability of First-Trimester Medical Abortion

Beverly Winikoff

Introduction

Recent scientific developments and clinical investigation have opened a new world of medical abortion. As a result, there has been an explosion of scientific, public and political interest in the promise and problems of this technology. While some see it as a way to easy, effective, safe and accessible abortion services, others have raised caution ranging from sceptical to hostile. Questions have been raised over the safety, efficacy and feasibility of this technology in various cultural and clinical contexts, and about the extent to which women would use medical methods of abortion.

Aspects of acceptability in abortion services

For a new medical technology to become widely used, it must be acceptable to the consumers and providers of medical services, and be feasible to administer. Acceptability is much more important with more elective procedures. Contraception and induced abortion are two areas in which consumer preference may be especially salient, since most of the services are both elective and provided to healthy patients. The problem of defining acceptability research was first confronted in regard to the development of contraceptive technology and family planning services. Concepts of acceptability have been evolving since the mid-1970s and have been applied to medical abortion in scattered studies over the last 15 years. Before reviewing the information developed by those studies, it is helpful to review the meaning of acceptability and acceptability research.

Acceptability research takes place at the intersection between clinical, psychological and marketing research. Studies generally reflect the academic training of the researcher conducting the work. Acceptability was defined initially by the World Health Organization (WHO) as 'a quality which makes an object, person, event, or idea attractive, pleasing, or welcome' [1]. Acceptability research has not only been about qualities of various technologies but also about the perceptions, attitudes and behaviours of people. Rather than being a quality, acceptability is an interaction or product of: (i) the values of individuals; and (ii) their perceptions of the attributes or qualities of particular products. This approach, combining values and perceived characteristics, was employed in a study of perceptions of family planning services by Severy and McKillop [2] who noted that 'the combination of values and perceived features of family planning services may be viewed as the reasons for women's choice'.

Values are prized characteristics that individuals seek in the products or services they choose. The attributes of specific products are matched by individuals against their ideals. Insofar as the attributes of a technology are perceived to correspond or lead to valued outcomes, these products will be desired, preferred or 'acceptable'. Whatever affects either values or perceptions can, therefore, affect acceptability. Factors highly influential in shaping values and perceptions include:

1   ethnicity, nationality or culture;
2   class or education;
3   personality;
4   experience.

The objective reality of the item being evaluated and the alternatives available also influence perceptions. The value of a medical technology is modified according to the locally available alternatives.

Previous research on contraception and abortion has identified some of the values that appear repeatedly as important components of acceptability [3,4].

1   Efficacy. The desire for induced abortion represents an attempt to solve a particularly difficult and stressful problem: unwanted pregnancy. Thus, there is a high value placed upon efficacy.

2   Safety/freedom from side effects. These are highly valued in virtually all medical and surgical interventions but particularly in contraception and abortion, since patients are healthy, often young and perhaps anticipating future reproduction.

3   Freedom from pain. This is a self-evident, strongly held preference which is particularly important when there are alternatives with lower anticipated pain.

4   Ease and convenience. This refers to both accessibility of the service and the method itself. Many women seeking abortion have household, childcare or employment obligations that they do not wish to disrupt. More

generally, these values may refer to the desire for minimal inconvenience.

5   Gentleness/non-invasiveness. This may relate to both anticipated pain and the preservation of body integrity. It reflects the desire that the procedure should be less threatening and less destructive—of either the woman or the embryo—than other methods. Therefore, with respect to abortion, it may also have a connotation of 'more moral'.

6   Privacy. Women are particularly concerned with privacy when dealing with a problem relating to sexual behaviour and intimate relationships. There may also be the need for secrecy because of the real or presumed disapproval of others. Physical privacy, as in protecting the body from exposure to strangers in a threatening environment, may also have a high value. Thus, 'privacy' may have several different meanings in relation to abortion techniques.

7   Autonomy. Some women value very highly the ability to manage their lives and bodies. Methods associated with loss of consciousness may be particularly unwelcome.

8   Affordability. This is a key ingredient to acceptability which has not often been studied with respect to medical technology, because treatment is generally provided free in clinical investigations. Cost affects the acceptance of new technologies.

How medical abortion 'fits the bill' or corresponds to these values is determined by women's perceptions of the characteristics of the technology. Perceptions of the attributes of a method are strongly influenced by personal, community and medical characteristics. They are also influenced by the alternatives and what kinds of service-delivery requirements surround those methods.

Studies of medical abortion have assessed very different regimens as technology has evolved. Drugs have included antiprogestins and prostaglandin analogues, both separately and in combination. The route of delivery has varied, including oral, vaginal and intramuscular administration, and side effects have ranged from minimal to extremely distressing. In addition, service-delivery variables are not constant: women can be treated as in-patients or out-patients, or are self-treated at home. These differences may have a substantial impact on the perception and acceptability of the methods.

In clinical practice, the alternative surgical abortion options vary. For example, vacuum aspiration can be provided as an in-patient or out-patient procedure under general or local anaesthesia. Thus, individuals must assess the characteristics of medical abortion against a shifting frame of reference.

Regardless of the drugs or procedures used, the following character-istics are intrinsic to medical compared to surgical abortion:

1   a slightly lower efficacy;
2   a longer procedure;
3   more experience by the patient of bleeding and the expulsion of products of conception;
4   more difficulty in combining the procedure with other desired procedures for fertility regulation such as intrauterine contraceptive device (IUCD) insertion or sterilization.

If patients object strongly to these attributes, the method may be re-jected. Improvements can only be made with new advances in technology.

Several other characteristics appear to be intrinsic, but are dependent on service-delivery choices, including:

1   more visits than for surgical abortion;
2   more or less pain than with surgical abortion; this depends on the type of anaesthesia used in surgery, and the dose and type of prostaglan-din used for medical abortion;
3   no admission to hospital.

How acceptability is studied

Acceptability can be examined in several ways [4]. Useful concepts include:

1   primary acceptance (whether the method would be used if offered, regardless of alternatives);
2   comparative acceptance (a test of the adoption of a technology in the context of other available choices);
3   re-use/recommendation (whether individuals would use it again and/or recommend it to others);
4   side effects or complaints.

These issues can be studied through questions oriented to the potential user as a consumer; e.g. 'Would you use or prefer X? If not, why not? Would you use it again or recommend it to others?' And so on. Questions like this form a basis for the assessment of acceptability. Such a study design would rely heavily on interviews with users both before and after the experience of medical abortion. This technique provides information on what users think of the product's attributes before and after use, as well as whether experience is consonant with expectations. While eliciting information through patient interview is common to all accept-ability studies, other methodological issues in study design are variable.

Researchers need to decide not only when to assess acceptability but also how to design the studies. Several methodological problems exist.

Comparative trials

To those who perform clinical trials, a comparative trial always seems more scientific. While this may be so, there are unique challenges in assessing a new technology. Generally, a comparative trial tests a new method against an established method. Both users and providers may have well-formed ideas about the risks, benefits and characteristics of the more standard method but perhaps nebulous or erroneous impressions of the new technology. These can be favourable or unfavourable. Personal bias, hearsay and unverified speculation may have more impact on attitudes about the new method than about the already familiar technology. In addition, providers may give realistic and specific information about the usual procedure but may not be so accurate about the newer one. This may create bias in choice or unrealistic expectations of the newer method. The attitudes of users about newness and risk-taking may become more important in both method choice and method evaluation.

Randomized studies

Trials of drug therapy rely heavily on random allocation of patients into groups, comparing, for example, the best available therapy and a new therapy. The ideal is a double-blind study in which neither patient nor prescriber knows which drug is received. This allows unbiased comparison of the side effects and efficacy of the two therapies and identifies which of the two methods would be more acceptable if a similar population of patients were assigned to a method. The equivalent of this situation would occur if a health service needed to choose only one technology for first-trimester abortion.

Conversely, a group of patients who chose one procedure from the alternatives is likely to be different from a random sample of the population. Characteristics of each method will preferentially attract a different group of users. Thus, the results of a random allocation trial may not represent the reactions of the women most likely to use the method once it becomes available as a choice. Thus, the trial's results may be valid but not generalizable to the women likely to use the method.

Randomization, of course, means that women who enrol in a study must be willing to accept any of the procedures in the trial. If a woman has an aversion to one of the study methods, she will not enrol in the study for fear of being assigned to a treatment she could not accept. Such refusals of treatment have occurred in random allocation studies [5], indicating that randomized study populations do not represent the full range of women who will be candidates for the methods under study. Again, this does not influence validity but limits extrapolation to particular populations.

Study characteristics

The study *per se* is distorting; there is always an effect of the research process on the results. Any study filters the type of people who enrol and, therefore, affects the representativeness of the group being studied. A person who volunteers for a study needs to be willing to tolerate the extra burden of the study. Such persons also may be willing to accept more onerous regimens and may not reflect the dissatisfaction that any related inconveniences might elicit in a general population. Those who choose to enter the trial may be especially averse to some feature of the standard method or especially excited by some aspect of the new method.

If subjects are allowed to choose among several methods, including the usual treatment, those who choose the standard method may be very different from the general population of users: for some reason, they have enrolled in a study when they could have received the same method without doing so. Finally, study conditions sometimes impose many more visits than necessary in a normal clinical situation. This can also affect acceptability.

Women who have had induced abortions and who volunteer to test medical abortions may not be representative. Those who opt for medical methods in trials may have been especially dissatisfied, disappointed or unhappy with the results of the surgical procedure, and may reflect a biased comparison of the two methods when asked to compare them.

Studies of user acceptability

The existing literature on acceptability of medical abortion is small. Since 1979, 12 published studies have evaluated the acceptability of medical abortion methods in the first trimester (Table 9.1). The work comes from seven cultural environments, none in developing countries. In addition, the number of patients in each study is small—only one study has cohorts of over 100 patients.

As medical abortion regimens have evolved, the methods studied have changed in important ways. There is a wide range of side effects and, therefore, patient reactions because of the variability in methods studied. The two earliest studies used prostaglandin vaginal suppositories alone. Later, oral mifepristone was used alone or in combination with a prostaglandin. The prostaglandin was administered vaginally, intramuscularly or orally. A combination of mifepristone and a vaginal suppository was evaluated in seven studies; mifepristone plus injectable prostaglandin in one; mifepristone plus oral prostaglandin in one other; and mifepristone alone was studied in two.

Of the 12 studies, two were of one method only, five involved patient choice of medical abortifacient, four involved random allocation and one used both patient choice and random allocation. Only seven of the 12 studies report on regimens that are approved for regular clinical use, and most of these used vaginal suppositories for the prostaglandin.

Eligibility was restricted to patients with early pregnancies (< 42 days) in two studies. Three studies allowed enrolment to 49 days, two studies up to 56 days and four studies through 63 days of amenorrhoea. One study only states that the women requested a medical abortion in very early pregnancy. Since the experience of medical abortion can be quite different at different gestational ages, reactions may have been affected. There were also varying exclusion criteria, producing groups with both unknown and obvious similarities. For example, Rosen et al. studied only women who had complete abortions [6] or prior deliveries [5]. Grimes et al. [13] studied women without a pregnancy test, half of whom turned out not to be pregnant.

The number of visits required of patients differed from study to study; some required as few as two visits for a medical abortion, and two studies required seven [8,11]. The number of interviews varied as did their timing relative to the treatment (Table 9.2).

Yet, because of consistent findings under such variable circumstances, several general conclusions are possible (Table 9.2).

Rosen and her colleagues in Sweden [5,6,17] designed studies to test acceptability in patients randomly allocated to vaginal prostaglandin or vacuum aspiration. The hospital was well known for its work on medical abortion and, thus, attracted patients interested in that method, not necessarily representative of the population of women seeking abortion.

In the earlier study [6], the first 30 patients using each method who had complete abortions were evaluated. Consequently, failure as a reason for method dissatisfaction was not registered. Differentials in success

Table 9.1 Studies of acceptability of first-trimester medical abortion

Country	No. studied	Methods	Recruitment	Allocation to method	Length amenorrhoea	Total no. visits	Other comments	Reference
Sweden	30	Vacuum aspiration with diazepam and cervical block	Patients admitted to hospital's regular abortion service	Random	≤ 56 days	3 +	Acceptability study only for women who had complete abortions with method	[6]
	30	0.8–1 mg 16, 16-dimethyl PGE_2 vaginal suppository, every 3 h × 4				3 +		
Sweden	18	Vacuum aspiration	Patients admitted to hospital's regular abortion service	Random	≤ 49 days	2 +	No women admitted to study unless one full-term delivery prior	[5]
	18	PGF_2 vaginal suppositories in hospital every 6 h × 2						
	17	PGE_2 vaginal suppositories at home				2 +		
England	100	Mifepristone 600 mg, then gemeprost* vaginal suppository at 48 h	First 100 who accepted method from women referred for abortion	One method	≤ 63 days	5		[7]
Hong Kong	19	Vacuum aspiration	From women requesting abortion at a family planning association. Surgical patients referred	Patient choice after information on both methods	≤ 49 days	2		[8]
	23	Mifepristone followed by vaginal suppository* on day 4				7		
Scotland	37	Vacuum aspiration/general anaesthesia	Regular abortion patients, agreed to be interviewed. Abortion patients offered opportunity to try medical abortion in a study	Medical method patients had chance to be part of a study	≤ 63 days	3		[9]
	54	Mifepristone then gemeprost* vaginal suppository				4		
Denmark	25	Vacuum aspiration/general anaesthesia	Patients referred for abortion	Random	≤ 42 days	3		[10]
	25	Mifepristone 600 mg				3		
Sweden	43	Dilatation and vacuum aspiration; heavy sedation	Women requesting abortion by the specific method used	By patient choice within medical guidelines. Research environment for medical abortion	9–12 weeks	2	In group 1, only women who wished to come for a 2-week post-procedure visit were enrolled	[11]
	40	Vacuum aspiration/local anaesthesia			5–8 weeks	2		
	45	Mifepristone then gemeprost* vaginal suppository			Very early	7		

Country	n	Method/anaesthesia	Population (early abortion at one of six clinics in France)	Randomization/choice within clinical context	Gestation	No. of visits	Comments	Ref.
	107	Vacuum aspiration/local anaesthesia	early abortion at one of six clinics in France			3–4	were freely available without enrolling in study. None was an experimental abortion method	
	251	Mifepristone 600 mg then sulprostone 0.25, i.m. after 48 h				4–5		
USA	8	Mifepristone, 600 mg	Women with delay in menses ≤ 10 days. No pregnancy test	Not applicable† (one method)	< 42 days	4	Half of patients in each group were not pregnant	[13]
	8	Placebo				4		
Scotland	94	Mifepristone then gemeprost suppository* at 48 h	Referred by GP for abortion. Most arrived expecting a medical method	Not stated in regard to the drug. Randomized (ward vs. sitting room) for location of PG treatment	≤ 63 days	5	Purpose was to study preference for ward vs. sitting room as place for abortion	[14]
	86	Mifepristone (various doses) then oral misoprostol 600 µg at 48 h						
Hong Kong	99	Mifepristone 600 mg then vaginal suppository* on day 3	From women requesting abortion at family planning association	Patient choice after information on both methods	≤ 49 days	2	Vacuum aspiration patients were referred to a hospital for the procedure	[15]
	45	Vacuum aspiration				5		
Scotland	73 chose	(a) Mifepristone 600 mg then gemeprost 1 mg vaginal suppository (b) Vacuum aspiration/general anaesthesia	Women requesting abortion eligible for both medical and surgical methods	Women who agreed to be randomized were assigned; those who declined randomization received method of choice	≤ 63 days	Surgical, 2 Medical, 3	Randomization offer preceded offer of choice	[16]
India	250	(a) Mifepristone 600 mg then oral misoprostol 400 µg (b) Vacuum aspiration/general anaesthesia	Women who came to clinic requesting abortion	Patients eligible for either method could choose the method to use	≤ 56 days	Surgical, 2 Medical, 3		B. Winikoff et al., unpublished data
Cuba	250	(a) Mifepristone 600 mg then oral misoprostol 400 µg (b) Vacuum aspiration/general anaesthesia						
China	299	(a) Mifepristone 600 mg then oral misoprostol 400 µg (b) Vacuum aspiration/topical anaesthesia						

*16,16-Dimethyl-trans-Δ_2 PGE$_1$ methyl ester.
†Randomization with respect to placebo. Acceptability trial is really of *one* method.
GP, general practitioner; PG, prostaglandin.

Table 9.2 Results of studies of first-trimester acceptability of medical abortion

Type of medical abortion	No. and assignment of patients	Interviews	Attitude to medical abortion prior to treatment	Positive aspects post-treatment	Negative aspects post-treatment	Would use again	Reference
PG vaginal suppository	30 (R)	(a) Prior to first appointment with doctor (b) after treatment, prior to discharge (c) 2 weeks later	More favourable to medical than surgical abortion	Better than expected Easier than expected More harmless than expected	Higher scores on pain and bleeding than surgical patients	Not reported	[6]
PG vaginal suppository (hospital) PG vaginal suppository (home)	18 (R) 17 (R)	(a) Prior to first appointment with doctor (b) 2 weeks later, prior to follow-up examination	Hospital preferred by 15% of sample Home preferred by 65% of sample Medical abortion more natural Some felt safer in hospital Home more comfortable Home more private Possibility of partner support at home	Generally met positive expectations	Pain/bleeding led some to prefer surgical	Yes, 64%	[5]
Mifepristone + PG vaginal suppository	100 (C/L)	(a) 7 days post-treatment (b) 14 days post-treatment (c) 28 days post-treatment	64% of those offered method agreed to try it	95% complete abortion	Over 50% required analgesia after PG	Yes, 88% Unsure, 3% No, 9% (due to failure 3%, due to pain, 6%)	[7]
Mifepristone + PG vaginal suppository	23 (C/S)	(a) Before treatment (b) 8 days post-treatment (c) 15 days post-treatment (d) 43 days post-treatment	*Acceptors* Less trauma, 38% More natural, 22% Felt doctor preferred, 13% Fear pain in surgery, 11% *Refusers* Not as effective, 38% Long process/many visits, 28% Surgery convenient quick, 18% Want to do abortion quickly, 16%	*Day 8* Relieved, 30% Natural, 21% Safe, 14% Convenient, 9%	*Day 8* Doubt complete abort, 9% Inconvenient visits, 4% Sad, saw abortion, 4% *Day 43* Bled too long, 11%	Yes, 91% No, 9% 96% would recommend to friends	[8]
Mifepristone + PG vaginal suppository	54 (C/L)	(a) 2 days before treatment (b) 1 week after treatment (c) 4 weeks after treatment	Not reported	Liked: awareness of process; more in control; avoiding anaesthesia; more discreet	More negative assessment if: younger; nulliparous; needed more analgesic; saw products of conception	Yes, 75% Previous abortion experience (n = 13), 77% prefer medical	[9]
Mifepristone	25 (R)	1 week after treatment	Not applicable	Rated acceptable by patients classified as 'uncomplicated' cases	20% of 'uncomplicated' cases reported side effects—all mild	All four patients with previous abortion preferred medical method	[10]
Mifepristone + PG vaginal suppository	45 (C/L)	2 weeks after treatment	Not applicable	*Week 2* Positive assessment, 87% Expressed relief, 40%	*Week 2* Bleeding heavier than menses, 65% 'Much pain', 44%	Yes, 81% Most women would choose method used this time for next time	[11]

Method	N	Timing	Reasons	Satisfaction / preferences	Side effects / negatives	Recommendation / use again	Ref
Mifepristone + PG, intramuscular	251 (C/U)	(a) Prior to selection of method (b) 2 weeks after treatment	*Acceptors* Less trauma, 67% Less dangerous, 29% Less risk future pregnancy, 27% *Refusers* Less trauma, 53% Less failure, 36% Less dangerous, 29% Less risk future pregnancy, 16% *Acceptors valued*: newness, efficacy, lack of invasiveness, possibility of verifying expulsion, naturalness of the process	63% wanted to see what had been expelled. Large majority satisfied	12% some dissatisfaction (increased with complication or failures). Women felt need for rest/sleep after procedure. Some found method not so quick and easy as expected		[12]
Mifepristone (or placebo)	16 (C/L)	4 weeks post-treatment	Believed in efficacy Preferred medical to surgical	Liked privacy. Liked non-invasive technique	Some had side effects of pain, nausea but these were similar in placebo group	Generally, yes Three with previous abortion preferred medical method	[13]
Mifepristone + PG vaginal suppository Mifepristone + oral PG	94 (not reported) 86 (not reported)	At time of discharge after PG visit	Not reported. Majority came requesting medical method	Majority preferred sitting-room treatment. 60% of oral PG group needed no analgesia. 99% were satisfied	More pain in vaginal suppository group. More analgesia in vaginal suppository group	95% would recommend to friend all women with prior surgery abortion (n = 41) were satisfied	[14]
Mifepristone + PG vaginal suppository	99 (C/S)	(a) Before treatment (b) 8 days post-treatment (c) 15 days post-treatment (d) 43 days post-treatment	*Acceptors* Fear of surgery, 81% Convenient for work, 41% Less injury to body, 21% Fear of general anaesthesia, 11% *Refusers* Surgery quick, 82% Too many visits/long procedure, 69% Worry over efficacy/side effects, 11%	*Day 8* Relieved/felt good, 28% Convenient/safe, 20% Avoided surgery, 12%	*Day 8* Painful, 11% *Day 43* Too time consuming, 11% Bleeding too long, 10%	Yes, 85% No, 11% Unsure, 4% 70% of those with prior surgical abortion felt medical was better	[15]
Mifepristone + PG vaginal suppository	73, choice 99, randomized	(a) At the time of choice (?) (b) 2 weeks after treatment	*Agreed to random assign (54%)* *Chose medical (20%)* Fear surgery/anaesthesia, 59% More natural, 21% Surgery 'too fast', 21% Want to be conscious, 8% *Chose vacuum aspiration (26%)* Medical abortion 'too slow', 40% Wanted to be unconscious, 39% Fear adverse effects of medical abortion, 23% Lived further from clinic	More positive ratings among those who chose the procedure than those assigned to it	More painful than surgery both among those who chose and who were assigned to it	*Would use same method again* Chose medical, 95% Chose surgical, 90% Assigned surgery, 87% Assigned medical, 74%	[16]

C/L, choice to be in study of one method; C/S, personal choice among methods in study; C/U, personal choice among usual clinical services; PG, prostaglandin; R, random assignment.

rates were thus erased as possible reasons for preference of one method over another.

Prostaglandin treatment was by far the preferred method prior to the procedure in both medical and surgical treatment groups. Women treated with medical abortion increased their preferential rating of it after the abortion and valued the 'naturalness' of the method and privacy during treatment. However, they gave negative evaluations regarding pain and the duration of treatment. They also reported more bleeding.

The most striking finding of the study was the enormous increase in the acceptability of surgical abortion among surgical patients who appreciated a quick and painless procedure. Post-treatment, most of the patients in this group switched to a preference for vacuum aspiration. Women in both groups were enthusiastic about the hypothetical possibility of a self-administered method. Women in the prostaglandin group became even more positive toward such a possibility after the experience of medical abortion.

A later study [5] compared surgical abortion to both medical abortion in the hospital clinic and medical abortion at home. A specific intent was to assess acceptability of a home abortion remedy. Initially, home treatment was a stated preference of 69%, and medical methods were preferred by 84% of the women enrolled. In fact, when the study was randomized, four patients found their assigned method to be so unacceptable that they withdrew from the study and changed methods. Of these women, two switched out of home treatment (one each to hospital prostaglandin treatment and vacuum aspiration) and two switched into home treatment (one each from hospital prostaglandin treatment and vacuum aspiration).

Success rates were high for both treatments (97% for medical abortion and 100% for surgical), but duration of bleeding was longer for the medical group (about twice the number of days). There was also a substantial incidence of vomiting and diarrhoea. Neither side effect occurred in the vacuum aspiration group. Analgesic injections were required by 39% of the hospital treatment group receiving prostaglandin, but only 6% of the home treatment group. No surgical patients required analgesia after the dose given at surgery. Women did not change their positive attitudes toward medical abortion after their experience of it. Vacuum aspiration patients were enthusiastic about the surgical method.

In the two studies combined [17], 81% of patients who experienced prostaglandin treatment had preferred medical abortion initially and 78% preferred it after treatment. Among vacuum aspiration patients, however, while only 38% preferred surgery before treatment, 69% preferred it after the experience. Most patients stated that they would select the method that they had used if they needed a repeat abortion. This preference was slightly stronger among the medical group than among the surgical group (75 versus 68%). Conversely, a slightly larger number of women in the medical group (16 versus 13%) said that they would prefer and recommend the method they had *not* used.

Most of the medical abortion users who switched preference did so because of pain and/or amount or duration of bleeding. Some reacted negatively to the length of the procedure. A substantial portion (31%) of the surgical patients persisted in a preference for medical treatment, because it was more natural, involved less risk of infection and required no hospital admission. Surgical patients who preferred surgery cited a quick, easy procedure with no pain.

Hill *et al.* [7] studied 100 women using mifepristone plus a vaginal suppository. Only 64% of the women offered the method agreed to try it instead of the routine surgical abortion. About half of those who declined ascribed their reluctance to the length of the trial and the required follow-up. About half stated that they would prefer to be asleep during the procedure. Of the women interviewed after the procedure, 88% would use the method again, 9% would not, while 3% remained unsure. Of the 9% who would not, one-third were dissatisfied because of method failure, and two-thirds claimed that the method had been too painful. All 18 patients with previous surgical abortion experience preferred the medical abortion.

In a 1991 study, Tang [8] reported on a trial of mifepristone plus vaginal prostaglandin suppository versus surgical abortion. Women were allowed to choose their method, and the final sample included 23 who chose a medical abortion and 19 who chose vacuum aspiration. Reasons given for choosing medical abortion included: (i) that it would produce less trauma to the body (38%); (ii) it was a more natural means (22%); or (iii) patients perceived physician preference for the method (13%). Fears about aspects of surgery were also prominent: fear of pain (11%), fear of general anaesthesia (5%) and rejection of hospitalization (9%). The women said that medical abortion was easy, referring to the ease of taking medication as compared to hospitalization and surgery. Nonetheless, most were not favourably disposed toward the idea of using a medical method at home. Reasons given for not choosing medical abortion included worries about efficacy or side effects (28%), the length of the abortion procedure (18%) or desire to get the abortion over quickly

(16%). Almost two-thirds of the patients who were requesting a repeat abortion chose to use surgery a second time rather than switch to medical abortion.

Reactions to the medical therapy were assessed at three points in time. At each assessment, a substantial number of patients (30–50%) expressed their relief or stated that they felt good. At 43 days post-treatment, patients liked the medical therapy because it was 'natural' or like menstrual regulation (39%). Negative comments included that the bleeding was too long (11%) and that the visits were inconvenient (9%). (This study's protocol for medical abortion required seven visits.) Almost all of the women experiencing medical abortion (96%) would recommend it to friends. Two of the 23 medical abortion patients would not use it again. These two were not among the three method failures. In the surgical group, all women said they were satisfied with their method.

Single women found mifepristone more convenient as it did not require an overnight stay, and they could go to work as usual. Thus, they would not have to explain an absence at home or at work. These women were also afraid surgery might have an effect on their future fertility. Conversely, married women often chose surgery because childcare obligations meant they could not afford the time for the treatment schedule of the medical abortion, and they did not have as many worries about future fertility. In addition, the authors speculate that experience of childbirth may have made surgical intervention more acceptable.

Tang *et al.* [15] extended this work in a second study, enrolling 144 women of whom 99 (69%) chose medical abortion with mifepristone plus prostaglandin vaginal suppository and 45 (31%) chose vacuum aspiration. Younger, single and nulliparous women preferred the medical method. Reasons for choice of the medical method were remarkably similar to the previous study, including: fear of surgery (81%) or general anaesthesia (11%); less injury to the body (21%); and convenient for work (41%). Surgery was preferred because it was quick and convenient (82%) or because patients did not like the number of visits or length of the medical abortion process (69%) or were worried about drug efficacy and side effects (11%).

Almost all women who tried medical abortion would use it again (85%), including four of the 12 women for whom the method had failed. Of the 27 women who used medical abortion and had previous experience of surgical abortion, 70% felt that medical abortion was better. At the final evaluation (43 days after treatment), the most common reaction was relief (38%), but others complained that the procedure took too long (11%) or that there was too much bleeding (10%).

Urquhart and Templeton [9] assessed psychiatric morbidity and acceptability following medical and surgical abortion. The medical abortion method was mifepristone followed by a vaginal prostaglandin suppository. The medical abortion patients chose their method, but surgical patients were recruited from the usual clinic patient population. The clearest finding of this study is a large decrease in anxiety and depression after successful abortion using either method.

When asked if the same method would be acceptable again, 75% of the medical abortion and 94% of the surgical patients agreed that it would. Women tended to be less positive toward medical abortion if they were younger, nulliparous, had a failure or problems with the procedure or saw the products of conception. Patients cited as positive features the awareness of what was happening, feeling more in control, a more natural and more discreet method and no anaesthesia. Of the 13 women who had had a previous abortion, 77% said that they preferred the medical alternative.

This is the one study that shows higher preference for their method among the patients in the surgical group than in the medical group. This may be partly due to study design. Patients experiencing medical abortion were recruited for a clinical trial, whereas the vacuum aspiration patients were recruited after having experienced the usual surgical service. The patients using medical abortion might have had higher expectations for the new treatment under study. The composition of the two groups was not comparable. Nonetheless, in both groups, the large majority of the women were satisfied and would use again the treatment they had experienced.

Legarth et al. [10] conducted a random assignment study in Denmark using surgical abortion with general anaesthesia and mifepristone alone. Mifepristone patients reported both more pain and longer bleeding than did the vacuum aspiration patients. However, women who experienced uncomplicated medical abortion spent fewer days in bed than women who experienced an uncomplicated vacuum aspiration. Both groups rated their method as acceptable, but the mifepristone group 'evaluated the procedure more positively'. Four women in the mifepristone group had had previous abortions, and all preferred the medical procedure.

One unusual feature of the study is a high rate of serious complications. Three of 25 vacuum aspiration patients developed pelvic inflammatory disease (PID), and another had a uterine perforation requiring emergency laparotomy. Six of 25 mifepristone patients had incomplete abortions treated by surgical evacuation, three of whom developed PID.

Even with such high failure and complication rates, women found the procedure acceptable.

Holmgren [11] conducted interviews with women who underwent either vacuum aspiration, dilatation and aspiration, or treatment with mifepristone and gemeprost vaginal suppository. Women were interviewed about the acceptability of the abortion experience about 2 weeks after treatment. The large majority gave positive evaluations: 88% of those using early vacuum aspiration 72% of those undergoing later dilatation and vacuum aspiration and 87% of those experiencing medical abortion.

Medical abortion patients reported more pain and evaluated the blood loss as heavier than women who experienced surgery. Nonetheless, 40% of the medical abortion patients were relieved not to have needed a surgical procedure. As in other studies, most women (70–80%) reported that if another abortion were necessary, the same method would be preferred.

Bachelot et al. [12] is the only study that compares the acceptability of non-experimental methods in a general clinic population. It reports on the choices of nearly 500 women who came for abortion in six French clinics. The available choices for women requesting early abortion were medical abortion (mifepristone then intramuscular prostaglandin), vacuum aspiration under general anaesthesia and vacuum aspiration with local anaesthesia. Amenorrhoea had to be < 42 days at enrolment in order for all of the interviewed women to be eligible for medical abortifacient treatment by 49 days, including the 1-week waiting period required by French law.

Women's initial choices favoured the medical method (64%). Some women expressed no preference among the methods offered. After women consulted with physicians, the procedures performed were: (i) medical abortion, 59%; (ii) vacuum aspiration with local anaesthesia, 31%; and (iii) vacuum aspiration with general anaesthesia, 11%. Generally, women who elected the medical method or surgery with local anaesthesia had higher educational levels, higher occupational class and more often had ethnic/cultural backgrounds from North America or Europe. More of the women who initially had no preference or preferred general anaesthesia came from Africa and South America.

In order to gauge their impressions of the characteristics and acceptability of the methods, 86% of the women were interviewed after their treatment. Valued characteristics most significantly associated with medical method selection included: (i) newness of the method; (ii) efficacy; (iii) reduced invasiveness of the method; (iv) possibility of seeing the expulsion; and (v) 'naturalness' of the method.

Women who elected for vacuum aspiration tended to value the guarantee of medical precautions, the reduced waiting period and the proven reliability of the method. Substantial proportions of women in all groups placed high value on methods that were less traumatic, less dangerous, more effective and safer for future pregnancies. The possibility of failure was less important among those who chose the medical method and avoidance of trauma less important among those who chose vacuum aspiration under local anaesthesia. Worry about risk to future pregnancy was more important for women who chose medical abortion.

Most of the women who chose the medical method of abortion knew that they would choose this method before they arrived at the clinic (68%) whereas only half as many surgical patients had a preference for surgical abortion before arrival. Women who used the medical abortion method were characterized by wanting to see what was expelled and a desire to control the situation. They also expressed the need for more rest after the procedure.

At interview, most women in all groups expressed satisfaction with their chosen experience. There was more dissatisfaction, however, among the medical abortion group (12%) than the surgical group (4%). Women appear to have heard about the new method as a 'magic' one but later felt the abortion was 'not so easy and quick' as expected. Satisfaction decreased when abortion was unsuccessful and when more side effects were recorded.

The rate of follow-up in the groups was different: 94% of the medical abortion patients returned for interview, but only 78% of the vacuum aspiration/local anaesthesia and 71% of the vacuum aspiration/general anaesthesia did so. Women dissatisfied with their treatment may not have returned for the extra visit. This would bias the results.

In order to take account of patient preference for method of abortion in study design, Henshaw et al. [16] carried out a study that combined both patient choice and random allocation between medical (mifepristone followed by prostaglandin vaginal suppository) and surgical (vacuum aspiration under general anaesthesia) abortion methods. Women who were eligible for both methods were asked if they were willing to be randomly assigned a method, and those who were not were given their choice. Most women (53.7% of the total) were willing to be assigned and were allocated to medical (27%) or surgical (26%) treatment. The rest were given the method for which they expressed a strong preference: surgical abortion, 26%; and medical abortion, 20%.

Women who chose surgery lived significantly further from the clinic, and this may have affected their choice of method because of the extra visits required for the medical procedure. Medical abortion was assessed as 'too slow' by 40% of the women who chose surgery, and 39% preferred to be unconscious during the procedure. Some (23%) also feared adverse physical effects from a medical procedure. Those who preferred the medical procedure expressed fear of surgery or anaesthesia (59%), felt medical abortion was 'more natural' (21%) and that surgery was 'too fast' (21%).

Acceptability was similar and extremely high in both medical and surgical abortion patients who chose their method. Only 4% of each group would certainly choose the other method if another abortion were necessary; 95% of medical patients and 90% of surgical patients would choose the same method again. Vacuum aspiration (under general anaesthesia) was rated as less painful, but in all other aspects the two methods were rated equally.

This was not true of the women assigned a method. Among these women, medical abortion ranked lower on six of 12 features. Most women would choose the same procedure again, but the rates were lower than for those who chose their method and lower for the medical (74%) than for the surgical (87%) group. Gestational age was the only predictor of dissatisfaction among women assigned to medical abortion: 95% of those who rated the procedure unacceptable had had the abortion at 50 or more days gestation. At earlier gestational ages, there were no differences in acceptability among the women allocated randomly to medical or surgical abortion. Conversely, gestational age did not have any impact on acceptability among the women who chose their own method of abortion.

The authors recommend that eligible women who express a preference for method of abortion be accorded their choice regardless of length of gestation. The study demonstrates the importance of the existence of choice for women with different preferences and the fact that the process of choice may be associated with higher overall satisfaction.

It is interesting to speculate on how many women might have expressed a preference for a method if the first option presented had been choice rather than random assignment. In a slightly different study design (Winikoff *et al.*, unpublished data), women eligible for both methods were given a choice and only those who were undecided were randomly assigned a method. In this study of over 1300 patients in three countries, only 1% of patients did not express a preference between medical and surgical abortion and were therefore assigned a method.

Thong *et al.* [14] in Scotland studied 180 women choosing medical abortion to determine preferences in aspects of service delivery. The women were apparently participating in another study as well, since they received one of four different doses of mifepristone followed by either vaginal gemeprost (52%) or oral misoprostol (48%). Route of administration of prostaglandin does not appear to have been by patient choice.

Place of treatment with the prostaglandin was randomized to a sitting-room with out-patient atmosphere or a more formal hospital ward. Women were interviewed about their experience prior to discharge. Most women would have preferred treatment in the sitting-room (77% of those assigned there and 69% of ward patients). Treatment at the same time as other women, in either setting, appeared to strengthen the stated preference for sitting-room treatment. Virtually all the patients were satisfied with their medical abortion experience; one woman was 'unsure' and 95% would recommend it to a friend. All 41 who had had a surgical abortion previously were satisfied with the medical regimen.

This work suggests that individualized options need to be available. Some women in the sitting-room wanted to lie down, so some provision for this was needed. About half of the women would have wanted a partner or friend with them, but a slightly larger group wanted no one. It should be possible to accommodate both preferences. One-quarter of the women expressed preference for a home abortion, an option that is not yet available.

Grimes *et al.* [13] report on a different sort of acceptability study. They enrolled women interested in medical abortion, in a randomized manner, to use mifepristone alone or a placebo. The delay in expected menses could be no more than 10 days, and there was no pregnancy test prior to enrolment. In effect, this study tested a medical version of 'menstrual regulation'. Effectiveness was higher with mifepristone than with placebo, but side effects did not differ. In fact, two of four women who were pregnant and received drug reported passing tissue as did two of four women who were not pregnant and received placebo. Women expressed a favourable impression of the effectiveness of the drug, lack of side effects, privacy of not having to come to an identified abortion facility and convenience. They stated a preference for a medical regimen if another abortion were needed and would recommend it to friends.

Virtually all of the work assessing acceptability shows a strong interest in medical methods among women requesting abortion (about two-thirds of patients). While Bachelot's study [12] gives some indication that women in France who come from developing countries have less interest in this method, other information from developing countries suggests the opposite [4,18].

In all studies, women are overwhelmingly positive about any method that safely and effectively resolves the problem of unwanted pregnancy. Many authors have noted the sense of relief that women feel after abortion [8,9,13,15,19,20]. Those women for whom a method fails are more often dissatisfied with it since around 95% of eligible women will have a successful outcome with a medical method [21–23], the 5% failure rate can have only a small impact on overall levels of dissatisfaction, although for any one woman the experience of failure may be unacceptable.

Generally, both prolonged bleeding and multiple visits may be associated with dislike of the medical method. Similarly, the type of prostaglandin used and its side effects will be important in the overall experience. Oral misoprostol, one of the newer developments in medical abortion regimens, promises lower levels of pain and cramping than vaginal suppositories or intramuscular prostaglandins.

Several studies [9,12] document higher disappointment with medical than surgical abortion. This may be because the method is new and has been oversold in the press or by medical personnel with little experience of it. As the method becomes better known, expectations may become more realistic. Conversely, some women may be more likely to be unhappy with medical than with surgical abortion. Paradoxically, the medical abortion method seems to produce greater levels of high satisfaction along with slightly greater levels of dissatisfaction. In these studies, women who have experienced both procedures rate the medical abortion procedure higher [9,10,14,15].

What the acceptability of medical abortion will be in clinical practice remains unclear. As one illustration of the importance of context, Rosen [17] interviewed non-abortion as well as abortion patients for their preference of medical or surgical abortion. The non-patient group was evenly divided about which technology they would prefer for abortion if the need arose, but the patient group, currently seeking an abortion, preferred medical abortion (74 versus 26%).

Acceptability to providers

The issue of provider acceptability has been much less frequently addressed than patient acceptability. Nonetheless, women will not have the opportunity to choose medical abortion if the technology is rejected by providers, programme managers and policymakers. Availability of abortion services is clearly an important determinant of whether women will be able to use the services they desire [24].

Providers have clear preferences for different abortion technologies. With respect to second-trimester abortion, providers seek to distance themselves from an unpleasant procedure: physicians prefer medical abortions (where they need not be present at the expulsion of the fetus), and nurses prefer dilatation and evacuation (D & E) procedures (where the physician does the 'distasteful' surgery) [25]. Some have held that medical abortion in the second trimester is morally preferable to surgery [26]. Such considerations are less likely to be important with respect to early abortion. In fact, since earlier abortions are more acceptable to medical professionals [27], a medical method that allows very early abortion (even earlier than vacuum aspiration) may be particularly preferred by providers.

Provider attitudes toward abortion depend on many characteristics including personality and values [28,29]. Women providers tend to be more likely to provide abortion services than male providers [30]. Thus, if women providers share women patients' enthusiasm for medical methods, this may increase the availability of medical alternatives.

The service-delivery environment will also influence the acceptability of a new method. Reimbursement policies of various government and insurance entities will be important. Where there is harassment of abortion providers, the possibility of providing abortion services less visibly than in a surgical clinic may be appealing. Conversely, the burdens of provision of information and counselling to patients may be higher with a medical method. The anxieties of patients waiting for an abortion to take place, perhaps over a period of days to weeks, may also place more demands on providers and may reduce their enthusiasm for the method [31]. Providers may also be more nervous about the possibility of undetected ectopic pregnancy and the loss to follow-up of women with failed or incomplete medical abortion procedures.

Providers are also strongly responsive to the well-being of their patients. Thus, any method that works well and is safe and comfortable is of interest. When it is obvious that many patients would prefer the method, provider interest will grow.

Conclusion

Unwanted pregnancy is a serious and stressful problem for women and all those involved. Technologies that afford safe and effective abortion are very well accepted and provide relief from a great difficulty.

Many women fear surgery and will try to avoid it. Substantial apprehension exists about general anaesthesia during surgery, yet some fear that local anaesthesia may not prevent pain. This leads to a high demand for a medical abortion alternative.

An 'easy' abortion procedure is highly valued. Some women consider that the quick and definitive surgical alternative is easier; some find that swallowing a pill is 'easier'.

Privacy is greatly valued in the sense of both keeping the abortion secret and of preserving bodily autonomy and modesty. Medical abortion technology can meet this need more easily than surgical abortion, especially if the surgical alternative mandates hospital admission and absence from home.

The high values placed on privacy, autonomy and the wish to be at home create a demand for a self-administered home treatment for early abortion. A safe and effective regimen for this would be acceptable and an important development for many women.

Failure of an abortion method is frequently a cause for dissatisfaction, but both medical and surgical modalities now provide such a high degree of success that this will be infrequent. Conversely, if a method becomes known in the community as less reliable, it will probably be unpopular.

Pain and gastrointestinal disturbances are clearly problems with the use of some prostaglandins. Even these side effects, however, do not cause rejection of medical abortion with these drugs, because other characteristics of the method are valued by many women. Newer medical abortion regimens using misoprostol may provide substantially more comfortable experiences for women.

The prolonged bleeding experienced by some women using medical abortifacients is unpleasant and inconvenient. If this could be reduced, the method would be viewed even more favourably.

A regimen requiring many visits is likely to be less acceptable, but many women will agree to a number of visits simply to have the opportunity to choose a medical alternative. Two or three visits seem to pose no special burden to women already able to avail themselves of existing services. However, programme planners should reduce the number of mandated visits to the fewest possible. Improvements in technology may also be able to help if the antiprogestin and prostaglandin can be formulated to be taken at the same time.

Given a choice between surgery and any of several medical abortion methods, most eligible women appear to prefer the medical method. Satisfaction with the experience is extremely high. When measured against surgical procedures, women generally report more satisfaction, willingness to use again and to recommend to others. At the same time, however, the size of the dissatisfied minority is often larger than among surgical patients. This may be due to unrealistic expectations about a new technology.

New service-delivery approaches to medical abortion might better serve the needs of certain women and the constraints of specific service-delivery environments. For example, the suggestion of Grimes *et al.* [13] that it may be possible to develop a 'medical menstrual regulation' regimen deserves attention. This could be especially appropriate in certain developing countries where menstrual regulation is already a well-developed health service.

New approaches to the delivery of the two-drug regimen might also be considered. Mifepristone is a very safe drug with few side effects. Problems, when they occur, are much more likely in association with the administration of prostaglandin. Hence, broadening the availability of the mifepristone while maintaining medical oversight after prostaglandin administration may be reasonable. This might increase both accessibility and comfort by allowing women to start the procedure at home and complete it at a health care site.

Medical abortion provides a choice for women in a domain where previously there was none. Many will avail themselves of this new option. Not only is medical abortion acceptable, but for some it is markedly preferable. The task now is to improve the technology and make the service delivery even more convenient and responsive to women's needs.

References

1 Marshall J. Acceptability of fertility regulating methods: designing technology to fit people. *Prevent Med* 1977; 6: 65–73.
2 Severy LJ, McKillop K. Low-income women's perceptions of family planning service alternatives. *Fam Plann Perspect* 1990; 22: 150–157.
3 David HP. Acceptability of mifepristone for early pregnancy interruption. *Law Med Health Care* 1992; 20: 188–193.
4 Winikoff B, Coyaji K, Cabezas, E *et al.* Studying the acceptability and feasibility of medical abortion. *Law Med Health Care* 1992; 20: 3.
5 Rosen AS, von Knorring K, Bygdeman M. Randomized comparison of prostaglandin treatment in hospital or at home with vacuum aspiration for termination of early pregnancy. *Contraception* 1984; 29: 423–435.
6 Rosen AS, Nystedt L, Bygdeman M, Lundstrom V. Acceptability of a nonsurgical

method to terminate very early pregnancy in comparison to vacuum aspiration. *Contraception* 1979 19(2): 107–117.

7 Hill NC, Ferguson J, MacKenzie IZ. The efficacy of oral mifepristone (RU 38,486) with a prostaglandin E$_1$ analog vaginal pessary for the termination of early pregnancy: complications and patient acceptability. *Am J Obstet Gynecol* 1990; 162: 414–417.

8 Tang GW. A pilot study of acceptability of RU 486 and ONO 802 in a Chinese population. *Contraception* 1991; 44: 523–532.

9 Urquhart DR, Templeton AA. Psychiatric morbidity and acceptability following medical and surgical methods of induced abortion. *Br J Obstet Gynaecol* 1991; 98: 396–399.

10 Legarth J, Peen UB, Michelsen JW. Mifepristone or vacuum aspiration in termination of early pregnancy. *Eur J Obstet Gynecol Reprod Biol* 1991; 41: 91–96.

11 Holgrem K. Women's evaluation of three early abortion methods. *Acta Obstet Gynecol Scand* 1992; 71: 611–623.

12 Bachelot A, Cludy L, Spira A. Conditions for choosing between drug-induced and surgical abortions. *Contraception* 1992; 45: 547–559.

13 Grimes DA, Mishell DR Jr, David HP. A randomized clinical trial of mifepristone (RU 486) for induction of delayed menses: efficacy and acceptability. *Contraception* 1992; 46: 1–10.

14 Thong KJ, Dewar MH, Baird DT. What do women want during medical abortion? *Contraception* 1992; 46: 435–442.

15 Tang GW, Lau OWK, Yip P. Further acceptability evaluation of RU 486 and ONO 802 as abortifacient agents in a Chinese population. *Contraception* 1993; 48: 267–276.

16 Henshaw RC, Naji SA, Russel IT, Templeton AA. Comparison of medical abortion with surgical vacuum aspiration: women's preferences and acceptability of treatment. *Br Med J* 1993; 307: 714–717.

17 Rosen AS. Acceptability of abortion methods. *Baillières Clin Obstet Gynaecol* 1990; 4: 375–390.

18 Coyaji B. Safe motherhood and RU 486 in the Third World. *People* 1990; 17: 13–15.

19 Urquhart DR, Templeton AA. Acceptability of medical pregnancy termination (letter). *Lancet* 1988; ii: 106–107.

20 Zolese G. Psychiatric morbidity and acceptability following medical and surgical methods of induced abortion (letter). *Br J Obstet Gynaecol* 1991; 98: 1312–1313.

21 Silvestre L, Dubois C, Renault M, Rezvani Y, Baulieu E, Ulmann A. Voluntary interruption of pregnancy with mifepristone (RU 486) and a prostaglandin analogue. *N Engl J Med* 1990; 322: 645–648.

22 Ulmann A, Silvestre L, Chemama L *et al*. Medical termination of early pregnancy with mifepristone (RU 486) followed by a prostaglandin analogue. *Acta Obstet Gynecol Scand* 1992; 71: 278–283.

23 Peyron R, Aubény E, Targosz V *et al*. Early termination of pregnancy with mifepristone (RU 486) and the orally active prostaglandin misoprostol. *N Engl J Med* 1993; 328: 1509–1513.

24 Richards JM Jr. Ecology of abortions in the United States since 1973: a replication and extension. *Pop Environ* 1984; 7: 137–151.

25 Kaltreider NB, Goldsmith S, Margolis AJ. The impact of midtrimester abortion techniques on patients and staff. *Am J Obstet Gynecol* 1979; 135(2): 235–238.

26 Lilford RJ, Johnson N. Surgical abortion at twenty weeks: is morality determined solely by the outcome? *J Med Ethics* 1989; 15: 82–85.

27 Evans MI, Drugan A, Bottoms SF *et al*. Attitudes on the ethics of abortion, sex selection, and selective pregnancy termination among health care professionals, ethicists, and clergy likely to encounter such situations. *Am J Obstet Gynecol* 1991; 164: 1092–1099.

28 Bourne JP. Abortion: influences on health professionals' attitudes. *Hospitals* 1972; 46: 80–83.

29 Bourne JP. Health professionals' attitudes about abortion. In: Lewit S, ed. *Abortion Techniques and Services*. Amsterdam: Excerpta Medica, 1972: 136–140.

30 Weisman CS, Nathanson CA, Teitelbaum MA, Chase GA, King TM. Abortion attitudes and performance among male and female obstetrician-gynecologists. *Fam Plann Perspect* 1986; 18: 67–73.

31 Greenslade FC, McLaurin K, Leonard A, Winkler J, Bhiwandiwala P. Technology introduction and quality of abortion care. *J Women's Health* 1993; 2: 27–33.

10 Abortion Controversies: Ethics, Politics and Religion

Ruth Macklin

Introduction

Probably no issue at the intersection of medicine, ethics and law is more controversial and more difficult to resolve than the issue of abortion. There are several reasons for this, reasons that are more political than they are matters of ethical principle. The first reason is that, unlike many ethical issues in biology and medicine, the abortion debate is not limited to scholars and health professionals, but has engulfed entire societies. A case in point is the ongoing debate in the USA, despite the fact that a constitutional right to abortion was established by the US Supreme Court in 1973 and upheld in 1992. Candidates for public office feel compelled to take a stand on abortion. In the legal and regulatory sphere, there is constant activity in state and federal courts, in bills introduced into legislatures and in regulations promulgated by governmental agencies. Media coverage of opponents of abortion actively picketing and blocking access to clinics keeps the issue before the public eye.

A second reason for the intractability of the abortion issue is the ideological character of the debate. Spokespersons for opponents of abortion adopted for their side the label 'pro-life', thereby implying that anyone willing to allow abortion is 'anti-life'. Supporters of the right of women to have an abortion, for their part, selected a label that reflects the cherished Western value of freedom to choose, calling themselves 'pro-choice'. The ideological battle lines of the controversy are thus drawn with one side charging the other with being against life in slogans that proclaim 'abortion is murder', and the other side contending that foes of abortion are against free choice and the right of women to control their own bodies. When ethical positions assume the characteristics of an ideology, rational argumentation is no longer possible. The fundamental stakes in this debate are revealed by the use of rights language by the opposing factions: 'right to life' and 'right to choose'.

A third reason for the impossibility of reaching agreement about the ethics of abortion stems from roots of the pro-life position in religious beliefs and practices.

Abortion and religion

Although opponents of abortion do not always identify the religious underpinnings of their views, a demographic analysis links the anti-abortion movement with particular religions and denominations, chiefly Roman Catholicism and fundamentalist groups of other major religions, including Islam and Christianity. However, sects other than the fundamentalist branch of Islam do permit abortion for a wide range of reasons during the first trimester of pregnancy [1]. According to one account, 'an examination of statements by religious leaders and scholars leads to the conclusion that no major religion, with the possible exception of Roman Catholicism, has a unified position on the matter of induced abortion' [2].

Despite common perceptions to the contrary, within Islam different sects have different opinions. According to Muslim theologians, the fetus becomes ensouled at the end of 120 days. Before that time, there is variation among the different sects regarding the timing and reasons for permissible abortion. The Haneefiyah allow abortion before ensoulment but there must be a permissible reason, one of which is pregnancy in a lactating mother. Theologians from the Malekeyah sect dislike induced abortion prior to the 40th day of pregnancy and prohibit it thereafter. The Hanabliyah theologians consider abortion 'rather loathsome', while the Zaidiyaa theologians permit abortion unconditionally prior to quickening. Even within sects there is variation; for example, some Shafeihah theologians allow induced abortion before the 120th day of pregnancy but others prohibit it. The one thing Muslim theologians do agree on is that after a period of 4 months from the date of conception, abortion is the taking of a life. However, even that limit may be set aside if the woman faces a medically determined risk of death [2].

Confusion about the permissibility of abortion according to the Islamic religion is understandable in light of the different positions adopted by these various sects. But, misleading statements by some writers on Islamic views about abortion are also responsible for generating confusion. One contributor to an international conference on ethics and human values in family planning presented the Islamic position as being much more uniform than the above-noted survey indicates. Contending that Islam views abortion as conflicting with the sanctity of human life, Hathout inquires whether the term 'human life' includes the intrauterine phase.

'According to the teachings of Islamic jurisprudence on the rights of the fetus, it does' [3]. Hathout dismisses the views of Islamic juridical writers from 'olden times' who 'thought that until the mother felt quickening the fetus had been a lifeless flesh, and to them quickening meant the instillation of life' [3]. Introducing modern science to support the contention that Islam views human life as beginning with conception, he invokes the 'genetic pattern that is characteristic of the human race at large and also of a unique individual', concluding that 'life begins with the fusion of a spermatozoon with an ovum to form the fertilized ovum or zygote' [3].

Introduction of modern scientific knowledge to buttress the position that 'human life begins at fertilization' is a tactic used also by supporters of Roman Catholic theology. A leading scholar in this field contends that, 'the positive argument for conception as the decisive moment of humanization is that at conception the new being receives the genetic code. It is this genetic information which determines his characteristics. A being with a human genetic code is man' [4]. Although contemporary Catholic teachings appear united in their opposition to abortion, this has not always been true. It is a common misconception that the Church's current position is the result of 2000 years of unchanged teaching [5]. The current view of the majority in the Church hierarchy—that induced abortion is a serious sin and grounds for excommunication—has only been a part of official Church doctrine since the *Apostolicae sedis* of Pope Pius IX in 1869. Before 1869, most theologians held that the fetus did not become ensouled, and consequently was not a human being, until at least 40 days after conception and in some cases later [5]. Even today, a minority of Catholic theologians believe that abortion is permissible in the early stages of pregnancy [5].

Up to AD 600, major theologians argued that abortion carried out in the earliest stages of pregnancy was not homicide. St Augustine saw 'actual human life as beginning at some point after the fetus has begun to grow' [5]. That was the mainstream position of the Church at the time, although other theologians held that abortion was homicide at any point. St Augustine did not consider abortion homicide, but he still condemned it. This condemnation stemmed not from a view of the moral status of the conceptus but rather from the fact that the necessary connection between the sexual act and procreation is broken. This is the same ground on which the Catholic Church condemns contraception. A theological debate continued over the years on the question of whether or not abortion is homicide. A collection of canon law that was accepted as authoritative within the Church from AD 1140 to 1917 included the statement that 'abortion was homicide only when the fetus was formed' [5]. St Thomas Aquinas held that abortion is not a sin of homicide until the fetus is ensouled and thus a fully human being. Nevertheless, St Thomas upheld the Church's opposition to contraception, and to abortion as a form of contraception, as both were held to be sins against marriage [5]. The distinction is an important one, since a sin against marriage is a 'sexual sin' in the Catholic teachings, constituting a separation between the sexual act and the procreative act. This is an entirely different basis for condemnation of abortion than a sin equating abortion with homicide.

The history of the Catholic Church reveals a growing centralization of power in the Vatican and a corresponding increasing influence of the Pope as the authority in Catholic theology. Before the modern era, different Catholic theologians held different views on many topics, and no one position was wholly authoritative. In 1864, a Jesuit theologian wrote in total opposition to abortion based on the concept of potentiality: to kill a potential human being is tantamount to killing an actual human being [5]. This idea gained support, and in 1869 Pius IX stated that all abortion is homicide, at any stage of pregnancy, and requires excommunication. As centralization of power in the papacy became established, dissent and theological debate were increasingly stifled. It thus appears that political factors operating within the Roman Catholic Church contributed to the emergence of the current united front opposing abortion. The doctrine of papal infallibility was also instituted during the reign of Pius IX, but that doctrine actually applies to very few papal declarations. In fact, abortion is *not* included as an infallible teaching under this doctrine. This limitation on the doctrine of papal infallibility is widely misunderstood by Catholics [5].

Despite the anti-abortion stance taken by the Roman Catholic magisterium and the anti-abortion rhetoric of spokespersons for fundamentalist Protestant sects, it remains true that many people on the pro-choice side are deeply religious. Although Orthodox Judaism stands in opposition to abortion, other branches of the religion, like most Protestant denominations, contend that abortion is a decision that must be left to the conscience of pregnant women. Before the 1973 Supreme Court decision in the USA, which guaranteed constitutional protection to women seeking abortions, Protestant clergy and Jewish rabbis deliberately broke the law by participating in a broad network called the Clergy Consultation Service, which counselled pregnant women and referred them to physicians who would perform abortions [1]. Once abortion was legalized in the USA, however, the most visible activities of religious groups have been those of the Catholic bishops and fundamentalist Protestants galvanized in efforts to overturn pro-choice laws.

If it is impossible to argue about the rightness or wrongness of fundamental religious convictions, so too will it be impossible to mount a rational argument about an ethical position that is deeply rooted in a religious world view. Dogmatic adherence to an ideology, whether religious or secular, tends to make people unwilling to argue rationally in defense of their position. Frances Kissling, President of the organization Catholics for a Free Choice, observes that the Catholic Church 'does not put forward an absolute prohibition on the taking of life in a reasonable wide range of other circumstances' [1]. Nevertheless, in the matter of abortion the Church sees 'only one value—fetal life', a position that lies 'outside the pale of respectable debate' [1].

Religious groups opposed to abortion have laid claim to the moral agenda. This is most evident on the international scene with the activities of the Catholic Church. In a 3-week conference at the United Nations, preparatory to the 1994 International Conference on Population and Development, the Vatican campaigned vigorously to exclude abortion from family planning services. Along with a few countries including Argentina, Benin, Guatemala, Honduras, Malta, Morocco and Nicaragua, the Vatican objected to wording in the draft Programme of Action plan that included the terms 'reproductive rights', 'reproductive health', 'family planning' and 'safe motherhood'. The objection was based on the suspicion that those terms were code words sanctioning abortion [6].

The intense involvement of fundamentalist Protestant sects in the anti-abortion movement in the USA provides further evidence of efforts by religious conservatives to capture the moral agenda. A television evangelist, Jerry Falwell, proclaimed that 'Satan has mobilized his own forces to destroy America by negating the Judeo-Christian ethic, secularizing our society, and devaluing human life through the legalization of abortion and infanticide' [7]. However, ethics is not solely the prerogative of religion. Secular ethics provides a basis for making moral judgements, criticizing existing or traditional practices and justifying enactment of laws and policies. Although ethics and religion often overlap and yield the same judgements or conclusions with respect to right and wrong, secular ethics can be a useful tool for evaluating particular religious doctrines on principled moral grounds.

Ethical analysis: rights and personhood

One major difference between religious and secular ethics lies in their differing methodologies. A prominent approach to secular ethics relies on the use of principles. A leading principle of bioethics is *respect for persons*. This principle rests on the premise that human beings have dignity and deserve respect. Another version of the principle is *respect for autonomy*, starting with the presumption that mature human beings possess autonomy, that is, the capacity for self-rule, for making reasoned decisions and engaging in actions that affect themselves, their family and others who surround them. The ethical principle of respect for persons is the criterion by which coercion is judged a moral wrong, especially paternalistic forms of coercion, in which people are forced to do things ostensibly for their own good or welfare. It is also the principle that underlies the doctrine of informed consent in medical practice.

Respect for persons is the ethical principle most closely associated with the value of individual rights. To recognize human beings as worthy of respect dictates respect for their dignity, their privacy and their liberty. The language of rights is usually reserved for the most important human values, since moral rights are often backed up by courts or embodied in legislation, in which case they become legal rights. But, even when rights are not specifically guaranteed by laws, their importance is signalled in statements and declarations of various sorts. An example is the international statement claiming the existence of reproductive rights that was agreed upon by the representatives of 136 governments in the World Population Plan of Action in Bucharest in 1974: 'All couples and individuals have the basic right to decide freely and responsibly the number and spacing of their children and to have the information, education and means to do so'. As is true of other examples, the rights enumerated in this statement of reproductive rights imply the existence of correlative duties on the part of some agency, most probably a government, to guarantee their fulfilment. In the political debate carried on first in the USA and then in other countries, feminists adopted the phrase 'a woman's right to control her own body', thus specifying a right into which the government, a religious authority or even the woman's own husband may not intrude. 'The right to control one's own body' is another way of describing the right to self-determination.

The underlying basis for the woman's reproductive right is the right to liberty. The principle of liberty dictates that individuals have a right to freedom of decision and action, to the extent that their actions do not interfere with the rights of others. Opponents in the abortion controversy do not disagree on the soundness of that fundamental ethical principle itself. But, they disagree profoundly over its application: foes of abortion claim that the act of terminating a pregnancy does interfere with the rights of another (the fetus), while advocates of a woman's right to procure an abortion deny that killing a fetus is a violation of rights. Thus, in the abortion controversy, the alleged rights of the fetus are pitted against the rights of the pregnant woman.

It is often thought that if we could only resolve the question of the 'personhood' of the fetus, we could settle the ethical debates surrounding abortion once and for all. However, the initially promising path of trying to ascertain whether a fetus is a person and therefore possesses rights, is of little use, because there is no prospect for agreement on criteria for personhood. The view that people hold regarding the morality of abortion typically determines the position they take on whether the fetus should be construed as a person. The answers offered at opposite poles of this debate are that: (i) personhood begins at conception, and so a very early embryo has rights; and (ii) that personhood begins at the moment of birth or later, thus disqualifying all prenatal life from the category of personhood.

In between these two extremes lies a range of other criteria for personhood, some of which are matters of traditional belief, while others have been introduced more recently as a result of scientific developments. An example of the former is 'quickening', the time at which a pregnant woman first feels fetal movement. Another example is 'animation'. St Thomas Aquinas and early Christian authors talked about 'ensoulment'—the time at which the embryo or fetus becomes infused with a soul. An example of a criterion that relies on modern scientific knowledge is the presence of electroencephalographic (brainwave) activity. Viability is still another point between conception and birth that many people hold to be the time at which the fetus acquires moral standing. Despite the fact that the US Supreme Court declined to define personhood in *Roe* v. *Wade*, the case that established a constitutional right to abortion in the USA, the ruling in that case accorded political significance to viability. The Court used viability as a place to draw a line beyond which the State may interfere with a woman's 'right to privacy'.

Yet another approach to the personhood of prenatal life has been termed the 'developmental' view. This approach denies that there is a single point or a sharp line that distinguishes personhood from an intrauterine existence that lacks moral standing. A final strategy for defining personhood makes use of the potentiality principle. It is simply the *potential* for developing into an adult human being that confers on a fertilized ovum the moral status of a full-fledged adult.

The end result of these definitional disputes is that proponents of choice advocate freedom and equality for women, and therefore propose a strict definition of personhood, one that is difficult to meet. Opponents of abortion tend to favour sex-appropriate social roles and an idealized, traditional family, and therefore adopt a very lenient definition of personhood, one that allows a zygote to qualify as a person.

It is no less controversial to bypass the intermediate step of defining personhood and go directly to ascribing rights to an embryo or fetus. The language of rights can generate confusion. A deeply cherished right in free societies is the right to life, which prohibits innocent people from being killed by the State and promises State protection against other threats to the lives of citizens. However, the 'right to life' has taken on a new meaning since being adopted by groups with an anti-abortion political agenda. By casting their moral position in terms of a 'right to life' these groups make it appear that anyone who favours a woman's right to an abortion must therefore reject the proposition that people have a right to life. The confusion stems from applying a general moral claim asserting the 'right to life' to a highly controversial area like abortion.

The position that human life acquires moral standing from the moment of conception is an article of religious faith for some people and an absurd proposition for others. The latter group finds it impossible to construct a rational defence of the assertion that a cluster of cells attached to the lining of the womb should be granted the rights normally accorded to living children and adult human beings. Yet, despite the lack of any similarity between the properties of a conceptus and those of a woman, man or child, opponents of abortion contend that human life deserves protection from the moment of conception.

A consequentialist ethical analysis

One of several ethical principles applicable to abortion is *respect for persons*. Another leading principle of bioethics is *beneficence*. This principle obligates individuals to seek to bring about good consequences of their actions; or, perhaps more accurately, to strive to bring about a preponderance of favourable over unfavourable consequences. This principle applies to the policies of governments, to the behaviour of doctors and other health professionals and to all citizens. The principle of beneficence has always been central to medical practice, as it obligates physicians to recommend treatments or procedures likely to have the most beneficial health outcomes for their patients.

Both in the literature on abortion and in the political arena, the debate in the USA has been carried out almost exclusively in the language of rights. Yet, consequentialist ethical arguments, those that appeal to the good and bad results of actions or social practices, provide a respectable, alternative mode of ethical analysis. The long history of women's death and disease from self-induced abortions, along with data about the persistence of morbidity and mortality resulting from clandestine abortions, are well-documented harmful consequences of anti-abortion policies. These consequences affect not only women, but also the children they bear and the entire society in countries where population growth strains monetary and natural resources. Thus, the negative consequences of restricting access to safe abortion are a compelling factor to consider in an ethical weighing.

Compared with the rights-based framework in which the debate is typically cast in the USA, the focus in many nations is on the consequences of permitting or prohibiting abortion. This point was emphasized by Sai and Newman [8]:

> The ethical arguments about abortion are complex, although often presented simplistically. Often debated is a woman's 'right' to control over her body and to refuse to carry to term a pregnancy she does not want. However, not often considered is the ethics of withholding the benefits of a technology which is less hazardous than carrying a pregnancy to term. Nineteenth-century anti-abortion laws were generally designed to save women from the dangerous, and often experimental, surgical procedures of the time. However, this reason is no longer valid, and today the effect of applying anti-abortion laws is to increase rather than reduce risk to women's lives and health.

The problem is especially acute in developing countries. An estimated 70 000 or more Third World women die every year as a result of botched abortions [9]. In most African countries, where safe abortion is either not available or legally restricted, illegal abortion is the only solution for women with unwanted pregnancies. Complications of these abortions include sepsis, haemorrhage, infection, uterine perforation and secondary infertility [10]. In Nigeria, a review of maternal deaths in one hospital over a 13-year period revealed that abortion was one of the three major causes of death [11].

Similar reports from Latin American countries document that most abortions are performed in sordid and clandestine conditions and that physicians use medicines such as hormone injections to induce menses, or unsafe curettage that can be harmful to women's health [12]. A study on the use of misoprostol (Cytotec) by Brazilian women revealed that for all the low-income women interviewed, the main reason they gave for using misoprostol was that it would not kill them. For these women, part of the reality of their lives was a fear of dying from an abortion, a lesson they learned from real-life experience [13]. The negative consequences of enforcing restrictive policies on abortion are not limited to risks to the lives and health of women, but extend also to the infants and children they bear. Close spacing of children produces more high-risk pregnancies, premature births and low-birthweight infants. The very large number of 'street children' (millions in Brazil alone) is a clear testimony to another dramatic consequence of unwanted pregnancies [14].

It is instructive to compare the consequences for women's lives and health in countries that have changed their abortion laws in the past few decades. Legalization of abortion has tended to reduce maternal mortality, while making laws more restrictive has had the opposite effect. For example, in the former Czechoslovakia, abortion laws were made less restrictive during the 1950s, and abortion-related mortality fell by 56% and 38% in the periods 1953–57 and 1958–62, respectively. In contrast, in Romania, a restrictive abortion law was enacted in 1966, resulting in a sevenfold increase in deaths from abortion. The abortion mortality rate per million women rose from 14.3 in 1965 to 97.5 in 1978 [15].

Reports from developed as well as from developing countries, and assessments by experts in the field of reproductive health throughout the world, leave no room for doubt that women will continue to seek to end unwanted pregnancies regardless of legal or religious prohibitions. Restrictive abortion laws and practices have well-documented negative consequences for women, as evidenced by the high rates of mortality and morbidity resulting from unsafe abortions. In light of such consequences, what ethical justification can opponents of abortion provide for their position?

The only defence is to grant a higher status to fetal life than to the life and health of the woman in whom the fetus is lodged. A theological hierarchy of values removed from real-world concerns accords higher status to fetuses than to women and adolescent girls whose life and health is endangered by unsafe abortions. Policymakers whose views are dictated by religious or traditional values in their country ignore these dire consequences for women, reflecting the low esteem in which women continue to be held. From an ethical perspective, the principle of beneficence yields the undeniable conclusion that legal prohibition of abortion and lack of access to safe abortion results in an overall balance of negative consequences and is therefore morally wrong.

Justice and access to abortion

The most prominent disagreements in the abortion controversy focus on the rights of the individual woman and the permissible role of government in restricting those rights. Nevertheless, questions of social justice are also ethical concerns, whether they involve women's access to information about abortion services, having access to the services themselves or government funding for abortions for poor women. One formulation of the relevant principle of justice holds that all persons within a given society deserve equitable access to goods and services that fulfil basic human needs.

A country might have liberal laws pertaining to abortion services, such as those in developed countries like the USA, that guarantee women the right to procure an abortion up to the time of fetal viability. But, if the government does not provide financial assistance to poor women who seek an abortion, the legally guaranteed right to abortion turns out to be empty. Ample evidence exists to show that restrictive policies on abortion adversely affect more coloured and poor women than white, middle-class or wealthy women. This serves as a reminder that rights presuppose corresponding obligations on the part of persons, agencies or governments to act in ways that enable those rights to be realized. The principle of justice is violated when health services are available only to those with the ability to pay.

A few examples are illustrative. In the USA as of early 1992, only 13 states out of 50 paid for abortions for low-income women. It is reported that counsellors at abortion clinics hear stories every day from desperate women—of rape victims unable to pay for an abortion, of poor women who use money intended for their children's food to pay for an abortion and of women unable to procure an abortion because of referrals and delays resulting in their being past the legal limit [16].

The principle of justice mandates that all individuals who need them should have equitable access to health services that are available to others. A precondition for access is information about the existence and nature of the services. In developing countries, poor women disproportionately bear the burden of restrictive abortion laws and inadequate or non-existent public services. Furthermore, wealthy women in any country can afford to travel to other countries where abortion is legal.

In Mexico, physicians who work in both the public and private sectors provide abortions for their private patients but decline to do the same procedure for patients in the public hospital, even in places where abortion has been decriminalized. The explanation for this dual system is that physicians are paid on a fee-for-service basis by their private patients, but for their work in the public hospital they receive a fixed salary. Financial motivation is thus capable of overriding whatever moral qualms these doctors may feel about performing abortions.

A group of women's health advocates in Chile described ways in which laws prohibiting abortion are flouted. They said that women with money can circumvent existing laws and guidelines (as is true almost everywhere). This group pointed out that although there are many laws, there are also many loopholes. They cited a Chilean saying: 'The law is born, but the loophole is born at the same time'.

Attitudes and practices in some developing countries

The interplay of culture, religion and law varies from one country to another. The following account of attitudes and practices regarding abortion provides a context in which to understand the barriers to safe, legal abortion in several developing countries.

Bangladesh

Bangladesh is an interesting case study, demonstrating a blend of political and religious opposition to legalizing abortion, and at the same time, a widespread practice of menstrual regulation (MR), which is a variant of vacuum aspiration carried out in the first few weeks following a missed menstrual period.

Maternal mortality in Bangladesh is very high, nearly six per 1000 live births. More than 25% of deaths are due to complications of abortion induced by untrained providers using traditional methods that include insertion of sticks, painful abdominal massage and use of indigenous medicines [17]. A survey conducted in 1978 estimated that 800 000 abortions are performed annually in Bangladesh, resulting in about 8000 deaths each year.

MR services were first introduced in 1974, and since then MR training programmes have been established throughout the country. Despite the success that the introduction of MR has achieved in providing safe abortion services to Bangladeshi women who are eligible and know about MR, barriers to safe, legal abortion remain. Availability of this service has been limited mostly to educated and younger women. For instance, MR may only be performed up to 8 or 9 weeks of gestation. Despite the ready availability of MR services from trained providers, studies show that about one-third of the women seeking MR at official centres are refused, mainly because the pregnancy is too advanced [18]. The majority of those women then turn to traditional abortion providers. There is insufficient knowledge on the part of women about the duration of pregnancy up to which MR may be performed and where services can be obtained. In addition, many illiterate women lack the knowledge to ascertain the duration of their pregnancy, and women and family planning workers alike are confused about precisely how to count the duration of pregnancy.

Still other barriers of a sociocultural nature exist. Properly carried out, MR requires a pelvic examination for accurate estimation of the length of gestation and also a second pelvic examination to ascertain that the induced abortion is complete. But, for very many Bangladeshi women, a pelvic examination is considered to be an 'invasive' procedure. It is a reason for many women not to seek clinical services but, instead, use traditional herbal and other methods [19]. Although abortion in later pregnancy is treated with moral condemnation, MR has nevertheless gained wide acceptance as a method of abortion in early pregnancy [20].

Against this backdrop, the ambivalence with regard to official legalization of abortion in Bangladesh is curious, if not paradoxical. The Penal Code of Bangladesh was enacted at the end of the nineteenth century. Under the penal law, abortion is illegal except when performed to save the life of the woman [21]. The Bangladesh National Population Policy tried to legalize early abortions on broad medical and social grounds, but failed in that attempt [21]. Despite the legal prohibition of induced abortion however, the Bangladesh Government has encouraged the introduction of MR as an integral part of family planning. The explanation for this apparent paradox is that MR is determined not to fall within the purview of Section 312 of the Penal Code, the provision that prohibits abortion, because as MR is routinely practiced, pregnancy is not actually established. A 1979 report of the Bangladesh Institute of Law and International Affairs states that pregnancy is, 'an essential element of the crime of abortion but the use of menstrual regulation makes it virtually impossible for the prosecutor to meet the required proof' [21]. Thus, the paradox remains: Bangladesh has not given any legal sanction to the practice of MR, but the government has nevertheless encouraged the practice of MR in recognition of the deaths due to incomplete and septic abortions performed by untrained providers.

The Philippines

Abortion is illegal in the Philippines and strongly opposed by the dominant Catholic Church, many politicians and devout citizens. The Philippine Constitution, drafted in 1986, contains a clause protecting the rights of the unborn as a matter of State policy. Efforts are continually being made to increase penalties for performing abortions, including a proposal of the death penalty for physicians.

Despite all this, among many rural women abortion before 3–4 months of pregnancy is not held to be wrong. According to a social scientist conducting research at the grass-roots level, one does not hear women saying 'it is a sin' or 'it is against God's teaching', with reference to either contraception or abortion. There appear to be no feelings of guilt among many rural women who seek and obtain abortions, at least from traditional healers. The procedure is viewed more as 'bringing down menstruation' than as killing a human life.

Traditional healers use non-invasive methods of abortion, such as herbal concoctions, which they believe are effective. Potions are administered after a missed menstrual period. If this procedure is done three times and fails to bring on menstruation, the pregnancy is viewed as 'meant to be' and the traditional healers do not advance to more invasive means. However, women themselves sometimes seek other illegal and unsafe means of abortion following these failed attempts.

Mexico

Mexico is a study in contradictions. Down to the exact wording, the Mexican Constitution incorporates the reproductive right asserted in the 1974 Bucharest World Population Plan of Action: 'All couples and individuals have the basic right to decide freely and responsibly the number and spacing of their children and to have the information, education and means to do so'. However, the statement of this right in the Mexican Constitution is in stark contrast to reality. Abortion remains illegal everywhere in Mexico, although it has been decriminalized in some states and liberalized somewhat more in a few regions. A group of legal scholars and practising attorneys outlined the key points about the existing legal, political and social situation in Mexico as follows.

1   The Penal Code permits abortion in cases of rape and when the woman's life is in danger. The Catholic Church in Mexico is *not* actively campaigning against these legally permitted exceptions to the Church's general prohibition of abortion.

2   Attempts to legalize abortion through legislation have failed because legislators tend to overestimate the power of opposition groups and, therefore, fail to take the necessary steps to push the legislation through. Although there are vocal, conservative groups in some states, they are not a strong force everywhere in Mexico and legislative efforts could very well be successful.

3   Current law in Yucatan includes six different reasons for allowing abortion, including economic grounds. Despite this liberalization, the Church is not attacking Yucatan's abortion law. It is not clear why the Church has refrained from active opposition to the liberalized law in that state.

4   The attitude in Mexican society toward maternity is important. This is not simply a matter of the Church and its authority. The bond between mother and child is very powerful, and this creates fear in the population. One of the reasons the society opposes abortion is that legalization would appear to question *all* maternity.

This group of legal scholars and practising attorneys reported the problem with seeking legislative reform of abortion laws in Mexico. No one wants to discuss it; conservative voices in the legislature remain loudest. So, even though most of the people in Mexico believe that reproductive decisions are a private matter, it is still impossible to get the laws changed. It was speculated that male legislators are reluctant to liberalize laws stemming from a traditional attitude of wanting to control women's sexuality.

A women's activist group reported on a workshop they conducted for physicians from different states in Mexico. Physicians at that meeting reported that in 50% of the states from which they came, laws had already been changed to allow abortions for reasons relating to women's health or for genetic anomalies diagnosed prenatally. Nevertheless, despite these changes in the law, many doctors acknowledged that a barrier to performing abortions lay in the physicians' own beliefs. The physicians seemed uninterested in the fact that there were laws in existence that protected them; rather, their own moral views appeared to be the determining factor in their willingness to perform abortions. It emerged that one of the chief motives driving the physicians' behaviour was their fear of being looked upon as an 'abortionist'. Another worry the physicians voiced was the need to pay blackmail so that the police would remain silent. The clear message from that workshop was that doctors do not want to hear about the *laws* regarding abortion; they see the issue in terms of their relationship with their patients.

Chile

A somewhat different picture emerged from a conference with physicians in Chile. When the view that 'life begins at conception' was characterized as a religious precept, one physician objected, claiming that it is a *moral* view that is not necessarily accompanied by a particular religious faith. That reply poses the interesting question of whether moral views having their roots in a religious doctrine should still be characterized as 'religious' views when held by people who claim not to derive their moral viewpoint from that religion. It is undeniable that countries or cultures in which the predominant religion has for many years been Roman Catholicism continue to have restrictive or prohibitive laws regarding abortion, and this reflects the attitude of politicians and much of the population.

A group of women's health advocates told stories about how women were treated when they were admitted to the hospital following known or suspected induced abortions. Although some physicians do treat such women well, many do not. Physicians could get into trouble for not denouncing women who tried to induce abortion. Some physicians actually perform a dilatation and curettage (D & C), but then, for the record, say that the woman had come to the hospital with an incomplete abortion. It sometimes happens that a woman's own family denounces her for having an induced abortion. It was noted, however, that there are few women who actually have been jailed for attempting an abortion.

At another meeting in Santiago, one woman told the story of a patient who was brought to the hospital *in extremis* after a self-induced abortion. Although the patient was dying and in urgent need of medical attention, the physician refused to help her, saying that if a doctor tried to heal a patient who had committed a sin, the physician would also be implicated in that sinful behaviour. This case illustrates how strong religious or ideological views can lead to flawed ethical reasoning. It may well be ethically acceptable for a physician who is opposed to abortion on moral or religious grounds to refuse performing the procedure (with possibly rare exceptions, such as saving the life of the woman if there is no other physician available). However, this case did not involve a physician performing or assisting in an abortion but rather treating a patient who had made the attempt herself. So, the physician could in no way be viewed as implicated in the patient's earlier act.

Argentina

In public hospitals in Argentina, there is a 'protocol' for dealing with suspected abortions. The hospital is supposed to register with the police all cases of induced abortion. Some women 'confess' to having had an induced abortion, but most do not. The 'rule of the game' followed by women is not to confess, but physicians claim that they need to know whether the abortion was induced in order to provide the proper mode of treatment. However, in cases where women do not 'confess', physicians do not make a report to the police because they have no evidential basis for such a report.

It is worth remarking on a situation in which women who are hospitalized are asked to 'confess' a crime. Physicians are placed in the role of agents of the state, inquisitors of their patients and informers to the police. This situation is highly inimical to the physician–patient relationship and requires physicians to act knowingly and deliberately against the best interest of their patients. The language of 'confession' may be appropriate in the relationship between priests and penitents. It is most commonly the language of police investigations conducted on behalf of governments. A system in which physicians are asked to seek 'confessions' from patients and report the information to the police is a deeply unethical system.

Conclusion

As one writer observes, 'Those who oppose abortion claim to have religion, tradition and law on their side. However, if abortion is a key to women's reproductive health, it is necessary to talk about the ethics of abortion from a woman-centred perspective' [22].

The claim that religion is on the side of opposition to abortion is true of some religions but surely not all. Moreover, it is important to recall that the dictates of any specific religion are binding only on its adherents. In any society in which not all people believe in the same religion, a principle of religious freedom and toleration requires that the precepts of one religion—even the dominant one—not be imposed on those who are not adherents. Although orthodox and fundamentalist religions tend to treat ethics and religion as completely coincident, most religions treat the two as overlapping but not identical spheres.

The claim that tradition is on the side of opposition to abortion may well be true, but what follows from that observation? Not everything that exists according to tradition is, by that token, ethically acceptable or desirable. To resist change because of traditional beliefs or practices is a philosophical error. The error lies in concluding that, because a state of affairs has existed in the past, it ought to continue into the present and future. The flaw in that reasoning can easily be seen by reflecting on the fact that manifestly unjust social institutions, such as slavery and colonialism, would still be with us if history and tradition served as an infallible moral guide. Moral progress requires a critical evaluation of past practices and institutions. Of course, many social practices and institutions will withstand such critical evaluation, but others will not.

The claim that law is on the side of opposition to abortion simply points out the obvious truth that many countries have laws that prohibit abortion. But, laws can be repealed, modified and amended. Laws can be changed for ethical reasons and to eradicate injustices, as in the case of abolition of slavery, dismantling of apartheid, granting women and black people the right to vote and providing guarantees of civil rights and civil liberties.

The three leading principles of bioethics—respect for persons, beneficence and justice—together provide an ethical mandate for guaranteeing to women throughout the world a legal right to safe abortion. The fact that some well-organized religions, some powerful political groups and many entrenched rulers are opposed to reform of restrictive abortion laws does not make their position morally right. 'Might makes right' is a political slogan best left in the dustbin of history.

Acknowledgement

Much of the information for developing countries reported in this chapter was collected during site visits as part of a project on ethics and reproductive health supported by the Ford Foundation.

References

1 Kissling F. Religion and abortion: Roman Catholicism lost in the pelvic zone. *Women's Health Issues* 1993; 3: 132–137.

2 Serour GI. Antiprogestins: ethical issues. In: Kamal GM, ed. *Proceedings of the International Symposium on Antiprogestins*. Dhaka: Bangladesh Association for Prevention of Septic Abortion, 1992: 87–94.

3 Hathout H. Ethics and human values in family planning: perspectives of the Middle East. In: Bankowski Z, Barzelatto J, Capron AM, eds. *Ethics and Human Values in Family Planning*. Geneva: CIOMS, 1989: 222–237.

4 Noonan JT Jr. An almost absolute value in history. In: Gorovitz S *et al.*, eds. *Moral Problems in Medicine*, 2nd edn. Englewood Cliffs: Prentice-Hall, 1983: 303–308.

5 Hurst J. The history of abortion in the Catholic Church. *Conscience* 1991; 12: 1–17.

6 Chira S. Abortion is divisive issue at population talks. *New York Times* 1994; April 24: 18.

7 McKeegan M. The politics of abortion: a historical perspective. *Women's Health Issues* 1993; 3: 127–131.

8 Sai FT, Newman K. Ethics and human values in family planning: Africa regional perspective. In: Bankowski Z, Barzelatto J, Capron AM, eds. *Ethics and Human Values in Family Planning*. Geneva: CIOMS, 1989: 143–166.

9 Maternal Health and Safe Motherhood Programme. *Abortion: A Tabulation of Available Data on the Frequency and Mortality of Unsafe Abortion*, 2nd edn. Geneva: World Health Organization Division of Family Health, 1993.

10 Mashalaba NN. Commentary on the causes and consequences of unwanted pregnancy from an African perspective. *Int J Gynecol Obstet* 1989; 3 (Suppl.): 15–19.

11 Unuigbe JA, Oronsaye AU, Orhue AAE. Abortion-related morbidity and mortality in Benin City, Nigeria 1973–1985. *Int J Gynecol Obstet* 1988; 26: 435–439.

12 Toro OL. Commentary on women-centered reproductive health services. *Int J Gynecol Obstet* 1989; 3 (Suppl.): 119–123.

13 Arilha M, Barbosa RM. Cytotec in Brazil: 'at least it doesn't kill'. *Reprod Health Matters* 1993; 2: 41–52.

14 Pinotti JA, Faúndes A. Unwanted pregnancy: challenges for health policy. *Int J Gynecol Obstet* 1989; 3 (Suppl.): 97–102.

15 Hagenfeldt K. Ethics and human values in family planning: European and North American perspectives. In: Bankowski Z, Barzelatto J, Capron AM, eds. *Ethics and Human Values in Family Planning*. Geneva: CIOMS, 1989: 184–207.

16 Hurdles increasing for women seeking abortion. *New York Times* 1992; March 15: 1 and 18.

17 Akhter HH. The scientific basis of antiprogestins. In: Kamal GM, ed. *Proceedings of the International Symposium on Antiprogestins*. Dhaka: Bangladesh Association for Prevention of Septic Abortion, 1992: 33–36.

18 Kamal GM. Menstrual regulation service provisions in Bangladesh. In: Kamal GM, ed. *Proceedings of the International Symposium on Antiprogestins*. Dhaka: Bangladesh Association for Prevention of Septic Abortion, 1992: 5–9.

19 Kabir S, Germain A. Is RU 486/PG in its current form likely to be appropriate for women in Bangladesh? In: Kamal GM, ed. *Proceedings of the International Symposium on Antiprogestins*. Dhaka: Bangladesh Association for Prevention of Septic Abortion, 1992: 48–57.

20 Rahman S. Acceptability and feasibility of RU 486 in Bangladesh. In: Kamal GM, ed. *Proceedings of the International Symposium on Antiprogestins*. Dhaka: Bangladesh Association for Prevention of Septic Abortion, 1992: 64–66.

21 Huda S. The legal implications of the use of antiprogestin drugs. In: Kamal GM, ed. *Proceedings of the International Symposium on Antiprogestins*. Dhaka: Bangladesh Association for Prevention of Septic Abortion, 1992: 82–86.

22 Berer M. Making abortion safe and legal: the ethics and dynamics of change. *Reprod Health Matters* 1993; 2: 5–10.

11   A Woman's Legal Right to Choose

Rebecca J. Cook & Bernard M. Dickens

Introduction

Recorded history reflects the dominant pattern of patriarchy [1]. Men were the hunters, food gatherers and providers, while women bore and reared children. Social norms were conditioned by environments, in that nomadic peoples had to control pregnancies since women in advanced pregnancy could not travel with speed or safety [2]. In contrast, pastoral residents of fertile lands, such as the Fertile Crescent of the Judeo-Christian Holy Land, accepted a duty to be fruitful and multiply. High rates of infant mortality encouraged repeated pregnancies, and competition among family, tribal and racial groups was more successful where numbers were greatest. Maternal mortality due to excessive childbearing was accepted and often attributed to divine will and, in response to this fact, men created laws that permitted polygamy.

Patriarchy attributed to men the role and status of masters of their families. It made men the architects of practices to promote childbirth which they protected through rules, given force through religious and secular precepts, that became laws. The prohibition of abortion was important among these, because men desired children as a personal tribute to their manhood and to enhance their family and tribal authority. The harmful consequences of primitive and unskilled abortion practices reinforced the wisdom of restrictive rules.

Limited knowledge of reproductive biology conditioned rules that identified pregnancy at some point after conception or at a woman's first identification of fetal movement, the stage of 'quickening'. This was the point to which the Anglo-Saxon customary or common law attached significance. Conversely, the much older biblical Old Testament defined different measurements from conception at which abortion was prohibited, and this influenced Jewish, early Christian and Islamic laws (see Chapter 10).

Patriarchal legal systems controlled a woman's right to choose abortion, but were less vigilant of women's control and induction of regular menstruation. From early times, the folk medicine accessible to women contained means to induce menstruation when it was delayed. Whether delay was due to conception or other causes, women could choose whether to employ the herbal, manipulative or other means known to them by which to restore menstruation, perhaps by the termination of an existing early pregnancy, before legal systems became engaged. In time, however, advancing knowledge of reproductive biology, religious condemnation of women's health care knowledge as witchcraft and the growing prestige and monopolistic influence of organized medicine foreclosed this choice. Recognizing the association between abortion and menstrual induction, legislation increasingly prohibited the use and advertisement of means to restore menstruation or achieve contraception. The first legislation in the English-speaking world that prohibited abortion was enacted in 1803 [3]. In 1869, the Roman Catholic Church moved its long-standing condemnation of abortion back from 40 days after conception to apply from the point of conception itself, even if this is before the time of ensoulment [4]. The effect was to preclude a sexually active woman's choice not only of abortion but of reproductive self-determination.

Types of legal systems

Women's rights to choose abortion are governed by local legal systems [5–8], which fall into one of three general classes.
1   Comprehensively codified laws, in which any right must have its basis in a code provision.
2   Judicially developed systems, in which judges declare customary or common law. Such law is subject to amendment and partial codification by legislatively enacted laws, which will be interpreted by the judiciary.
3   Religious law, revealed to and declared by religious authorities.
    Until quite recent times, women had no influence within legal systems. They were not found among the codifiers of laws, within legislatures that enacted codes in codified systems and *ad hoc* legislation in non-codified systems, nor among the secular and religious judges that declared customary law, interpreted legislation and determined the relationship between legislated and customary laws. Women's exclusion was based on custom and convention, on legislation that explicitly excluded women and on legislation that failed to include women, which male judges interpreted to exclude women [9]. Men were satisfied that, as husbands, fathers, conscientious citizens and devout interpreters of divine intentions, they could represent and protect the interests of women, all of whom lacked

the intellect and temperament to become engaged in the affairs of men. There was no choice of a woman that a man could not exercise better.

The three systems of law rarely operate in a pure form. Comprehensively codified or civil law systems,* such as those based on the French Code Napoleon, are subject to changing understandings of their provisions, so that new meanings emerge without legislated reform of the Code itself [10,11]. Similarly, common law systems show that many influences affect customary understandings, and there is continuing tension and interaction between common law and legislation [12]. Judges may read legislation as prevailing over previous common law, or as intended to fit within the general law, providing detail but not fundamental reform. Religious laws may be derived from a singular, perhaps infallible authority, but in, for instance, the Islamic tradition, there is no central authority and authoritative interpreters of Islam follow several schools of thought whose conclusions on particular matters may differ (see Chapter 10). Religious legal systems coexist with secular laws, usually created by legislation, as many matters of social and industrial functioning have no religious content, such as laws governing on which side of the road vehicles are driven.

State legal systems, whether based on civil, common or religious law, function within the framework of international law. Domestic systems determine whether international treaties, such as human right treaties, are automatically incorporated into domestic law and prevail over it, or whether treaties must be adopted by state legislation in order to take legal effect as domestic law. The relationship between state law and international law may be a source of legal disagreement, since states may claim the sovereign right to determine the influence of international law, while international law may claim that states exist only subject to the rules of international law, and can discharge state functions only under international law.

Types of laws

Constitutional law

The most important legal framework within a state is its constitution.

---

* Confusingly, 'civil law' is used in three senses: (i) civil law in contrast to Anglo-Saxon common law; (ii) civil law, concerned with compensation, in contrast to criminal law, concerned with punishment; and (iii) civil law of general citizens in contrast to military law.

When the constitution is in a written form, which is usually the case with exceptions such as the UK, constitutional declarations and documents frequently state the highest ideals to which a country commits itself, and the rights and privileges that its citizens enjoy. Modern constitutions tend to refer to the provisions of leading international human rights instruments. Constitutional law determines the relationship between centralized and decentralized governmental authority and determines governmental powers and spheres of individual privacy or self-determination. It also determines the source and scope of criminal law, police powers of investigation, authority to prosecute alleged violations of law, state responsibility for public health and, for instance, state responsibility for, and private access to, hospital and other health services.

In countries where constitutional rights attract considerable attention, the issue of whether the right to choose abortion is constitutionally protected is of great significance. If the right is so protected, political majorities in legislative assemblies may be unable to interfere with the right without first achieving a constitutional amendment. This invariably requires a higher level of political consensus than routine legislation, and is exceptionally difficult to achieve in many countries.

Constitutions often incorporate categories of human rights principles, including those derived from the right to liberty and security of the person and the right to sexual non-discrimination. Constitutions may not contain specific terms that define how far government may penetrate private and family life, and how far individual bodily integrity is protected against actions of government agents, but courts that interpret the constitution may define how governmental powers and individual rights relate to each other under constitutional provisions. For instance, the famous 1973 US Supreme Court abortion decision in *Roe* v. *Wade* found that the USA constitution included a protected area of personal privacy that federal and state legislatures could not invade by compelling a woman to continue an unwanted pregnancy.

Criminal, non-criminal (civil) and administrative law

A distinction is commonly recognized between offences against the state, which endanger the welfare of society itself or of protected interests within the state, and offences that violate the interests only of individual persons. The former are described as criminal offences and the latter as civil wrongs or delicts. Because of public interests in religious, moral and social values regarding the protection of the lives of women and unborn children, laws prohibiting women's choice of abortion have historically fallen within the scope of criminal law. Agents of the state usually prosecute criminal offences, and offenders who are convicted are liable to punishment, for instance by imprisonment or liability to pay fines.

For civil wrongs or delicts, private persons will usually first seek settlement without going to court. If court judgements are obtained, they will normally provide financial compensation to injured parties for any expenses, pain or indignity that they can prove they have suffered. Exceptionally, civil courts, perhaps with juries, may award punitive or exemplary damages, which are a quasi-criminal sanction. For instance, in May 1994, a civil jury in Texas ordered two anti-abortion groups, Operation Rescue and Rescue America-National, to pay more than $1 million in punitive damages to a Planned Parenthood clinic for forcefully disrupting clinic services [13].

Some legal systems in addition have a body of administrative law providing for the regulation of state agencies and protection of individual rights separately from criminal and civil law. Other systems have developed a body of administrative law by selective use of the principles and procedures of criminal and civil law. Administrative law governs, for instance, the provision of medical services, licensing of facilities where medical procedures may be conducted, the licensing of medically and otherwise qualified personnel to undertake health-related procedures and eligibility for state funding of procedures. State authorities concerned with licensing within the health professions, private professional bodies and hospital corporations that give status to licence-holders, members or employees may be bound by principles of administrative law in their decision-making procedures regarding licensure, membership and employment.

Where powers of administrative agencies are created by or consolidated in legislation, the enactment may provide only the general purposes of the powers and the broad framework for their exercise. Legislation may empower subordinate bodies such as branches of government to fill in details for implementation of the purposes and application of the framework. Such details may be expressed in subordinate legislation, variously described as regulations or bylaws. Because courts will presume that legislatures did not intend to bestow on subordinate bodies the whole power of the legislature itself, they will find regulations and bylaws valid, provided that they are compatible with the purposes of the legislation they are designed to implement, and are made in accordance with the expressed and implied conditions set by the legislature.

Non-compliant regulations will be struck down as void. Accordingly, subordinate legislation whose purpose or effect is to frustrate the legislative intention to make abortion services available will be of no legal effect.

Practitioners who disregard regulations or act inconsistently with them and are subject to legal proceedings for their violation, will make a good legal defence by showing that the regulations never had the force of law. Similarly, people and bodies that the courts find to have sufficient interest may be granted standing to initiate legal proceedings to have the regulations declared void. For instance, regulations introduced in Nova Scotia, Canada, purporting to ensure safe conduct of medical procedures but intended simply to prevent establishment of a private abortion clinic were found to be void [14].

Legislation

Legislation is law-making by politically motivated bodies, having power under constitutional law to make law by positive enactments. Most legislatures claim democratic authority under constitutional law since most countries are created as democracies, but most democratic constitutions provide for suspension of democratic legislatures, for instance during military or other emergencies.

Governmental and other political agencies are frequently fearful to address abortion. The issue compels them to confront and resolve the commonly experienced contradiction that, while official positions of public and religious authorities oppose abortion, procedures are known to be widely undertaken, especially where means of contraception are similarly opposed. Ministries and departments of health know the heavy burden that unskilled abortion imposes on the scarce obstetrics and gynaecology services of public hospitals [15].

The pragmatism of legalizing abortion in order to make it safe and save hospital costs and women's lives is resisted by the need to subscribe to principles such as the sanctity of unborn life and to uphold religious doctrines and institutions that teach the wrongfulness of abortion. Accordingly, the legislative process is torn between pragmatism and principle, and this is a common source of individual and party political conflict that governments frequently prefer to avoid.

Where legislation is proposed that is intended to be not simply prohibitive and punitive but to provide conditions under which procedures may lawfully be undertaken, law-makers have to settle a frequently complicated set of issues such as the conditions—medical, social and otherwise—under which abortion is legitimate, places where procedures may be undertaken and how such places may be publicized, appropriate personnel who may administer services and their qualifications and, for instance, age and marital status of eligible women and whether they may obtain services confidentially and without the approval of third parties. Legislation on abortion tends to be isolated from the legal setting in which other medical services may be requested and provided, and it tends to include features that would be objectionable if applied to other medical procedures, including those related to other reproductive choices such as vasectomy.

Judicial decisions

Courts are empowered to interpret and apply legislation, including legislated comprehensive codes and *ad hoc* enactments in non-codified legal systems. In the latter, they also declare customary law that fills gaps left by legislation, and decide how legislation fits within the general legal framework. For instance, they may rule that legislation has superseded customary or common law, that words in legislation either embody or amend understandings of the same words in customary law or that legislation is to be interpreted compatibly with or as subordinate to customary law and not change it.

Judges may take initiatives to apply interpretations that reflect changes in common understanding of legislation, customary law or the relationship between the two. For instance, judges in a number of countries accept the growing influence of human rights law found in national constitutions and international human rights treaties, particularly when their countries have made international commitments to be bound by such treaties and to respect them in their domestic practice. For example, the French Conseil Constitutionel upheld France's liberal abortion law as consistent with the principle of liberty contained in the Declaration of the Rights of Man and of the Citizen [16], and the Constitutional Court of Austria sustained the legality of Austria's liberal abortion law and stated specifically that it did not violate the European Convention on Human Rights [17]. More recently, the Court in the Hague held that there was no conflict between the liberal Dutch abortion law and state subsidization of abortion clinics and the obligations of the Netherlands as parties to the International Covenant on Civil and Political Rights and the European Convention on Human Rights [18].

In religiously based legal systems, judges may hold office through training in secular law or by virtue of their rank within religious institutional structures. They may invoke divine revelation and the opinions of religious authorities to apply the law in particular cases. Religions vary in the extent to which they accommodate variations in interpretations of sacred texts and among the statements of perhaps historic religious leaders.

In judicial systems that apply the doctrine of strict precedent, which gives effect to the ethical principle of justice that like cases be treated alike, decisions of higher courts on points of law create precedents that lower courts are legally obliged to follow. This system offers greater certainty of what decisions lower courts will reach, but denies lower courts the flexibility, for example, to invoke international human rights provisions with which the judgements of higher national courts are inconsistent. It is common that courts of the highest authority, whose decisions bind lower courts, are not themselves bound by their own decisions. If they were to be so bound, legislation would be required to amend their decisions. Even though not bound, however, courts of the highest authority do not usually interpret the same law differently in the short term. They may eventually depart from their earlier decisions, but tend to move through incremental evolution rather than through landmark reversals of historic judgements.

Within the limits of precedent and by conservative evolution, judges apply abortion law by giving effect to constitutional law, by interpreting the meaning of valid legislation, by determining the significance of principles of customary law in non-codified legal systems and by assessing the role and appropriate influence of international human rights obligations.

Decisions of trial courts are not themselves precedents, but they may have considerable and sometimes even immense influence. For instance, legal systems based on the English common law have accepted the interpretation of criminal abortion legislation rendered in the instruction on the law given to a jury at the Central Criminal Court in London, England in 1938 in the *Bourne* case [19]. The judge recognized the distinction between criminal and non-criminal abortions, and found that abortion procured to save a woman's life or her health, including mental health, at risk of serious compromise through continuation of pregnancy, was non-criminal and accordingly not punishable. Almost all countries of the British Commonwealth whose legislation is derived from or influenced by the historic English legislation that expressed only the prohibition of abortion have accepted the *Bourne* decision as their relevant law [20]. However, their politicians, medical professions and lay public frequently omit this fact from their discussions of abortion, which they treat as criminal in all circumstances [21].

International human rights law

International human rights conventions, such as the International Covenant on Civil and Political Rights, often create or recognize the jurisdiction of special tribunals, such as the Human Rights Committee, that give effect to their terms. At the regional level, the European Commission of Human Rights and the European Court of Human Rights were established by the European Convention on Human Rights. Similarly, the Inter-American Commission of Human Rights and the Inter-American Court of Human Rights were established by the American Convention on Human Rights.

International human rights tribunals may find that states that are parties have violated applicable international human rights conventions on a variety of grounds. State legislation may be inconsistent with treaty obligations, decisions of state courts may uphold violations of, or fail to respect, rights protected under such conventions, governmental agents may have acted in ways that violate conventions or states may have violated their responsibilities to protect human rights against the conduct of private persons within state jurisdiction.

The European Commission on Human Rights has upheld UK legislation under which abortion choice is available to women under liberal terms [22]. However, this Commission has also found restrictive legislation in the former West Germany not to be in breach of the European Convention on Human Rights [23]. In a more recent ruling, the European Court of Human Rights found that the Irish government's ban on counselling women about where to find abortion abroad violates their right protected by the European Convention to receive information [24,25].

It has been seen that through the constitutions of some countries, international treaties take direct effect in domestic law, but that in others conventions have no direct effect unless and until they are nationally legislated to take domestic effect. Nevertheless, state courts may anticipate how international tribunals would apply international conventions, and themselves apply the conventions indirectly through state courts so as to give them effect and prevent their states from being held liable by international tribunals. National courts may suppose that their states intend to comply with and not to violate their international commitments, and may recognize the evolution in international law through which individuals have legal status, and states are internationally accountable for protection of the human rights of individual persons within their jurisdiction [26].

Abortion laws

Abortion has normally been regulated through criminal law provisions of either customary or religious origin. In the present century, most countries' prohibitions of abortion are contained in legislation that objects to abortion in principle, expressing philosophical preferences for contin- uation of pregnancy over elective termination. Many criminal codes have located abortion within their sections on crimes against morality, sometimes with additional provisions restricting communication of knowledge of contraceptive means and of methods of inducing menstru- ation. These laws reflect a patriarchical conditioning of morality, in which women's interests in health and self-determination have no recognition. Criminal laws traditionally had no provisions, for instance, against spousal rape, men's abandonment of their wives and families or their irresponsible imposition of life- or health-endangering pregnancies, such as those that are very closely spaced.

The presence of legal regulation of abortion within countries' criminal codes or legislation is rarely questioned, particularly where religious systems have identified protection of the unborn as an important element of the sanctity of human life. With harmful effects on women's right to choose abortion, and in many cases on women's very survival, such religious systems have not given the same regard to women's survival of pregnancy and childbirth, or reacted as vigorously to the deaths of an estimated 500 000 women each year worldwide from pregnancy-related causes that safe abortion could reduce [27]. The characterization of objectionable abortion as criminal equates deliberate termination of embryonic and fetal life with termination of the life of a born person. This equation also indicates that the crime warrants severe punishment.

A historic body of evidence confirms, however, that women seeking abortion and many who assist them in gaining access to abortion, are conscientious, responsible people whose motives are not socially deviant [28]. These women seek to protect the well-being of the existing children for whom they are responsible, and to maximize their ability to provide for future children. They also strive to achieve responsible balances in discharging the duties they find they owe to others such as children, husbands, parents and parents-in-law. Because women tend to be the primary caregivers to dependent members of their families, including extended families, they frequently have to strike balances between competing interests, and may find that the interests of unborn children are not appropriate to prevail in every case. It is pretentious of legislators and of religious and other social leaders to believe that their resolutions of these sensitive dilemmas in accordance with impersonal doctrines are superior to those that women strike in the circumstances of their own families.

Prevailing experience in Canada confirms that criminal abortion legislation is unnecessary to protect the symbolic and practical values represented by the concept of the sanctity of human life. Canada's restrictive Criminal Code provision on abortion was declared unconstitutional by a Supreme Court decision in early 1988 for violation of human rights [29], and a legislated proposal to replace it with a better attuned criminal law provision failed. In the years since Canada has been without a criminal prohibition or regulation of abortions performed by physicians, no evidence has emerged that the rate of abortion has risen, or that women are having abortions on irresponsible or trivial grounds. On the contrary, since the decision on abortion is no longer directed by criminal law but is governed by each woman's moral conscience and ethical judgement, the climate of ethical decision-making has improved, and the status of women has risen as they have become recognized as legitimate and responsible moral agents. It appears that the presence of criminal abortion legislation denies women this status, and denies societies the opportunity to acknowledge women's significance as such.

Criminal legislation on abortion, whether contained in comprehensive national or criminal codes of law or in more specific legislation that fits within systems of customary law, can be generally assessed within three classes, namely, basic, developed and advanced laws [12]. Basic laws provide the range of punishment for illegal abortion and usually lack any definition of what constitutes abortion or any distinction between legal and illegal abortion. No country compels a woman in imminent danger of death from continuation of pregnancy, such as from ectopic pregnancy, to continue the pregnancy. Devoutly Roman Catholic countries accommodate the legality of medical procedures that terminate such pregnancies under the doctrine of double effect, which permits inadvertent but unavoidable moral harms when the goal of conduct is to achieve a transcending virtue, such as saving human life. Nevertheless, basic laws reflect none of this understanding, but simply condemn and punish illegal abortion.

Developed law more explicitly distinguishes between legal and illegal abortion, usually providing that abortion is lawful when undertaken for the bona fide purpose of preserving a pregnant woman's life or her enduring physical or mental health. In some countries, developed laws have been directly legislated, but in many others basic laws have been developed by judicial decisions, such as the *Bourne* decision [19], that have provided details of abortions that are legally justified, or that are at least excusable and not punishable under the prohibitive criminal law. A simple version of a developed law is Section 240 of the Penal Code of Kenya, which qualifies a basic prohibitory section of the Code by providing that [30]:

> A person is not criminally responsible for performing in good
> faith and with reasonable care and skill a surgical
> operation. . .upon an unborn child for the preservation of the
> mother's life, if the performance of the operation is reasonable,
> having regard to the patient's state at the time and to all the
> circumstances of the case. Preservation of life is accepted to
> include the quality of life, meaning physical and mental health.

Advanced law positively provides that abortion is lawful when a woman chooses the procedure under specified indications. Legislation incorporating advanced laws is not uniform, but treats abortion as lawful in such cases as danger to the pregnant woman's life or physical or mental health, pregnancy from rape or incest, predictable gross physical or mental abnormality of a child if born, the harmful effect of childbirth upon the health or welfare of a woman's existing child(ren) and family and, for instance, failure of a routinely employed contraceptive method. Advanced laws may also address such procedural matters as the required qualifications of abortion practitioners, facilities where abortions may be performed, stages of pregnancy at which abortions may be performed on given indications, requirements of second or psychiatric medical opinions and, for instance, subsequent contraceptive counselling.

The graduation from developed to advanced laws is one of legal specificity, but not necessarily one of increasing liberalization. Many instances of advanced legislation are more restrictive in their terms or effects than instances of developed laws, and developed laws may be less accommodating than basic laws in jurisdictions where physicians are trusted to apply their judgement in good faith in response to women's requests. In others, physicians' claims of aborting women whom they feared would commit suicide are unquestioned, particularly when reinforced with psychiatric opinions, so that legislation that is basic in its terms is applied in a liberal fashion. There is also unsavoury evidence that doctors who decline to perform abortions in public hospitals under advanced laws are not prosecuted when they perform procedures in their private practices for fee-paying patients [12] (see also Chapter 10).

A growing tendency in abortion legislation internationally has been towards explicit liberalization, at first narrowly changing basic to developed laws on grounds of preservation of women's lives and health, and then moving to more accommodating advanced laws. A common pattern has emerged to decriminalize early abortion unconditionally, for example in the first trimester of pregnancy, and to introduce, for instance, indications such as health of the woman or risk of fetal malformation or handicap later in gestation [31]. In Europe, traditionally Roman Catholic countries such as France [32], Italy [33], Portugal [34], Spain [35] and more recently Belgium [36], have introduced liberal provisions to accommodate women's choice. Elsewhere, formerly colonized or subjugated countries including Botswana [37], Ghana [38], Zambia [39], Zimbabwe [40], India [41], Indonesia [42–44], Malaysia [45] and Barbados [46], that had preserved the restrictive laws that their former colonizers had applied to them but later abandoned in their own systems, have modernized their laws by adopting liberal provisions of their own creation or based on those adopted by their former colonizers [20].

A number of countries of Eastern Europe, such as Albania [47], Bulgaria [48] and Romania [49], that have reappraised their domestic laws following political changes on the demise of the Soviet Union, have enacted liberal abortion legislation, including decriminalization. A counter-tendency has also arisen, however, where the Roman Catholic Church has become a stronger political force, such as in Poland [50–53]. A similar influence in the new balance of domestic power in the reunified Germany has resulted in more restrictive law becoming applicable to the former East Germany. Church influence in Latin America and, for instance, the Philippines, has attempted to maintain criminal restriction of abortion choice through both prohibitive legislation and constitutional provisions declaring human life to be recognized and protected 'from conception'. These provisions do not necessarily afford unborn life more protection than, or priority over, the life of a pregnant woman, but encourage abortion opponents to limit women's choice. Liberalizing attempts have been thwarted in several countries including Chile, Colombia and Nicaragua by the same influence. The result has been less to promote childbirth over abortion than to maintain unsafe abortion rather than allow safe abortion [54].

Future legal challenges

The transition to health-based law

Placing the legal control of reproductive choice within the body of a state's criminal law is not only demeaning to women's status as responsible moral agents, but dysfunctional to protect women's health. Equally significantly from the perspective of reducing the incidence of abortion, it is also dysfunctional to minimize abortion rates themselves. There is compelling evidence from, for instance, the Netherlands and Scotland, where liberal abortion laws are associated with low rates of abortion because of wide availability of family planning services and sex education [7], that approaches that emphasize individual health and welfare reduce the frequency of unwanted pregnancy and abortion. Promotion of contraceptive practice more effectively reduces recourse to abortion than does the strict enforcement of criminal prohibitions against women seeking abortion services and health professionals delivering them. Reducing the incidence of unwanted pregnancy serves both women's choice and the reduction in abortion rates.

Unreflective continuation of historic patterns of resisting women's choice of abortion through criminal laws places this medical procedure within a psychological, sociological and symbolic context that deters rational analysis of the causes of unwanted pregnancy, hampers ethical exercise of abortion options and obstructs determination of the effects of unsafe abortions on both women's health and use of public health care resources. Locating responses to women's requirements of abortion choice outside the context of crime and punishment and within the context of health and welfare offers the prospect of focusing attention on pragmatic as well as doctrinal features of each country's experience of abortion. Unfortunately, moralistic condemnation of abortion, particularly when inspired by religious perceptions, is often allied with condemnation of family planning practices. Both are seen as illicit human interventions in the mystical divine plan for the future of humanity. In also resisting availability of contraceptive services, however, campaigns against abortion are self-perpetuating, because they are self-defeating.

The challenge of responding to abortion through laws directed to choice in family planning and the promotion of reproductive health is that such laws may appear to place pragmatic over ethical considerations. Accordingly, the ethics of promoting and protecting women's moral agency, and of facilitating women's protection of their family and reproductive interests in a manner consistent with their own individual values, merits attention (see pp. 207–209). It has been shown that family planning programmes promote maternal and infant health by drawing women into health care systems and providing them with access to medical information and counselling, which fosters responsible reproductive and family based decision-making. Evidence also shows that family planning services increase women's use of antenatal care and of other health services not directly related to reproduction and, thus, indirectly enhance women's abilities to promote child and family health [55].

Abortion legislation *per se* does not influence abortion rates or reproductive health. South American experience confirms the frequent phenomenon that restrictive legislation can be associated with extraordinarily high rates of abortion [56], and the situation in the Netherlands shows that a very liberal abortion law can be associated with a low rate. Of greater influence on abortion rates is the quality of services available to accommodate reproductive health and choice. Abortion rates are incidental outcomes of reproductive health services, and legislation to promote reproductive health and self-determination will reduce women's need for abortion.

Legislation designed not simply to limit or to liberalize recourse to abortion but to address reduction of unwanted pregnancy and promotion of reproductive self-determination will include sections requiring provision of abortion at the earliest possible stage of pregnancy [57], provision of contraception to women and where possible their partners in the post-abortion phase [58] and, for instance, provision of contraception free of charge to high-risk groups such as adolescents [59].

A legislative framework for the development of comprehensive reproductive health services would be administrative rather than punitive. Countries would show seriousness in their concern about women's vulnerability to unwanted pregnancy by appointing an officer such as an ombudsperson to oversee delivery of reproductive health services, and to monitor such outcomes as rates of maternal mortality and morbidity, abortion rates, pre-abortion time delays and counselling and rates of unmarried adolescent pregnancy. In a setting of these concerns, liberalization or decriminalization of abortion law becomes one step among many in the promotion of reproductive health. Abortion rates indicate not personal moral failing but an administrative failing of reproductive health services and comprehensive sex education. Indeed, if countries were to address their abortion rates as a condemnation not of women's choice but of their reproductive health services, rates might serve a more positive role in the promotion of family health.

Medical advances

Many countries retain legislation restricting abortion that arose in the last century before sterile practice, when abortion was hazardous even in comparison to pregnancy and childbirth, which had high rates of maternal mortality and morbidity. In modern practice, early abortion is much safer than childbirth at its safest, and in many countries is undertaken on an out-patient basis. The relevance of modern law to reproductive health is challenged not only at the epidemiological level but also at the microscopic level, since improved knowledge of the biology of human reproduction has created refinements that marginalize crude repressive laws. Distinctions have become apparent between acting before and shortly following fertilization to prevent fusion or implantation, to which the historic crime of abortion was never applied.

Historic legislation often recognized that pregnancy itself could not be proven, due to biological uncertainties and destruction of evidence before the crime was identified, and therefore made the offence one of acting with intent to prevent continuation of any pregnancy, whether the woman was pregnant or not, although women themselves were usually punishable only if they were shown to be 'with child' [60]. Acting with intent to prevent conception or initiation of pregnancy following conception did not satisfy the intentional aspect of the crime of abortion. The law now draws an analogy between reproduction *in vivo* and reproduction *in vitro* to recognize that achieving fertilization is not the same as achieving pregnancy [61].

Modern recognition of the biological and technological realities of human reproduction opens the way to the law's enhancement of reproductive health. For instance, the abortion law of Italy mandates, 'the use of modern techniques of pregnancy termination, which are physically and mentally less damaging to the woman and are less hazardous' [62]. Even in the absence of such a provision in abortion legislation, the administrative systems under which delivery of health services is regulated should require that the least hazardous, optimally therapeutic procedures be employed to benefit patients. For instance, in many parts of the world, first-trimester abortions are still performed by dilatation and curettage which is not as safe as vacuum aspiration, and more costly [63–66]. Legal provisions on professional licensure, discipline, training and continuing medical education could be applied to ensure that medical practitioners are trained in the use of modern techniques, and legal provisions on the running and accreditation of hospitals and clinics could ensure that health practitioners are equipped to apply them. Similarly, legislation should be redesigned to accommodate the availability of non-surgical abortion, as the British Abortion Act of 1967 was amended to do in 1990 [67,68].

The development of non-surgical abortion through a so-called 'abortion pill' such as RU 486 (mifepristone) [69] advances prospective abortion practice in a manner that abortion law will be challenged to accommodate. Mifepristone requires the additional use of a prostaglandin to achieve abortion most safely and effectively and, like all medical techniques, it has a failure rate, side effects and contraindications [69]. When the technique is known to exist, but access to it is obstructed by legal barriers to safe practice, illicit markets and services will emerge through which women will use the technique outside safe limits. The resourcefulness women show in employment of drugs is evident in Brazil, where women who suspect unintended pregnancy take an orally active anti-ulcer prostaglandin analogue, misoprostol, to induce bleeding so that they can present themselves to hospital with 'spontaneous' abortions, the management of which requires uterine evacuation [70]. Criminal laws against abortion and illicit use of prescription drugs are all but powerless against such practices.

Drugs such as mifepristone may have multiple therapeutic uses, and it is unethical that they should be unavailable for those uses because of attitudes to abortion [71]. A potential use of mifepristone, which may in time eclipse its use as an abortifacient, is as a method of emergency contraception [72]. Emergency contraception may be medically prescribed within 72 h after unprotected intercourse, contraceptive failure or rape, and prevents fertilization or uterine implantation of a pre-embryo. The use of emergency contraception is thought to reduce the risk of unplanned pregnancy by 75% and halve the number of abortions [73].

Legislation primarily concerned with reproductive health and employment of best medical techniques would require that services such as emergency contraception be available, with the aim of reducing recourse to abortion. For instance, when contraceptive drugs are made available, recipients should be given information about emergency contraception by prescribing health professionals, pharmacists, package inserts or other appropriate instruction. Laws on professional licensure and competence could reinforce this obligation. Similar information would be part of post-abortion counselling. Public education on sexual matters and contraception should also publicize means of emergency contraception and of availability of early abortion where laws are accommodating.

Legal respect for human rights

It has been seen that criminal laws fit within national frameworks of constitutional law, and nations themselves derive their legal legitimacy from international law. A distinctive modern development in international law is its transition from being just the law of nations to becoming the law of humankind through recognition of the legal duty of states to protect the rights of human beings, whether they are their nationals or not. The international human rights framework provides the context within which abortion and related laws must be evaluated and by which the legitimacy of state conduct may be measured. By human rights standards, many instances of enforcement of laws restrictive of abortion choice, and the laws themselves, are suspect.

An approach to the conformity of abortion laws with human rights standards is to address not only what the laws prohibit, namely resort to and performance of abortion procedures, but also what they compel, namely involuntary continuation of pregnancy [74]. Involuntary imposition of the risk of pregnancy is normally severely punished under criminal laws, particularly through sanctions against rape, and analogous sensitivities would condemn enforcing involuntary continuation of pregnancy were it not for moralistic reasoning that women who voluntarily risk pregnancy through expressing their sexuality must bear the consequence of pregnancy. Respect for the sanctity of human life has not led to advocacy of legal power outside military service to compel persons to make bodily sacrifices for the survival of others, such as through bone marrow donations to children at risk of death from leukaemia [75]. Only pregnant women are required involuntarily to maintain the services of their bodies for the benefit of others [76]. Since men are not legally compellable to make sacrifices, for example of bone marrow or liver segments, for the survival of their children, legal powers to compel pregnant women to render bodily service to their children before birth may constitute discrimination against women on grounds of their sex, in violation of international human rights standards.

Distinctions between men and women based on differences in natural processes of human reproduction, that are claimed to justify compulsory continuation of pregnancy, tend to be dismissive or ignorant of women's interests and values, and insensitive to women's moral agency. The recognition of women as equally legitimate members of society with men, entitled to full participation in the evolution of their states' political, legislative, judicial and administrative institutions, is a goal of international human rights law. Laws that continue the silencing, marginalization, disempowerment and devaluation of women, including those inhibiting choice in abortion, are embarrassments to the claims of countries maintaining them that they respect human rights.

Laws on abortion that warrant reconsideration according to human rights standards include any that condition abortions of married or otherwise mature women on the consent of their relatives, notably husbands or parents. Equality should exist between the legal and pragmatic contexts in which men have resort to medical procedures such as vasectomy and those in which women may exercise abortion choice. Courts of highest authority have recognized that parents have no claim to regulate otherwise lawful contraception or abortion that their mature minor daughters seek [77]. Explicit legislation empowering a parental veto may satisfy constitutional standards in principle [78], but a veto is subject in operation to parental legal duties to provide their children with medically indicated therapeutic care. Spouses are normally legally obliged to provide or facilitate medically indicated care for each other, limiting the operation of laws conditioning abortion on husbands' approval, although such laws are suspect not simply on pragmatic grounds but upon principles of human rights law [79].

Similarly demeaning to respect for women's responsible moral agency and maturity are laws that explicitly impose a time period between a woman's request for abortion and its performance. So-called reflection delay requirements presuppose that women seek abortion unreflectively. Delivery of any such service requires patients' free and adequately informed consent, so that preliminary discussion and counselling should be offered according to routine standards of health care competency and hospital or clinic management. The emphasis that opponents of abortion choice give to reflection delays, elaborate information programmes for instance on fetal development and to abortion committee consideration of applications for the procedure shows that they are moralistically intended to obstruct abortion choice [80], in denial not only of women's best health care [81] but also of their legally protected human rights.

Provisions of human rights treaties that may be invoked in defence of women's rights to abortion choice and to access to family planning services that will reduce risks of unintended pregnancy, include the right to liberty and security of the person, the right to private and family life and the right to sexual non-discrimination. Reinforcing these basic rights that are part of human dignity are rights such as to the benefits of scientific progress and the right to health care. Distinctions are sometimes drawn between negative rights and positive rights. Negative rights are claims to be free from state intervention in pursuit of one's own preferences through employment of one's own resources. Positive rights are claims to be provided by others, notably the state itself, with resources through which to pursue individual preferences. It is usual for basic health care to be considered a positive right, although impoverished regions may lack means to deliver such care satisfactorily through public hospital and clinic services. Reproductive health services such as contraception, sterilization and abortion have been contested as positive rights on moralistic and political grounds, but the right to resort to such services is increasingly recognized to constitute at least a negative right, although abortion continues to be an exception.

National laws respectful of women's human rights would transcend the field of abortion and reproductive choice. They would reinforce women's protection against violence at the hands of their husbands and others, and remove legal discriminations such as against unmarried mothers that induce women to practice abortion, legally or illegally. Similarly, the positive use of law against practices that discriminate against women's access to fair employment opportunities and equal pay with men for work of equal value would fortify women's roles as providers for their families, and afford women economic means to care for the children they bear. Accordingly, human rights laws can apply in many ways to women's reproductive choice, and they are relevant not only to choice of abortion but also to the choice not to terminate pregnancies but to maintain them in order to give birth to children that enjoy the prospect of lives of adequate nutrition, care, well-being and dignity.

References

The abortion legislation cited in these references is reprinted and where necessary translated into English in the *Annual Review of Population Law* published by Harvard Law School and the United Nations Population Fund, or the *International Digest of Health Legislation published by the World Health Organization.*

1 Lerner G. *The Creation of Patriarchy.* New York: Oxford University Press, 1986.
2 Westermarck E. *Origin and Development of the Moral Ideas.* London: Macmillan, 1906.
3 Lord Ellenborough's Act, UK Statutes. 43 GEO. III Ch. 58.
4 Williams G. *The Sanctity of Life and the Criminal Law.* New York: Faber, 1958.
5 Boland R. Abortion law world-wide: a survey of recent developments. In: Bednarikova J, Chapman FC, eds. *Essays in Honour of Jan Stepan.* Zürich: Schulthess Polygraphischer Verlag, 1994: 89–106.
6 Cook RJ. Abortion laws and policies: challenges and opportunities. *Int J Gynaecol Obstet* 1989; 3 (Suppl.): 61–87.
7 Henshaw S. Induced abortion: a world review, 1990. *Stud Fam Plann* 1991; 22: 231–240.
8 United Nations. *Abortion Policies: a Global Review.* Volumes I, II and III. New York: United Nations, 1992, 1993, 1995.
9 *In the Matter of a Reference as to the Meaning of the Word 'Persons' in Section 24 of the British North America Act, 1867* [1928] Supreme Court Reports 276 (Supreme Court Canada) reversed in *Henrietta Muir Edwards* v. *Attourney General Canada* [1930] Appeal Cases 124 (Privy Council).
10 Knoppers BM, Brault I, Sloss E. Abortion law in francophone countries. *Am J Comparative Law* 1990; 38: 889–922.
11 David HP, Pick de Weis S. *Abortion in the Americas.* Washington, DC: Pan American Health Organization, 1992.
12 Cook RJ, Dickens BM. *Abortion Laws in Commonwealth Countries.* Geneva: World Health Organization, 1979.
13 Verhovek SH. Abortion foes ordered to pay clinic damages. *New York Times* 1994; May 10: A-1, A-16.
14 See the discussion in *R.* v. *Morgentaler* (1993) 107 Dominion Law Reports (4th) 537 (Supreme Court Canada) [1993].
15 Mpangile GS, Leshabari MT, Kihwele DJ. Factors associated with induced abortion in public hospitals in Dar es Salaam, Tanzania. *Reprod Health Matters* 1993; 2: 21–31.
16 Judgement of 15 January 1975, Conseil Constitutionel, Recueil Dalloz-Sirey [D.S.Jur.] 529, Journal Officiel, 16 January 1975.
17 Judgement of 11 October 1974, Constitutional Court of Austria, [1974] Erklärungen des Verfassungsgerichtshofs 221.
18 *Juristenvereniging Pro Vita* v. *De Staat der Nederlanden (Ministerie van Welzijn, Volksgezondheid en Cultuur),* 8 February 1990, Court, The Hague. Nederlandse Jurisprudentie, no. 43, 1990, entry 707, as summarized in *Eur Law Digest* 1991; 19: 179–180.
19 *R.* v. *Bourne* [1939] 1 King's Bench 687; [1938] 3 All England Reports 615.
20 Cook RJ, Dickens BM. *Issues in Reproductive Health Law in the Commonwealth.* London: Commonwealth Secretariat, 1986: 59–61.
21 Cook RJ. Clandestine abortions are not necessarily illegal. *Fam Plann Perspect* 1991; 23: 283.

22 *Paton* v. *United Kingdom*, 3 European Human Rights Reports 408 (1980).

23 *Bruggemann & Scheuten* v. *Federal Republic of Germany*, 3 European Human Rights Reports 244 (1977).

24 *Open Door Counselling and Dublin Well Women Centre* v. *Ireland*, 15 European Human Rights Reports 244 (1992).

25 Whitty, N. Law and the regulation of reproduction in Ireland: 1922–1992. *Univ Toronto Law J* 1993; 43: 851–888.

26 Cook RJ. International protection of women's reproductive rights. *New York University J Int Law Pol* 1992; 24: 645–727.

27 Abou-Zahr C, Royston E. *Maternal Mortality: a Global Factbook*. Geneva: World Health Organization, 1991.

28 *Report of the (British) Inter-Departmental Committee on Abortion* (Chairman: Norman Birkett), 1939: 37–40.

29 *R.* v. *Morgentaler* (1988) 44 Dominion Law Reports (4th) 385 (Supreme Court Canada).

30 *Mehar Singh Bansel* v. *R.* (1959) East African Law Report 813.

31 Cook RJ, Dickens BM. International developments in abortion laws: 1977–1988. *Am J Publ Health* 1988; 78: 1305–1311.

32 France. Law 79-1204 of 31 December 1979. *Journal Officiel de la République Française, Edition des Lois et Décrets* 1980; 1: 3–4.

33 Italy. Law 194, *Gazzetta Ufficiale della Repubblica Italiana*. Part I. 1978; 22 May (140): 3642–3646.

34 Portugal. Law no. 6/84 of 11 May 1984. *Diário da República*. Part I. 1984; 11 May (109): 1518–1519.

35 Spain. Organic Law no. 9 of 5 July 1985. *Boletín Oficial del Estado, Gaceta de Madrid* 1985; 12 July (166), text no. 14 138: 22 041.

36 Belgium. Law of 3 April 1990. *Moniteur Belge* 1990; 5 April: 6379–6380.

37 Botswana. An Act (no. 15 of 1991) to amend the Penal Code. The Penal Code (Amendment) Act, 1991.

38 Ghana. The Criminal Code (Amendment) Law, 1985. PNDCL 102, 22 February 1985.

39 Zambia. The Termination of Pregnancy Act no. 26, 1972. *Republic of Zambia Government Gazette, Acts Supplement* 1972; 13 October: 171–173.

40 Zimbabwe. Termination of Pregnancy Act 1977.

41 India. The Medical Termination of Pregnancy Act, 1971. *The Gazette of India Extraordinary*. Part II, section 1 1971; 10 August: 237–240.

42 Indonesia: 1992 Health Law.

43 Hull TH, Sarwono SW, Widyantoro N. Induced abortion in Indonesia. *Stud Fam Plann* 1993; 24: 241–251.

44 Djohan E, Inbdrawasih R, Adenan M, Yudomustopo H, Tan MG. The attitudes of health providers towards abortion in Indonesia. *Reprod Health Matters* 1993; 2: 32–40.

45 Malaysia. An Act (no. A727 of 1989) to amend the Penal Code (Federated Malaysian States, chapter 45), 19 April 1989. The Penal Code (Amendment Act) 1989.

46 Barbados. The Medical Termination of Pregnancy Regulations, 1983. Statutory Instruments. 1983/no. 62. *Supplement to Official Gazette No. 41 (Statutory Instruments Supplement No. 28)* 1983; 19 May.

47 Albania. Directive of 8 June 1991.

48 Bulgaria. Decree no. 2 of 1 February 1990. *Dăržaven Vestnik* 1990; 9 February (12): 4–9.

49 Romania. Order no. 605 of 27 December 1989, Ministry of Health.

50 Fuszara M. Legal regulation of abortion in Poland. *Signs* 1991; 17: 117–128.

51 Nowicka W. The new abortion law in Poland. *Plann Parenthood Eur* 1993; 22: 21–24.

52 Zielinska E. Recent trends in abortion legislation in Eastern Europe, with particular reference to Poland. *Crim Law Forum* 1993; 4: 47–93.

53 Rich V. Polish abortions. *Lancet* 1994; 343: 1090.

54 Paxman JM, Rizo A, Brown L, Benson J. The clandestine epidemic: the practice of unsafe abortion in Latin America. *Stud Fam Plann* 1993; 24: 205–226.

55 Pine RN. Achieving public health objectives through family planning services. *Reprod Health Matters* 1993; 2: 77–83.

56 *Clandestine Abortion: a Latin American Reality.* New York: Alan Guttmacher Institute, 1994.

57 Finland. Law no. 239 of 24 March 1970. *Suomen Asetuskokoelma-Finlands Författningssamling* 1970; 31 March (238–242): 482–484.

58 Iceland. Law no. 25/1975, 27 May 1975. *Annual Review of Population Law* 1976: 53–55.

59 Hong Kong. Offences Against the Person (Amendment) Ordinance no. 13 of 1981, 12 February 1981, *Annual Review of Population Law* 1981: 67–69.

60 Dickens BM. *Abortion and the Law.* London: MacGibbon & Kee, 1966.

61 Cook RJ, Dickens BM. *Emerging Issues in Commonwealth Abortion Laws, 1982.* London: Commonwealth Secretariat, 1983 (41–42).

62 Italy. Section 15 of Law 194, *Gazzetta Ufficiale della Repubblica Italiana.* Part I. 1978; 22 May (140): 3642–3646.

63 Tietze C, Lewit S. Joint Program for the Study of Abortion (JPSA): early medical complications of legal abortions. *Stud Fam Plann* 1972; 3: 97–119.

64 Cates W Jr, Grimes DA. Morbidity and mortality in the United States. In: Hodgson JE, ed. *Abortion and Sterilization: Medical and Social Aspects.* London: Academic Press, 1981: 155–180.

65 Grimes DA, Schulz KF, Cates W, Tyler CW. The Joint Program for the Study of Abortion/CDC: a preliminary report. In: Hern W, Andrikopoulos B, eds. *Abortion in the 1970s.* New York: National Abortion Federation, 1977: 41–54.

66 Greenslade FC, Leonard AH, Benson J et al. *Manual Vacuum Aspiration: a Summary of Clinical and Programmatic Experience Worldwide.* Carrboro: International Projects Assistance Services, 1993.

67 United Kingdom Human Fertilisation and Embryology Act 1990, enacting section 1(3A) of the Abortion Act 1967.

68 Morgan D, Lee, RG. *Blackstone's Guide to the Human Fertilisation and Embryology Act 1990.* London: Blackstone, 1991: 60.

69 Peyron R, Aubény E, Targosz V et al. Early termination of pregnancy with mifepristone (RU 486) and the orally active prostaglandin misoprostol. *N Engl J Med* 1993; 328: 1509–1513.

70 Barbosa RGM, Arilha M. The Brazilian experience with Cytotec. *Stud Fam Plann* 1993; 24: 236–240.

71 Macklin R. Antiprogestin drugs: ethical issues. *Law Med Health Care* 1992; 20: 215–219.

72 Glasier A, Thong KJ, Dewar M, Mackie M, Baird DT. Comparison of mifepristone

(RU 486) and high-dose estrogen and progestogen for emergency post coital contraception. *N Engl J Med* 1992; 237: 1041–1044.

73 Wentz AC. Waking up the US to the morning after pill. *J Women's Health* 1994; 3: 81–82.

74 Rubenfeld J. The right of privacy. *Harv Law Rev* 1989; 102: 737.

75 *McFall* v. *Shimp*, 10 Pennsylvania District Court. 3d 90 (Allegheny Cty Ct. 1978).

76 Thomson JJ. A defense of abortion. *Philos Publ Affairs* 1971; 1: 47–66.

77 *Gillick* v. *West Norfolk and Wisbech Area Health Auth.* [1985] 3 All England Reports. 402 (UK House of Lords for England).

78 *Hodgson* v. *Minnesota*, 110 Supreme Court. 2926 (1990) (United States).

79 Cook RJ, Maine D. Spousal veto over family planning services. *Am J Publ Health* 1987; 77: 339–344.

80 Amit D. Abortion approval as a ritual of symbolic control. *Women Crim Justice* 1992; 3: 5–25.

81 Report of the [Badgley] Committee on the Operation of the Abortion Law, 1977 (Canada) at pp. 66–67. Ottawa: Minister of Supply and Services, Canada.

Index